MAURICE BLANCHOT
AND THE LITERATURE OF
TRANSGRESSION

MAURICE BLANCHOT AND THE LITERATURE OF TRANSGRESSION

John Gregg

PRINCETON UNIVERSITY PRESS

PRINCETON, NEW JERSEY

COPYRIGHT © 1994 BY PRINCETON UNIVERSITY PRESS

PUBLISHED BY PRINCETON UNIVERSITY PRESS, 41 WILLIAM STREET,

PRINCETON, NEW JERSEY 08540

IN THE UNITED KINGDOM: PRINCETON UNIVERSITY PRESS,

CHICHESTER, WEST SUSSEX

ALL RIGHTS RESERVED

LIBRARY OF CONGRESS CATALOGING-IN-PUBLICATION DATA

GREGG, JOHN, 1954–

MAURICE BLANCHOT AND THE LITERATURE OF TRANSGRESSION / JOHN GREGG.

P. CM.

INCLUDES BIBLIOGRAPHICAL REFERENCES AND INDEX.

ISBN 0-691-03329-3

1. BLANCHOT, MAURICE—CRITICISM AND INTERPRETATION. I. TITLE.

PQ2603.L3343Z67 1994

843′.912—DC20 93-30911

THIS BOOK HAS BEEN COMPOSED IN LASER GALLIARD

PRINCETON UNIVERSITY PRESS BOOKS ARE PRINTED
ON ACID-FREE PAPER AND MEET THE GUIDELINES FOR
PERMANENCE AND DURABILITY OF THE COMMITTEE
ON PRODUCTION GUIDELINES FOR BOOK LONGEVITY
OF THE COUNCIL ON LIBRARY RESOURCES

PRINTED IN THE UNITED STATES OF AMERICA

1 3 5 7 9 10 8 6 4 2

Pour Dominique

"car nous sommes ce lecteur doublant un double et le
dédoublant en écriture par un acte de répétition qui sollicite,
vaguement, quelqu'un qui puisse le répéter à son
tour et à son tour se mettre en quête d'un
répétiteur peut-être définitif . . . "

Maurice Blanchot, *L'Amitié*

CONTENTS

ACKNOWLEDGMENTS   ix

A NOTE ON SOURCES   xi

Introduction   3

ONE
Literature and Transgression   10

TWO
Language, History, and Their Destinies of Incompletion   18

THREE
Blanchot's Suicidal Artist:
Writing and the (Im)Possibility of Death   35

FOUR
Mythical Portrayals of Writing and Reading   46

FIVE
Writing the Disaster: Henri Sorge's Journal   72

Silencing the Critics of the State   72
An Awkward Silence   83
The Crisis of (Mis)Representation   87
The Poetics of Writing the Disaster   98
Ink-Stained Pages   108
Sorge's "Fable" and Fragments on Narcissus   115
Sorge's Revolt   121

SIX
Flagrants Délits: Caught in the Act of Self-Reading   127

Discreet Violations of the Noli   127
Getting Started, Finishing Up: The Pro/Epilogue of
L'Attente l'oubli   132
Putting Their Story into Words   138
Perspectives of Authority   143
The Reversal   153
Flagrants délits   159
Qui parle?   162
De Man's Blind Spot   168
The Law of the Genre   171

CONCLUSION
Blanchot's Postmodern Legacy 173

NOTES 201

BIBLIOGRAPHY 233

INDEX 239

ACKNOWLEDGMENTS

I GRATEFULLY acknowledge the original publishers of the following sections of this book: "Blanchot's Suicidal Artist: Writing and the (Im)Possibility of Death" (chapter 3), published under the same title in *Substance* 55 (1988): 47–58, © 1988 by the Board of Regents of the University of Wisconsin System. Reprinted by permission. Portions of chapter 4 were published under the title "Theoretical and Fictional Portrayals of Reading in Blanchot" in *Dalhousie French Studies* 20 (1991): 75–87. Reprinted by permission.

A NOTE ON SOURCES

QUOTATIONS in French from Blanchot (and others) appear in the body of the text, and English translations have been provided in notes. Existing translations have been used whenever possible, although on occasion I have taken the liberty of slightly modifying them. All other translations from French sources (both Blanchot and others) were done by myself, with invaluable assistance from Dominique Froidefond, to whom I would like to express my thanks.

The following abbreviations have been used throughout to refer to the most frequently cited works by Blanchot and to their translations:

AC	*Après Coup*
CI	*La Communauté inavouable*
ED	*L'Ecriture du désastre*
EI	*L'Entretien infini*
EL	*L'Espace littéraire*
FP	*Faux Pas*
GO	*The Gaze of Orpheus*
IC	*The Infinite Conversation*
LS	*Lautréamont et Sade*
LV	*Le Livre à venir*
PAD	*Le Pas au-delà*
PF	*La Part du feu*
SL	*The Space of Literature*
SNB	*The Step Not Beyond*
UC	*The Unavowable Community*
VC	*Vicious Circles*
WD	*The Writing of the Disaster*

MAURICE BLANCHOT
AND THE LITERATURE OF
TRANSGRESSION

INTRODUCTION

DWELLING at the crossroads where two literary discourses meet, one critical the other fictional, Maurice Blanchot has pursued a rigorous meditation on reading and writing that has spanned more than four decades. His first collection of critical essays, *Faux Pas*, was published in 1943 and is composed of nearly sixty articles written originally for publication in the daily *Le Journal des Débats*. This assemblage is certainly the most eclectic of Blanchot's critical works, and the subjects of his articles—for the most part musings inspired by the latest releases of critical studies, translations, poetry, and fiction—range from da Vinci's *Notebooks* and the French baroque poets to Giono's rendition of *Moby Dick* and Camus's *L'Etranger*.

His second book of criticism, *La Part du feu*, appeared in 1949. Like the book that preceded it and the others that will follow—except for one, *Lautréamont et Sade*—it is comprised of pieces that first came out in periodicals, in this case *L'Arche* and *Critique*, the review founded by his close friend Georges Bataille. The second book contains half as many essays as the first one, but they are longer and more fully developed. He covers less territory in the subjects he treats, choosing to deal only with writers of the nineteenth and twentieth centuries (with the exception of Pascal), and we can begin to discern the emergence of a kind of literary pantheon, exemplary writers to whom he will incessantly return in his future discussions of what he calls the approach to the space of literature: Mallarmé, Kafka, Char, Hölderlin, and Nietzsche.

The next four books of criticism, *L'Espace littéraire* (1955), *Le Livre à venir* (1959), *L'Entretien infini* (1969), and *L'Amitié* (1971) are made up almost exclusively of pieces he wrote during his stint as a regular contributor to the *Nouvelle Revue Française* from 1953 to 1968. Of these, the first three constitute the core of Blanchot's theory of literature, and they are probably the best known of the works that form his critical corpus. Although they are compilations of previously published essays, they possess a thematic unity that the other collections do not: the essays are grouped into sections that have titles, and an implicit thread of argument ties these sections to each other in such a way that there is a sustained, progressive development throughout.[1]

Existing alongside these critical works is a somewhat lesser read (but no less impressive) narrative oeuvre which has evolved, roughly speaking, through three successive stages: the novels of the 1940s, the *récits* of the 1950s, and the fragmentary books (unclassifiable as purely narrative works) of the 1960s and 1970s.[2] With respect to the latter, *L'Attente l'oubli* is clearly more a narrative work than *Le Pas du-delà* or *L'Ecriture du désastre*, but the very fact that these works are nearly impossible to classify as either theoretical or narrative indicates that over the years the two complementary yet contradictory activities of critical and creative writing have tended to converge, resulting in a different kind of writing which, while not being totally indifferent to such categories as criticism and fiction, is irreducible to either of these categories and contests their ability to set up and define two different disciplines and orders of knowledge. If, in Blanchot's writing, these traditionally distinct activities have encroached on each other's territory, it is because their concerns are essentially the same: whether in the guise of novelist or critic, he seeks to plumb the depths of the mysteries of the origin of literature. As he explains in the preface to *Lautréamont et Sade*, one thing that as a critic he does *not* do is to submit a work he is discussing to value judgments, whereby a writer's success or failure could be measured against a set of standards extrinsic to the work imposed on the work by the critic:

> La critique n'est plus le jugement extérieur qui met l'ouvrage littéraire en valeur et se prononce, après coup sur sa valeur. Elle est devenue inséparable de son intimité, elle appartient au mouvement par lequel celui-ci vient à lui-même, est sa propre recherche et l'expérience de sa possibilité. (13)[3]

Blanchot portrays the critical impulse as a response to a demand made by the work that originates from within its most intimate recesses. The critic is thus a shadowy double of the writer who reenacts the latter's Orphic quest to arrive at the origin of the work. At stake in this quest for both figures is the potential apprehension of the conditions that render literature possible. Because it involves an uncovering of the fundamental principles that underlie the experience of literature, Blanchot's enterprise has a Kantian flavor to it, a perspective that he himself acknowledges: "de même que la raison critique de Kant est l'interrogation des conditions de possibilité de l'expérience scientifique, de même la critique est liée à la recherche de la possibilité de l'expérience littéraire" (*LS* 13).[4] Blanchot hastens to add, however, that the word *recherche* should not be associated unilaterally with the domain of the critic or theorist of literature; on the contrary, this activity belongs just as much to the province of creation: "Le mot recherche est un mot qu'il ne faut pas entendre dans son sens intellectuel, mais comme action au sein et en vue de l'espace créateur" (*LS* 13).[5]

The destinies of the writer and critic are thus inextricably intertwined, and the purpose of the present study is to elucidate some of the paradoxes inherent in this "étrange dialogue . . . de la parole critique et de la parole 'créatrice'" (*LS* 10).[6] To this end, I will first undertake (in chapters 1 through 4) an exposition of the major tenets of his theories of reading and writing as they are presented in his critical texts.

The first chapter concerns the affinity that exists between the thought of Blanchot and Bataille with respect to the notion of transgression, the theoretical paradigm that Blanchot borrows from Bataille in order to account for the economic relationships that link author, work, and reader. In the second chapter, we will examine Blanchot's characterization of the ontological status of the origin of language, which is inspired chiefly by Mallarmé and Heidegger. We will also consider the repercussions that such a notion of language has on classical theories of aesthetics as representation and the Hegelian model of history predicated on the closure of totalization. Chapter 3 contains a discussion of what is without a doubt the most fundamental theme that pervades all of Blanchot's thought, the relationship between literature and death, which is approached here from within the context of autobiographical forms of writing such as the journal. In chapter 4, we will take a look at the myths that Blanchot adapts primarily and most explicitly (but not solely) in his critical texts to portray the activities of writing (Orpheus) and reading (the resurrections of Jesus and Lazarus and Oedipus's encounter with the Sphinx). In each case, the mythical protagonist is involved in committing a transgression in the sense that Bataille gives to this term. We will also observe Blanchot the critic at work as he reads Kafka's *The Castle* in a manner faithfully consistent with his theoretical portrayal of reading.

In chapters 5 and 6, we will turn our attention to two representative works of fiction by Blanchot, *Le Très-Haut* and *L'Attente l'oubli*, respectively. In both of these works, Blanchot casts in the mode of fiction concerns that reside at the center of his critical enterprise. Besides the fragmentary structure of *L'Attente l'oubli*, the most striking difference between these two works is the almost complete elimination in the second one of the anecdotal elements that make of the first one a full-blown novel. The decision to examine works that come from two different periods will enable us to discern the shift that occurs in Blanchot's writing as he abandons in his search for a new poetics of statement the traditional form of the novel for a more experimental form based on fragmentation.

Le Très-Haut, his third and final novel published in 1948, is set in a modern capital city in the throes of a rapidly spreading epidemic and a political insurrection against a totalitarian regime. Because the book's main character, Henri Sorge, is engaged in the writing of a journal, an activity that he takes up to pass the time while on sick leave, we will be able to see how Blanchot depicts writing and reading (as a member of the State's bureaucracy, Sorge is a skilled exegete of the Law) in a narrative setting. Sorge's ambivalent attitude toward the conflicting exigencies of his writing and his work as functionary testifies to the inadequacy of political and aesthetic systems based on representation and implies a critique of the notion of Sartrean commitment, the posture that the intellectual/ writer can and ought to assume with respect to the regime in power.

L'Attente l'oubli, published in 1962, is a collection of fragmentary conversations that take place between a man and a woman in a hotel room. In telling the story of their encounter, Blanchot stages the problems contained in his theory of the *noli me legere*, which accounts for the rapport of estrangement that exists between the author and his work.[7] We will discover that the work's withdrawal from its author's purported mastery over it occurs not only after the work's completion but also at its very inception, an aspect of the *noli* that has generally been overlooked. Other questions that will receive our attention are the relationships that exist between creation and criticism and primary and secondary texts and the place that Blanchot reserves in his reenactment of the approach of/to the space of literature for subjectivity.

In the final chapter, I will attempt to situate Blanchot in the context of contemporary French critical theory by drawing some parallels between his thought and that of some of the leading figures of poststructuralism. More precisely, I hope to show how Blanchot's work and his theorizations of reading and writing can be said to emerge from within the postmodern condition as it is outlined by Jean-François Lyotard. I will also demonstrate how Blanchot heeds Nietzsche's call to overthrow Platonism, and I will compare Blanchot's critique of representation with those of Gilles Deleuze and Jean Baudrillard, specifically in connection with their respective discussions of the simulacrum. And, finally, I will entertain the notion that Blanchot's meditations on language and literature have contributed in a significant way to the analyses of discursive practices and power/knowledge networks pursued by Michel Foucault and to the elaboration of a deconstructive practice of reading espoused by Jacques Derrida.

Stated as succinctly as possible, the objective of this study is to ascertain how Blanchot's fiction constitutes a *mise en oeuvre* of the concerns he treats in his criticism. My overall approach is thus organized with respect to a fundamental opposition that makes a distinction between theory and practice. Although Blanchot's oeuvre taken as a whole is a hybrid corpus that lends itself to such an approach, to resort to this distinction is not without its problems, and before proceeding any further, some consideration of the validity of this opposition and of the way in which I make use of it is in order.

What is problematic about the theory/practice opposition is its fundamental undecidability as far as the ordering of the two terms with respect to each other is concerned. The ultimately unanswerable question as to which term has priority over the other places us squarely on the terrain inhabited by the age-old rivalry between two ways of knowing, art and philosophy. One perfectly reasonable point of view places practice above theory. To take a prosaic example, this logic underlies the proverbial saying: "Those who can't do teach." For a literary context, we might consider what Baudelaire says about poets and critics in his essay on Richard Wagner: "Il serait prodigieux qu'un critique devînt poète, et il est impossible qu'un poète ne contienne pas un critique" (1222).[8] By stating that every poet contains a critic and that poets make the best critics, he sets up an order of priority. Put a slightly different way, this ordering privileges the work of literature, the primary text, over the secondary, derivative activity of criticism. This model serves as the basis for Biblical exegesis, in which the relationship of the sacred text to commentaries of it is a consequence of another hierarchical ordering, the priority of the living word of God over its transcription in the sacred text.

The case can be made just as persuasively, however, for the opposite point of view, whereby theory has precedence over and even renders possible practice. This position owes much of its prestige to Kant, who maintained that theoretical knowledge was superior because it was achieved by a rigorous application of pure reason which was objective, disinterested, and unhindered by essentially irrelevant problems that sometimes crop up at the local level when attempts are made to put hard-won theoretical insights into practice. Baudelaire's statement about poets and critics applies here as well. After all, he insists that every poet does contain a critic, and he cannot conceive of a good poet who would be bereft of the critical faculty which plays an indispensable role in creative activity. It is certainly safe to assume that a creative writer does not inhabit a realm that excludes considerations of a theoretical nature. On the contrary, he approaches the work he is about to undertake with a certain set of general assumptions about what literature is or should be, and with another set of more specific assumptions such as what the laws of the genre he is composing are. There has to be some understanding of certain fundamental rules of the game before the game can begin.

What happens when we apply this distinction governed by a law of undecidability to Blanchot? In terms of the first interpretation of the opposition, his fiction, the creative writing of texts of his own, would provide him with a direct, unmediated experience of literature itself, and his criticism, the reading of works of others, would constitute an indirect, mediating analysis of this experience. In this instance, the experience of the composition of the work is elevated above that of the critical moment, which can only approximate retrospectively the intensity of the moment of creative inspiration.

It could also be argued that Blanchot's theory has precedence over his fiction. *L'Espace littéraire*, for example, is full of authoritative, self-adjudicating claims as to what true literature is, how literary language works, and what goes on during the activities of reading and writing. If this book constitutes a metadiscursive laying down of the laws that regulate the space of literature, his fiction can be seen as a series of experiments in which he attempts to create a new form of writing informed by an earlier theoretical meditation on what such art should entail.

Thus, both of the propositions contained in the reversible opposition of theory and practice hold true for Blanchot. Either the critical appraisal comes second and never measures up to the more immediate experience of the writer's encounter with the origin of his work that he tries to communicate, or the work, on the contrary, runs the risk of not being able to measure up to its theoretical origins. This undecidability can be articulated in terms of the setting up and the crossing of limits. According to the first proposition, the work of art is its own law; it exists on its own terms. The critical gaze that seeks to lay bare the secret internal functioning of the text would thus violate the work's integrity by not letting it be on its own terms, by forcing it to comply with a certain set of assumptions that orients the critical enquiry. If we assume, however, in accordance with the second proposition, that his critical texts correspond to the law, his fiction would constitute transgressions of the law, practical applications that fail to live up to the vision of literature that is more fully developed in the theoretical project. Blanchot's theory of the *noli me legere* provides us with an example of this quandary in condensed form. This law proclaims the inviolable sovereignty of the work, its stubborn resistance to appropriation by author and reader alike. Moreover, this law is codified in *L'Espace littéraire*, a corpus of laws (the second interpretation of the theory/practice opposition) dedicated to the proposition that the work is not subject to any laws that it does not initiate itself (the first interpretation of the opposition).

What Blanchot himself does not do is to maintain this opposition in order to claim a victory of the one over the other, a gesture accomplished by Hegel for whom art was a thing of the past, obsolete when compared to the prospect of absolute knowledge held out by philosophy. Nor is he a metasubject who moves carefreely from the one activity to the other, maintaining a position of mastery over each all the while. His literary history has projected him toward the writing of fragmentary books which escape generic classification and have the effect of erasing the boundaries traditionally thought to separate these activities into two clearly defined disciplines. Rather than being engaged in a dialectical struggle directed toward some future synthesis, creative writing and critical reading exist for Blanchot in a transgressive rapport of unarrestable circularity which undermines the pretensions of each to supremacy. The speech of passivity and worklessness always returns to undo the accomplishments of the transitive language of negativity both in his criticism *and* his fiction. This is so because Blanchot describes the scene of writing as an ontological domain in which the exigencies of impersonality, worklessness, and failure precede and condition the emergence of a subject capable of mastery and accomplishment in the regional economy of writing as power. Thus, it is more accurate to speak of the hybrid nature of each of Blanchot's works—whether narrative, critical, or fragmentary—rather than of the hybrid nature of his oeuvre taken in its entirety.

This incessant, circular movement of the setting up and tearing down of limits which takes place not only *between* the activities of creation and criticism but *within* these activities is precisely what I hope to delineate in this study. In so doing, I have adopted an attitude with respect to the theory/practice opposition which can be described as "strategic" in the way that David Carroll uses this word in his account of the relationship of mutual contamination that exists between the language of literature and that of philosophy:

> In this process of mutual transformation and subversion, there is really no reliable perspective on the question of the relationship of the various elements. No perspective or positioning can be considered to be more than strategic, a part of the conflict of forces and shifting boundaries between entities with no one perspective or position dominating the field. (*Paraesthetics*, 20)

The task that I have set for myself is to act as a mediator and to arrange a dialogue between his critical and narrative voices. I must, therefore, confess to leading Blanchot into temptation repeatedly, every time I induce him to violate his principle of the *noli me legere*, by using his critical texts to illuminate his narrative works. I am guilty of forcing him to read his own works, something that he has always claimed impossible to do and yet inevitably undertaken. Thus, readers ought to be aware that their decision to enter into the confines of this book will implicate them in the committing of a transgressive act. This is not an inappropriate pose to assume, however, when approaching the work of a writer for whom the essence of literature is expressed in the ancient story of another transgressor, the archetypal figure of the (post)modern writer, Orpheus.

ONE

LITERATURE AND TRANSGRESSION

IN AN autobiographical sketch written in 1958, Georges Bataille states in one brief sentence the event of 1940 that stands out for him the most (he speaks of himself in the third person): "Dès la fin de 1940, il rencontre Maurice Blanchot, auquel le lient sans tarder l'admiration et l'accord" (*Oeuvres complètes* VII: 462).[1] The friendship that developed between these two men over the next twenty years can be traced in the writings of each during this period. The role that Bataille accorded Blanchot in *L'Expérience intérieure*, the homage to Bataille that Blanchot placed at the end of *L'Amitié*, and their collaboration at *Critique* provide just a few examples of their intellectual affinities. According to Vincent Descombes, what the two share above all in their respective meditations on the human condition is the conviction that "the present 'discontent within civilization,' as Freudians say, is a symptom whose meaning is disclosed in the perspective of a discourse upon universal history, and not, as for Freud and his disciples, in one of familial psychology" (175–76).

The positions of both thinkers with respect to the sense of history are animated by a genuine attraction to certain concepts contained in the philosophy of Hegel and by a rejection of others. The most important notions that receive their critical attention are death, negativity, and the end of history. Hegel assimilates death to negation, the driving force behind the historical process of becoming, and treats it as the limit within which we all strive, the ultimate human horizon which is the source of our activity, mastery, and accomplishments. As Edgar Morin states, "Mort, Finitude, Détermination, Négativité, sont étroitement associées dans une philosophie rationnelle du devenir, où l'affirmation et la destruction du particulier fondent sans cesse un universel qui se réalise dans le mouvement même" (285).[2] Death motivates us to accomplish tasks and to gain mastery over the world in which we live. Christian theology justifies the presence of suffering and death in the world as necessary counterparts of redemption; the trials and tribulations that humankind must endure as a result of the fall carry hidden within them the promise of eternal life. Hegel's end of history, on the other hand, offers the prospect of totalization, the crowning achievement of the power of the negative. Whereas we do not accede to a state of immortality in a realm outside the world, we do arrive at a nonadversarial rapport with ourselves and nature. Alexandre Kojève, whose lectures on Hegel at the École pratique des hautes études between 1933 and 1939 had a profound influence on an entire generation of French intellectuals,[3] describes the scenario that awaits Hegel's last man at the end of history:

> Absolute knowledge, that is, Wisdom, presupposes the total success of Man's Negative Action. This Knowledge is possible only (1) within a *homogeneous* and *universal* State where no man is *exterior* to another, where there is no social *opposition* which is not suppressed, and (2) in the midst of a Nature that has been *tamed* by the labour of Man, and which, no longer *opposing* man, ceases to be *alien* to him. (Quoted by Descombes in his *Modern French Philosophy*, 28)

Hegel's view of history as a dialectical process that would culminate in the reconciliation of the subject/worker with the object/world is problematical for Bataille and Blanchot. They propose a different version of the end of history which originates in a reappraisal of death and negativity and a rejection of the notion that death can be totally assimilated to the power of constructive negativity. Man's ability to accede to the realm of the absolute would consist, says Blanchot, in his "pouvoir d'exercer totalement, c'est-à-dire de *transformer en action* toute sa négativité" (*EI* 304).[4] What becomes of the power of the negative, assuming that totalization has been accomplished? Is it used up entirely, "transformed into action" completely, after which it disappears? This very question prompted Bataille to write a letter to Kojève in 1937 in which he states:

> si l'action (le "faire") est—comme dit Hegel—la négativité, la question se pose alors de savoir si la négativité de qui n'a "plus rien à faire" disparaît ou subsiste à l'état de "négativité sans emploi": personnellement, je ne puis décider que dans un sens, étant moi-même exactement cette "négativité sans emploi" (je ne pourrais me définir de façon plus précise). (*Oeuvres complètes* V: 369)[5]

Bataille maintains that there is a dimension of negativity that persists in the wake of totalization, a useless remainder (a "part maudite") that serves no purpose once all there is to be accomplished has been accomplished through acts of power. Moreover, the surplus negativity forces open Hegel's model of history predicated on closure. The idea that we are incapable of investing all our negativity in constructive activity stems from an investigation into the act of dying itself. By reducing death to a concept that serves our desire for power and mastery, we lose the other, unthinkable side of death. Blanchot designates the characterization of death as a function of a historical process toward totalization as a "subterfuge" (*EI* 49); it cannot conceal the fact that the essence of death is to be found in its incompletion. There is a dimension to death that escapes our ability to mobilize it as an instrument of negativity. In the end, one who dies is powerless to do anything else except to wait passively for death's approach. In *Le Coupable*, Bataille expresses the dilemma: "La conscience est la condition de la mort achevée. Je meurs dans la mesure où j'ai conscience de mourir: cette conscience, en même temps, la mort la dérobe en moi" (*Oeuvres complètes* V: 241).[6] There is always some unfinished business whenever dying is concerned, and if the idea of death inspires anguish, it is because of the fear of being unable to die completely: consciousness is snuffed out before it has a chance to record death in its entirety. To be mortal is, therefore, to possess death as a source of possibility, but to die is to cease to be mortal, that is, to lose death as the power of the negative and to encounter it as an impossibility.

The necessity of according death a dual status led Bataille and Blanchot to modify Hegel's version of history as a dialectical process of becoming that would culminate in totalization, and in its place they propose an open-ended, repetitive, circular model of history whose movement they describe in terms of the institution and transgression of limits. Although the account of this movement has its origin in Bataille's work in his anthropologically oriented writings, it has more widespread applications: he also makes use of a much more abstract idea of transgression to describe the spiritual albeit atheistic exercise that he calls the "expérience intérieure," the adventure that awaits the final stage, humankind which cannot arrive at a state of satisfaction by transforming all its negativity into action. Furthermore, Blanchot borrows Bataille's abstract theory of transgression and utilizes it to define the rapports that form the literary economy of author, text, and reader. I will now delineate briefly Bataille's theory of transgression, and in so doing, I hope to show how the meaning of the term evolves as it moves from the context of his anthropological observations to that of Blanchot's presentation of the approach to the space of literature by a writer and a reader.

The points in Bataille's texts where constructive negativity, excess negativity, and transgression converge are his discussions of sacrifice. He considers the ritualistic performance of sacrifice to be the transgressive act par excellence. His characterization of it as "une rupture de la règle accordée par la règle" (*Oeuvres complètes* VIII: 108)[7] reveals the ambivalent nature of prohibitions: they not only establish limits that are to be respected but also make provisions for these limits to be violated under special circumstances. "L'interdit est là pour être violé" (72), he writes in *L'Erotisme*,[8] and in *La Littérature et le mal*, he states that "l'interdit n'en est pas moins une invite, en même temps qu'un obstacle" (21).[9] The sacrifice, which is authorized at periodic intervals when the prohibition of murder is temporarily lifted, is a perfect example of a legal crime. Bataille emphasizes the relationship of concealed solidarity between the law and its violation: the institution of a limit participates in the very violence it purports to do away with. He subscribes to the definition of sacrifice put forth by his mentors Hubert and Mauss as a procedure that consists "in establishing a means of communication between the sacred and profane worlds through the mediation of a victim, that is, of a thing that in the course of the ceremony is destroyed" (97). Prohibitions which regulate the interaction between the sacred and profane spheres of existence are ambivalent because of the fundamental ambiguity that resides at the heart of the sacred: it both attracts and repels, inspires love and horror. Hubert and Mauss consequently divide sacrifices into two categories. There are, first, sacrifices of communion by means of which the community seeks to assimilate the salutary qualities of the sacred. The purpose of sacrifices of expiation, the second type, is to purify the community by ridding it of sickness, death, malediction, or other unwanted, threatening impurities. In his examinations of primitive societies, Bataille remarks that the profane sphere of life governed in accordance with the exigencies of production, conservation and growth (the regional economy) could not thrive indefinitely on its own and that periodic violations of these principles during religious festivals (the general economy of worklessness and expenditure) are necessary so that it can reassert itself with renewed strength. Thus although transgressive behavior involves a disregard for the rules that are responsible for the smooth functioning of the regional economy, the infractions are tolerated only insofar as they stimulate and revive this economy. No transgression is ever complete; the law always survives the infraction because the latter is in the service of the former. Bataille explains the subordination of transgression to the law by saying that "c'est une aspiration à la destruction qui éclate dans la fête, mais c'est une sagesse conservatrice qui l'ordonne et la limite" (*Oeuvres complètes* VII: 313).[10]

As far as the particular transgression of sacrifice is concerned, a gift is offered by the worshipers to the divine, but it is not an act of purely disinterested giving; it is more like a bribe, and something is expected in return. Roger Caillois explains the contractual nature of sacrifices in *L'Homme et le sacré*: "Par le sacrifice, le fidèle s'en est fait le créancier, il attend que les puissances qu'il révère s'acquittent en exauçant ses voeux de la dette qu'elles ont contractée à son égard" (28–29).[11] Given Bataille's position regarding the dual status of death, however, it is impossible for him to view sacrifice solely in terms of an act of negativity subordinated to the well-being of the profane world of productive activity. One of the principal functions of sacrifices of communion is a prophetic one. The submission of the victim on the altar (in the case of human sacrifices) affords the other members of the community the opportunity to have a vicarious experience of death. The victim's example as the chosen one serves as an initiation to death and an illumination regarding their destiny as mortals. By witnessing the death of one of their own, the members of the community can have a different view of death from the one they would have on their own deathbeds. The sacrifice thus might be a way to overcome the dilemma of achieving a more complete consciousness of death, at least as far as the onlooking survivors are concerned. The ritualistic offices of the ceremony combined with the sympathetic identification of the witnesses with the victim conspire to give the witnesses a simulacrum of what the victim's and thus their own death might be like, and at the same time they survive, which enables them to take into account what has just transpired. In "Hegel, la mort et le sacrifice," Bataille states:

> In sacrifice, the sacrificer identifies with the animal struck by death. Thus he dies while watching himself die, and even, after a fashion, dies of his own volition, as one with the sacrificial arm. . . . Thus it is necessary, at any cost, for man to live at the moment when he truly dies, or it is necessary for him to live with the impression of truly dying. (Quoted by Derrida in *Writing and Difference*, 257–58)

Since the very nature of the sacrifice excludes the first option—the victim cannot live on at the moment of his death—the second option is the next best thing: to live on while having the impression of having died. The spectacle of the sacrifice gives the members of the community the impression of experiencing a death that is and is not their own. It is theirs to the extent that as survivors, their consciousness of the event will not be cut short by the consummation of the act. The insurmountable paradox inherent in sacrifice, however, is that it is not what it is; it does and at the same time does not accomplish what it promises. The immolation of the victim is surely complete, but personal appropriation of this death, whether by the victim or the surviving witnesses, is just as surely not complete. The potential for identification between the victim, the sacrificer, and the rest of the community resides in the principle of interchangeability. Theoretically any member of the community can assume either the role of sacred executioner or that of victim. The most extreme attempt to achieve a rapport of identification would require the concomitant death of the sacrificer, an absurd situation that Blanchot describes as "l'impossibilité de la mort dans sa possibilité la plus nue (le couteau pour trancher la gorge de la victime qui tranchait dans le même mouvement la tête du 'bourreau')" (*CA* 29).[12]

This impasse led Bataille to reconsider his views on sacrifice and eventually to reject the notion of community as fraternity founded on the concept of the members' "fusional assumption in some collective hypostasis" (Nancy 14). He abandoned the Rousseauistic position of one who nostalgically regretted the irrevocable loss of a community of presence in favor of the idea of a community based on the finitude of its members, not on their belief in the resurrectional powers of death thanks to which absolute immanence could be attained in a spiritual beyond. Sacrifice must be considered as unsuccessful in trying to bridge the gap between two worlds and to mediate the transition from life to death. What is supposedly an act of negativity, the systematic destruction of a victim, is in fact a transgression that fails to have mastery over death by rendering it personal, present, and possible.

It is precisely Bataille's approach to the question of the usefulness of sacrifice which signals the shift that this notion undergoes as it moves from the anthropological context to the abstract philosophical context of his "expérience."[13] It is the latter version of sacrifice and transgression that Blanchot takes over to describe the activities of writing and reading. The terms that Bataille uses to speak of sacrifice and transgression remain the same in both contexts. What differs is the emphasis he places on these terms. For example, in both situations he accords sacrifice the status of a failure, which has derogatory connotations as far as the anthropological presentation of the regional economy of power is concerned, based as it is on the successful completion of projects. In his philosophical use of the word, on the contrary, failure is a virtue. Far from being a reproach, failure is the primary exigency of transgression. Furthermore, Bataille's use of the expressions "regional economy" and "general economy" indicates what his priorities are. Rather than to subordinate transgression to the law, whereby illicit activities are tolerated only because they serve to strengthen the law, he makes of transgression the *general* economy, which precedes in essence and renders possible the regional economy. The general economy has ontological priority over the regional economy, which is a restricted instance of the former. To transgress limits is to enter a domain where power and mastery cease to be primary exigencies: this is the lesson that Bataille's meditations on sacrifice taught him. In "L'Expérience-limite," Blanchot explains this aspect of the abstract notion of transgression:

> *L'interdit marque le point où cesse le pouvoir*. La transgression n'est pas un acte dont, dans certaines conditions, la puissance de certains hommes et leur maîtrise se montreraient encore capable. Elle désigne ce qui est radicalement hors de portée: l'atteinte de l'inaccessible, le franchissement de l'infranchissable. Elle s'ouvre à l'homme lorsqu'en celui-ci, le pouvoir cesse d'être la dimension ultime. (*EI* 308)[14]

To transgress is to lose death as negativity, the source of power and mastery, and to encounter it as an impossibility. In addition, the approach to/of *le mourir* once the limits have been crossed involves a loss of personalized subjectivity:

"je" n'y parvient jamais, ni l'individu que je suis, cette particule de
poussière, ni le moi de tous qui est censé représenter la conscience absolue
de soi: mais seule l'ignorance qu'incarnerait le Je-qui-meurs en accédant à
cet espace où, mourant, il ne meurt jamais comme "Je", en première personne. (*EI* 311)[15]

Returning for a moment to the anthropological context, Bataille makes
the point that the subjects engaged in transgressive behavior during religious festivals undergo the same kind of dispossession of individualized
consciousness. In *Théorie de la religion*, he writes: "Il n'y a pas conscience
claire de ce qu'est *actuellement* la fête (de ce qu'elle est dans l'instant de
son déchaînement) et la fête n'est distinctement située dans la conscience
qu'intégrée dans la durée de la communauté" (*Oeuvres complètes* VII:
315).[16] Because of its involvement with the general economy, interiority
is transformed into an impersonal spontaneity which is not a self-identical
entity. Just as the significance of the events of the feast can only be partially assimilated into consciousness retrospectively, after the restoration
of limits, the notion of a self-coincident subject is an aftereffect produced
by interiority's desire to return to a point prior to its dispossession and to
regain what it lost in transgression. The integral subject of intentionality
is a restricted instance of consciousness that is at home in the regional
economy. It is merely one way—not the privileged one—that consciousness has of manifesting itself.

To transgress the law of the regional economy (the proposition that
death is constructive negativity and nothing else) is to embrace death as
an impossibility and to adhere to the very different "law" of the general
economy (the principles of expenditure, worklessness, failure, and loss of
the primacy of the subject). The law of the general economy, however,
does not remain in force forever, and it demands in turn to be transgressed, the consequence of which is the restitution of the law of the regional economy, which will inevitably be transgressed at some later time.

Transgression begins the moment that "power ceases to be the ultimate dimension," and what Blanchot says about writing a work of literature, that "l'oeuvre n'est jamais ce en vue de quoi l'on peut écrire (en vue
de quoi l'on se rapporterait à ce qui s'écrit comme à l'exercice d'un
pouvoir" (*EL*, 16),[17] can also be said of reading: it cannot be conceived
as an act of power. If the practice of literature is an endeavor that Blanchot privileges above all others, it is because nowhere else does the dual
status of death manifest itself so insistently. A book does possess a dimension of negativity whose impact in the world can be likened to that of
more direct forms of action: "Le livre, chose écrite, entre dans le monde
où il accomplit son oeuvre de transformation et de négation" (*PF* 305).[18]
And yet there is a dimension of the literary work that escapes any such

determination on account of the surplus negativity it carries within it, "l'entêtement de ce qui subsiste quand tout s'efface et l'hébétude de ce qui apparaît quand il n'y a rien" (*PF* 317).[19] What literature and sacrifice have in common is that they are both fictive approaches to death, and the drama that they reenact is an encounter with death whose primary exigency is not mastery but rather passive indecision.

Blanchot refuses to stop short at the reassuring view of death, and his literary effort is comprised to a large degree of the tearing away of the consoling illusions that culture has erected around death which allow us *not* to see death as it really is, as "ce qui n'arrive jamais à moi, de sorte que jamais je ne meurs, mais 'on meurt', on meurt toujours autre que soi, au niveau de la neutralité, de l'impersonnalité d'un Il éternel" (*EL* 327).[20] The role that Blanchot ascribes to culture is that of a massive cover-up: "Rendre à la mort une sorte de pureté a toujours été la tâche de la culture: la rendre authentique, personnelle, propre ou encore la rendre possible" (*EI* 269),[21] a task to which he is diametrically opposed. The purity that culture wants to find in death is, for Blanchot, an adulteration. Ironically, it is he who arrives at a purer, more complete notion of death by restoring to it its impurities, by insisting on the anonymous, noneventful character of what he calls *le mourir*, his formulation of Bataille's unemployable negativity. The function that he assigns to literature is, therefore, profoundly anticultural: to render death inauthentic, impersonal, and impossible, probably the most subversive moment of Blanchot's text. Art embodies the dual status of death, and literature is the one art in particular where this duplicity is the most evident. Why does literature have this dubious distinction? Because of the stuff it is made of, words.

TWO

LANGUAGE, HISTORY, AND THEIR

DESTINIES OF INCOMPLETION

BLANCHOT'S theory of language is informed principally by Mallarmé, who in "Crise de vers" divides linguistic activity into two domains, the *parole brute* and the *parole essentielle*. Use of the *parole brute* is comparable to exchanging money in the marketplace. It disappears after having served its purpose. It is thus the *result* of the exchange that is important and not the way in which the exchange is carried out. The *parole essentielle*, on the other hand, is strictly literary. Whereas the *parole brute* is uttered in view of accomplishing a transaction, the *parole essentielle* is not predetermined by any particular function to perform. The accent is placed on the way in which something is said and not on what is said. Poetic naming is different in another way as well: it does not fade into the result that it might provoke; it remains. What does disappear is the object that is named:

> Le mot n'a de sens que s'il nous débarrasse de l'objet qu'il nomme: il doit nous en épargner la présence ou "le concret rappel". Dans le langage authentique, la parole a une fonction, non seulement représentative mais destructive. Elle fait *disparaître*, elle rend l'objet absent, elle l'annihile. (*PF* 37)[1]

Nonliterary, everyday language participates in this destructive violence, but it differs from literary language by disappearing into the idea it evokes. The literary *parole* annihilates the object that it names and represents its absence in the form of an idea, but it does not end there; it does not dissolve completely into the meanings it creates. It becomes itself a thing and acquires the same dense, opaque materiality that any other object in the world has, "comme si les mots, loin de nous détourner des choses, devaient en être le décalque matériel: la sensualité du langage ici l'emporte et le mot rêve de s'unir aux objets dont il a le poids, la couleur, l'aspect lourd et dormant" (*PF* 45).[2] Literary language both creates an ideal absence (signification) and subsists as material presence (the rhythmical and sonorous qualities of words, the ink and paper of the book they are printed on). Poetic naming thus involves an oscillating movement between presence and absence. There is, first, the presence of an absence as the idea stands in for the nullified thing. This is followed by the absence of this presence as the idea becomes obscured by the materiality of language which seems to come to the aid of the thing that was destroyed by naming in the first place. The third stage of what Blanchot calls the "triple existence" of the literary *parole* again involves the presence of an absence, the appearance of a disappearance, but this time when the poem as a whole is considered. There is the physical presence of the printed poem on the page, but the movement of the poem, the succession of its images, suggests that it tends to its own extinction, an idea which is reflected by Mallarmé's obsession with the notion that poetry is the vain attempt of language to achieve silence and by his interest in the blank page, spaces, and margins as emblematic representations of silence.

Poetry is essentially an art of mobility, and the transition from one figure to the next that the reader of a Mallarmé poem experiences points more to the absence of an overall, grounding image than to the presence of one: "Non seulement, les figures sont raccourcies, placées de biais, diffuses, mais elles se succèdent selon un rythme assez rapide pour qu'aucune ne laisse à la réalité qu'elle circonscrit le temps d'exister, de nous devenir présente par son intermédiaire" (*PF* 40).[3] If a poem is the hovering back and forth between the ideal presence of the absent thing and the material presence of this ideal absence, what we have in the end is "une absence de mots et une absence de choses, un vide simultané, rien soutenu par rien" (*PF* 55).[4] In short, because each word is "un monstre à deux faces, réalité qui est présence matérielle et sens qui est absence idéale" (*PF* 328),[5] Blanchot defines the threefold existence of literary language as

> la poursuite sans relâche par laquelle les mots, grâce à leur valeur abstraite, détruisent la matérialité des choses, puis, grâce à leur puissance d'évocation sensible, détruisent cette valeur abstraite, et enfin, par leur mobilité, leur capacité de suspens, tentent de se volitaliser, de s'éteindre eux-mêmes derrière la réciprocité de leurs feux. (*PF* 70)[6]

It is worth noting that the source for this presentation of Blanchot's theory of language has been *La Part du feu*, and although the distinction between *parole brute* and *parole essentielle* is a constant in his theoretical vocabulary over the years, it is without a doubt in this particular book that he develops his theory of "la langue meurtrière" the most consistently, notably in the second essay on Kafka, the essay on Mallarmé, the two essays devoted to Jean Paulhan, and, of course, in "La littérature et le droit à la mort." "Le mystère dans les lettres" marks the second time that Blanchot took up problems posed by Paulhan's *Les Fleurs de Tarbes* (the first was published in *Faux pas* under the title "Comment la littérature est-elle possible?"), and his decision to borrow the title of the final section of "Quant au livre" indicates Blanchot's decidedly Mallarméan approach to these problems.

Paulhan's point of departure, too, seems to be so inspired: his distinction between Terror and Rhetoric sounds very much like Mallarmé's between the *parole brute* and the *parole essentielle*. The Terrorist position with regard to language that Paulhan deplores resembles Mallarmé's *parole brute* in that Terrorists consider language to be in the service of thought. Language's function, according to this view, is to communicate as faithfully as possible ideas or states of mind. Just as the *parole brute* disappears into the accomplishment of an act it was called on to perform, Terrorists strive for a transparent language whose words do not get in the way of what they are trying to express. They are fully aware, however, that words often *do* get in the way, that they are not always faithful servants of ideas, and the panic that they have unleashed in the garden of Letters contains the warning the language is not to be trusted. Terrorists spread the fear that language possesses treacherous powers, for instead of adhering faithfully to an idea they are supposed to express, "certains mots," as Paulhan observes in *Les Fleurs de Tarbes*, "trahissent une hypertrophie, aux dépens de l'idée, de la matière et du langage" (*Oeuvres complètes* III: 44).[7] The Terrorist writer is not on good terms with language, which is for Paulhan the chief characteristic of Terror. He explains the two points on which the perspective of the Terrorist rests:

> L'un est que la Terreur admet couramment que l'idée *vaut mieux* que le mot et l'esprit que la matière: il y a de l'un à l'autre différence de dignité, non moins que de nature. Telle est sa foi, et, si l'on aime mieux, son préjugé. Le second porte que le langage est essentiellement dangereux pour la pensée: toujours prêt à l'opprimer, si l'on n'y veille. La définition la plus simple que l'on puisse donner du Terroriste, c'est qu'il est *misologue*. (*Oeuvres complètes* III: 41)[8]

The Rhetorician is, on the contrary, a *philologue*. Instead of privileging the "pure" idea over potentially deforming linguistic expressions of it, he considers the materiality of language, the elements of language that serve to draw our attention to it and, therefore, to keep it from fading discreetly away into ideas, to be a source of thought rather than an obstacle to sincerity. In a word, logocentric Terrorists long for a language in which "le matériel verbal s'efface devant les idées ou les faits, se laisse aussitôt oublier,"[9] whereas the Rhetorician, the practitioner of what will later come to be called *écriture*, is in his element when "les mots ne se laissent point résorber, mais demeurent inséparables de l'état d'esprit qu'ils évoquent" (*Petite préface à toute critique* in *Oeuvres complètes* II: 281).[10]

Paulhan's distinction between Terror and Rhetoric led him up many a blind alley to some insurmountable paradoxes, one of the most telling of which he expressed in this proverbial, appropriately clichéd form (appropriate since Terrorists regarded clichés as unoriginal, insincere and thus inauthentic forms of expression on account of their repeatability): "Pensée d'auteur, mots de lecteur; mots d'auteur, pensée de lecteur" (*Oeuvres complètes* III: 65). The first half of this chiasmic formula states that for every author who is supposedly interested first and foremost in communicating thoughts and ideas, there is a reader who will be struck first and foremost by the style. A glaring example is philosophical writing. Who is concerned with transmitting ideas more than a philosopher, and yet what texts tend to be more obscure because of what a reader takes to be their excessive verbalism? The second half of the proverb says that the inverse is true as well: that for every author whose primary concern is form (a Valéry, for example, according to whom content was merely impure form) is a reader who wants to get to the heart of the themes and ideas in the text. This is the kind of self-contradiction that Blanchot delights in exposing, one more manifestation of what he calls the impropriety of literature.

What separates Blanchot and Paulhan, however, is that Blanchot places the impropriety at the *origin* of literature. Paulhan, on the other hand, uses the division of the word into its two elements, idea and matter, in an *a posteriori* analysis which isolates these two features of language which nevertheless cannot be considered as existing independently of each other. In his critique of Paulhan, Blanchot suggests that problems arise because Paulhan's dialectic is conceived after the fact of the existence of language, as one of its consequences. The problem is with analysis itself, for by dividing language into two components, idea and matter, and literary activity into two camps, Terror and Rhetoric, "il s'agit de composants qu'on isole momentanément pour les besoins de l'exposé analytique, mais qui n'existent pas isolés en dehors de cette analyse et qui ne sont donc justifiés à se rendre distincts que dans les limites de l'analyse" (*PF* 61–62).[11] Paulhan's problems arise because his opposition between Terror and Rhetoric does not hold up. It cannot, for as he plainly realized, no writer is either a complete Terrorist or a complete Rhetorician; the two tendencies inevitably interact. Blanchot overcomes the difficulty by strategically placing this play of differences at the origin of language, and in so doing, he is able to make a puzzling claim, one that runs contrary to popular opinion, that poetic language precedes everyday language: "En d'autres mots, dans la poésie, seule existe la tension qui unit les termes [idea and material form], et ces termes n'y sont distincts qu'en apparence et d'un point de vue postérieur, du point de vue du langage ordinaire qui, lui-même, s'est constitué à partir de la poésie" (*PF* 57).[12]

Thus, according to Blanchot, who follows Heidegger on this point, poetic language has ontological priority over everyday language. Poetry, viewed as the incessant movement back and forth between idea and matter, sense and sound, makes possible everyday language, in which this movement is arrested by common accord in the interest of getting things done. What counts in the poetic use of language is the relationship between these two terms, whereas the use of conventional language necessitates the suppression of one of the terms, the physical aspects of words, in favor of the other, meanings that are agreed upon in advance for the sake of accomplishing tasks. The relationship of the two terms preexists the decision to privilege the single term of signification. Poetry is, therefore, a neutral stage of language which provides for subsequent production of meaning.

By giving precedence to poetic language over ordinary language, Blanchot once again flouts the evidence proposed by common sense: that the poet is one who "par don ou par savoir faire créateur, se contenterait de faire passer le langage 'brut ou immédiat' au langage essentiel" (*EL* 47).[13] The poet does not start with the raw materials of conventional language and somehow, whether by talent, inspiration, or hard work, elevate it to the status of sublime art. The world of means and ends is not his starting point, and art does not come from the world. On the contrary, art expresses "des rapports qui précèdent tout accomplissement objectif et technique" (*LV* 288)[14] in the world. That poetic language precedes ordinary language is a corollary to the broader reversal that Blanchot effects on the commonly held view regarding the object and its image: "D'après l'analyse commune, l'image est après l'objet: elle en est la suite; nous voyons, puis nous imaginons. Après l'objet vient l'image. 'Apres' semble indiquer un rapport de subordination . . . Mais peut-être l'analyse commune se trompe-t-elle" (*EL* 28).[15] Blanchot proposes an aesthetics that rests on the opposite view. In the beginning is not the object which is subsequently represented in the form of an image. The object is not a purely integral original whose wholeness is compromised by reproductions of varying degrees of perfection. The object, on the contrary, is in excess over its own closure. It has the capacity to double itself, and the possibility of making copies is a consequence of this doubling. The splitting of an object into any number of imaginary representatives is not the result of an act of power but rather precedes and renders such an act possible. The image of the general economy is prior to the intramundane object of the regional economy; it is "le dédoublement initial qui permet à la chose d'être figurée" (*EI* 42).[16] The distance between the object and its representation is not the aftereffect of an intentional act; "l'éloignement est ici au coeur de la chose" (*EL* 347).[17]

Poetry precedes ordinary language because it is the inextrication of two components, one of which is privileged in everyday discourse. In a similar way, the image, the inextrication of both the original being of the object and possible useful applications of it, is ontologically prior to the object. On this subject, Blanchot's thinking resembles that of Heidegger in the latter's comparison of art and failed equipment in his essay "The Origin of the Work of Art." What works of art and broken tools have in common is their capacity to disclose the original being of things which has been covered up by their having been adapted to perform particular functions:

> Par analogie, on peut aussi rappeler qu'un ustensile, endommagé, devient son *image* . . . Dans ce cas, l'ustensile, ne disparaissant plus dans son usage, *apparaît*. Cette apparence de l'objet est celle de la ressemblance et du reflet: si l'on veut, son double. La catégorie de l'art est liée à cette possibilité pour les objets d'"apparaître", c'est-à-dire de s'abandonner à la pure et simple ressemblance derrière laquelle il n'y a rien—que l'être. (*EL* 352)[18]

Whereas Heidegger's later philosophy celebrates poetic language's powers of ontological revelation, it is more correct, in Blanchot's case, to speak of *ressemblance*, the duplicity of revelation in which "ce qui se révèle ne se livre pas à la vue, tout en ne se réfugiant pas dans la simple invisibilité" (*EI* 41).[19] Disclosure of being occurs neither as a visible, light-filled presence nor as an invisible absence of light. Being appears rather as the presence of an absence, what Emmanuel Levinas has designated as the *il y a*, the phenomenon of impersonal, anonymous being, an uneliminable moment of existence which is not conditioned by the negative: "Quelque chose qu'on peut ressentir quand on pense que même s'il n'y avait rien, le fait qu"il y a' n'est pas niable. Non qu'il y ait ceci ou cela, mais la scène même de l'être est ouverte: il y a" (*Ethique et infini*, 46).[20] In *De l'existence à l'existant* Levinas analyzes certain modes of existence—fatigue, laziness, insomnia—in which individualized consciousness is dispossessed by the incumbency of the *il y a*. Whereas deliverance from the ubiquitous *il y a* appeared to him in the form of an ethics, Blanchot insists on the impossibility of escaping it, and instead of being a diversion that lets us avoid encounters with the *il y a*, art leads us directly to it. In perhaps no other text is the link between art and the *il y a* more apparent than in his essay "Les deux versions de l'imaginaire," in which he likens images, the principal resource of art, to cadavers.

Blanchot defines the image as "ce qui nous est donné par un contact à distance" (*EL* 25).[21] Visual perception seems to put us in direct contact with the image, to eliminate the distance that separates us from it, although it is this very interval that constitutes and renders possible our contact with it. The image appears to be close at hand and someplace else at the same time. Cadavers share the same quality of both being and not being there:

> Ce qui est là, dans le calme absolu de ce qui a trouvé son lieu, ne réalise pourtant pas la vérité d'être pleinement ici. La mort suspend la relation avec le lieu, bien que le mort s'y appuie pesamment comme la seule base qui lui reste. Justement, cette base manque, le lieu est en défaut, le cadavre n'est pas à sa place. Où est-il? Il n'est pas ici et pourtant il n'est pas ailleurs; nulle part? mais c'est qu'alors nulle part est ici. La présence cadavérique établit un rapport entre ici et nulle part. (*EL* 348)[22]

The mortal remains that the dear departed left behind are present to us in the world, but the essential truth of the cadaver is that it is *not* of this world. This strangeness is overshadowed initially by the grief of the mourners who react emotionally to their sense of loss. Once sorrow has run its course, however, once the mourners come face to face with the fact that no human relationship with the departed is possible any longer, the strange, other-worldly inaccessibility of the cadaver makes itself felt in a most unusual way: it begins to resemble itself. It is commonplace at funerals to hear people remark "how good the body looks," a comment that attests to the resemblance achieved, thanks to the painstaking efforts of the undertaker, between the appearance of the corpse and that of the person when he was alive. Once again Blanchot does not exactly refute common belief, but by saying that the cadaver resembles *itself*, he ironically gives ontological priority to the corpse over the living person in a move consistent with his declaration that poetry preceded ordinary language and that the image preceded the object. It is insufficient to speak merely of the likeness of the corpse to the formerly living person, for there is something more than that at work:

> Oui, c'est bien lui, le cher vivant, mais c'est tout de même plus que lui, il est plus beau, plus imposant, déjà monumental et si absolument lui-même qu'il est comme *doublé* par soi, uni à la solennelle impersonnalité de soi par la ressemblance et par l'image. Cet être de grand format, important et superbe, qui impressionne les vivants comme *l'apparition de l'original, jusque-là ignoré* [my italics] . . . peut-être rappelle-t-il, par son apparence de souveraineté, les grandes images de l'art classique. (*EL* 350–51)[23]

The proof of the precedence of poetry over everyday language and of the image over the object lies, for Blanchot, in the notion of origin as a complex interrelation of terms which is irreducible to a single, simple, self-present, self-identical entity. Poetry as the irresolvable tension between sound and idea renders practical language possible, just as the image, an initial gap or fissure at the heart of the object itself, renders possible subsequent representations of it. And by shifting the resemblance of the cadaver away from the living person to itself, Blanchot stresses the neutral, impersonal nature of its being, which appears as "original" and "previously unknown." What had been known to all was a dissimulation of this being in the form of the social identity of the deceased when this person was alive. The anonymous being of the *il y a* is disclosed when the corpse recedes into its own image, which occurs when we cease to regard it in terms of the habitual and the everyday. Its existence as a particular *étant* is neutralized and in its place is affirmed "la possibilité d'un arrière-monde, d'un retour en arrière, d'une subsistance indéfinie, indéterminée, indifférente, dont on sait seulement que la réalité humaine lorsqu'elle finit, reconstitue la présence et la proximité" (*EL* 349).[24] Certain modes of existence and art bring us into fleeting contact with the *il y a*, but for the most part it tends to manifest itself as constructive negativity: "Dans la tranquillité de la vie courante, la dissimulation se dissimule. Dans l'action, l'action véritable, celle qui est travail de l'histoire, la dissimulation tend à devenir négation" (*EL* 343–44).[25] Poetry, images, and corpses let dissimulation, "l'informe lourdeur de l'être présent dans l'absence" (*EL* 351),[26] appear as such, whereas ordinary language, objects, and living beings dissimulate this dissimulation by seeming to transform it into the action of the negative.

One's identity in the world is but a regional instance of the general economy of being of the *il y a*, which is uncovered by the example of the corpse that resembles itself. Moreover, self-resemblance precludes identity which, as a suppression of irreconcilable differences, also belongs to the regional economy of being. The cadaver is not identical to itself; it is in excess over its identity: the image/cadaver does not represent an original object/person. What it does refer to is the fissure within itself, the lack of coincidence with itself which allows for the apparition of a residue of unemployable negativity. The cadaver constitutes a neutral region anterior to manifestation but which allows for the possibility of subsequent manifestation to take place. The presence of the cadaver defines the general economy of being as "a dimension irreducible to the discretion of the here and now, of presence and absence, identity and noncontradiction. The persistence of the cadaver describes a presence of the inactual, a presence of absence, as a fundamental possibility of presence itself in the economy" (Libertson 57).

Blanchot's theory of *ressemblance* places him squarely in a direction that modern philosophy has taken in response to the challenge issued it by Nietzsche, namely, that its task should be to overthrow Platonism. Gilles Deleuze explains the motivation behind Platonism that modern thought and literature have done so much to call into question:

it has to do with selecting among the pretenders, distinguishing good and bad copies or, rather, copies (always well founded) and simulacra (always engulfed in dissimularity). It is a question of assuring the triumph of the copies over simulacra, or repressing simulacra, keeping them completely submerged, preventing them from climbing to the surface, and "insinuating themselves" everywhere. (*The Logic of Sense*, 257)

According to Deleuze's appraisal, Platonism is motivated by a desire to distinguish and discriminate: to differentiate essence from appearance, the original from the copy, good copies from bad (simulacra). The good copy differs from the bad on the question of resemblance: "the copy truly resembles something only to the degree that it resembles the Idea of that thing" (257). A copy cannot be deemed good on the basis of a superficial, exterior resemblance; it must be of an interior, spiritual nature. Plato's mistrust of copies is evident in Book X of the *Republic* when comparing creation to imitation. His schema is composed of three terms: the *eidos*, the model or manifestation of the *eidos* in the world, and copies of the model. In the example of the production of a bed, there are three creators who correspond to these terms: the divine creator of the ideal form of the bed, the carpenter, and the artist who paints a picture of the carpenter's bed. The artistic imitation is criticized on several points. Painting is an imitation of things as they appear but not as they really are. The other triad mentioned in this section by Plato, that of the user, the producer, and the imitator, indicates who is in the best position of knowing the essence of the thing. In the case of a bed, someone who has slept in it is the closest to its ideal essence. The user of the bed occupies a position superior to that of the carpenter, for such a person can advise the carpenter as to any modifications in design that might need to be made. Image makers, on the other hand, create things that are twice removed from the truth and waste time that would be better spent on making originals.

If the task of philosophy is to overthrow Platonism, the target of this attack is the hierarchical order of the original *eidos*, the good copy, and the bad copy. "So 'to reverse Platonism' means to make the simulacra rise and to affirm their rights among icons and copies" (*The Logic of Sense*, 262). This reversal involves a rethinking of the rapport that has traditionally existed between identity and difference. The Platonic approach is "to think difference from the standpoint of a previous similitude or identity" (*The Logic of Sense*, 261). The essence of the *eidos* is the Same, identical to itself, against which copies can be measured up and judged good or bad, depending on their adherence to or divergence from this perfect original. Refusing the domination of the perfect original inaugurated by Platonism, the philosophy of difference has taken just the opposite approach: "to think similitude and even identity as the product of a deep disparity" (*The Logic of Sense*, 261). If anything can be pinned down as "original," it is not an identity but rather "une disparité de fond." On this point, Blanchot's affinity with the philosophers of difference becomes abundantly clear. When he posits poetry, in which "seule existe la tension qui unit les termes" (sound and sense) as prior to everyday language, what else is he doing if not claiming the latter to be "the product of a deep disparity"? Likewise, the image *qua* "dédoublement initial" is a "disparité de fond" which allows for the ulterior possibility of identity. Blanchot's contribution to the overthrow of the hierarchical order established by the Platonic theory of mimesis is his theory of *ressemblance* which contests the idea that an original precedes the copy and that the imaginary world of the artist flows from the source of the real. As Françoise Collin explains, it is the other way around: "La réalité n'est pas antérieure à l'irréel', n'est pas plus riche que sa 'copie'; il faudrait dire qu'au contraire, c'est l'irréalité qui est première et que sur elle, le 'réel' se compose" (*Maurice Blanchot et la question de l'écriture* 174).[27]

The Platonic system of ordering which enables good copies to be distinguished from bad ones was so conceived, as the philosophers of difference see it, in order to repress the *il y a*. Deleuze's discussion of the simulacrum confirms this, as does Derrida's analysis of writing and the *pharmakon* in "La pharmacie de Platon," and one of the main thrusts of the arguments is the necessity to differentiate between two modes of being, one which is regional, the metaphysics of presence, and the other which is general, the ontology of the *il y a*, "the formless weight of being, present in absence." These two modes of being are accompanied by corresponding conceptions of death. Hegel's humanizing reduction of death to the power of the negative belongs to the regional economy, whereas Blanchot's *mourir*, death as the inactual, impersonal excess of negativity, is part of the general economy of being. In terms of aesthetics, art as mimesis falls under the heading of the regional economy. Art as *ressemblance* belongs, on the other hand, to the general economy. There are, therefore, "two versions of the imaginary," depending on which economy or concept of negativity one takes into account:

> Ce que nous avons appelé les deux versions de l'imaginaire, ce fait que l'image peut certes nous aider à ressaisir idéalement la chose, qu'elle est alors sa négation vivifiante, mais que, au niveau où nous entraîne la pesanteur qui lui est propre, elle risque aussi constamment de nous renvoyer, non plus à la chose absente, mais à l'absence comme présence, au double neutre de l'objet en qui l'appartenance au monde s'est dissipée: cette duplicité n'est pas telle qu'on puisse la pacifier par un ou bien ou bien, capable d'autoriser un choix et d'ôter du choix l'ambiguïté qui le rend possible. (*EL* 357–58)[28]

Art does negate the real world and project us into a "higher," spiritualized plane of existence; this potential for evasion is indeed one of its principal attractions. And yet this version of art is not the only one, for art is irreducible to being the expression of a particular value or message. Literature is the art in which the duplicity of the origin, its irreducibility to an either/or situation, a reduction accomplished by Platonism, is the most evident because of its elemental components, words, "two-faced monsters" that can indifferently "change signs." If Plato excludes poets from his utopia, it is because of the duplicity of their medium, for words can function *both* as purveyors of truth *and* as harbingers of ambiguity. Thus there is a good form of writing that Plato admits—his own texts, which are faithful transcriptions of Socrates' living word—alongside of which there is a deep-seated mistrust of an art that allows an absent person to be (mis)represented by an impersonal text. Blanchot never denies the existence of the "good" version of literature as the power to transmit and record truth, nor does he ever tire of affirming that this version is but a partial explanation. In a remarkable sentence, Blanchot describes what the general economy of writing involves, when the writer has quit the world of the everyday for the essential solitude of the work:

> Ecrire, c'est disposer le langage sous la fascination et, par lui, en lui, demeurer en contact avec le milieu absolu, là où la chose redevient image, où l'image, d'allusion à une figure, devient allusion à ce qui est sans figure et, de forme dessinée sur l'absence, devient l'informe présence de cette absence, l'ouverture opaque et vide sur ce qui est quand il n'y a plus de monde, quand il n'y a pas encore de monde. (*EL* 27–28)[29]

Several things are worth noting here. Blanchot considers the traditional notion of the artist as demiurge to be obsolete: he replaces dynamic creativity, viewed as a happy combination of hard work, inspiration, and the power of the imagination, with a posture of passive indecision. The writer's indecision stems from the medium in which he or she works. Although writers may initially feel confident that they have control over words, and even if they think they know just what they want to say and how to go about it, they often feel the work slip away as they themselves become mesmerized by what they have written. The genial artist may "have a way with words," but for Blanchot, it is more a case of the words "having their way with the writer." When this reversal occurs, the writer "yields the initiative to words" and enters into a state of fascination. Fascination is not of the order of discursive knowledge, just as *la ressemblance* is not the revelation of something. It implies a temporary interruption of the habitual modes in which subjects perceive themselves and the world. One category that is provisionally set on end is that of personal identity:

Vivre un événement en image, ce n'est pas avoir de cet événement une image, ni non plus lui donner la gratuité de l'imaginaire. . . . Ce qui arrive nous saisit comme nous saisirait l'image, c'est-à-dire nous dessaisit, de lui et de nous, nous tient au dehors, fait de ce dehors une présence ou "Je" ne "se" reconnaît pas. (*EL* 357)[30]

Fascination breaks down the usual distinction between interiority and exteriority. When fascinated, writers are outside themselves, "beside themselves" when they give themselves up to the image, which provokes the transformation from the personal to the impersonal.

In addition to the phenomenon of depersonalization, fascination entails a rapport between words and things that differs, as we have seen, from that observed in everyday life. Whereas it has been argued that Platonic mimesis establishes a hierarchical order of *eidos*, model, and copy, to which correspond varying degrees of truth (or lack of it), Blanchot's *ressemblance* calls into question such an ordering by giving precedence to the copy over the original. Commonplace logic tells us that the artist moves from the real world of objects and events to their imaginary transposition in the artwork. Fascination, however, is a state in which this logic no longer holds sway. It is a state in which *ressemblance* replaces imitation, which explains why Blanchot says that "la chose redevient image" it *re*becomes an image, the image understood here, of course, as "the formless weight of being present in absence" and *not* as "la négation vivifiante, le travail idéal par lequel l'homme, capable de nier la nature, l'élève à un sens supérieur, soit pour la connaître, soit pour en jouir dans l'admiration" (*EL* 354–55).[31] Blanchot admits this latter "version of the imaginary," the view propounded by classical aesthetics, but only as a dissimulation of what he considers the essential trajectory to be: not as an elevation of the thing from the world to the canvas or book but rather a receding of the object into its own image and then into nothingness which persists as such.

One more point that Blanchot makes in this dense sentence is that fascination plays havoc with our conventional sense of time. Just as it contests the ontological principle of self-identity and the aesthetic notions of original and copy, fascination disrupts linear models of temporality which posit a beginning, a process of becoming, and an end. There is neither an *arche* nor a *telos* in the universe of fascination and resemblance, and repetition comes to take the place of dialectical progress.

That the persistence of anonymous being, which appears as the object recedes into its image, belongs to a temporality of incessant return rather than to one defined in terms of an absolute beginning and end is evident, for the uneliminable *il y a* is what there is "quand il n'y a plus de monde" and "quand il n'y a pas encore de monde." The end of history, when there is *no longer* any world, and the beginning of history, when there is *not yet* a world, overlap. They share the common denominator of the *il y a*, and the "end" is a return to the order of things as they were "in the beginning," which is to say that there never was a first time, nor will there ever be a last time. Hegel's eschatological history is just one of "two versions" of temporality—the reassuring one. The other version is provided by Nietzsche's law of the eternal return.

It is interesting to note that Blanchot speaks of the history of a work of art in the same terms as when he speaks of history in general. The same circularity is in effect, for the destiny of a work of art is to seek in vain whence it comes. Its end is to find its beginning. But there is no beginning. What does Blanchot mean, then, when he says that to write is to approach the center of the work and that "le point central de l'oeuvre est l'oeuvre comme origine, celui que l'on ne peut atteindre, le seul pourtant qu'il vaille la peine d'atteindre" (*EL* 56)?[32] What does the writer come up against as he approaches this elusive point in a state of fascination?

To answer these questions, it is not inappropriate to invoke the first chapter of the Gospel according to St. John: "In the beginning was the Word." Although he does not actually do so (in spite of the fact that he is inclined to parody Biblical verses and episodes), Blanchot might have rewritten this verse by saying, "In the beginning was the Murmur." Besides "le murmure," he uses a variety of other expressions to designate the same thing: "bruissement anonyme," "ressassement éternel," "flux ininterrompu et incessant de la parole non-parlante," "parole errante," and "parole du dehors," just to name a few. The writer has arrived at the heart of the space of literature when he has established a relationship with the incessant murmur, during which he first listens silently to it. Eventually he interrupts it, reducing it to silence by breaking his own silence. The task of the writer is to enter into "un rapport d'intimité avec la rumeur initiale. C'est à ce prix seulement qu'il peut lui imposer silence, l'entendre dans ce silence, puis l'exprimer, après l'avoir métamorposée" (*LV* 322).[33] When he interrupts the "rumeur initiale," he in effect imposes a limit on the interminable by putting it into written form. Blanchot explains the interruption of the murmur and the subsequent translation of it by the writer in this way: "Il faut lui imposer silence . . . Il faut qu'un instant elle [la parole errante] s'oublie, afin de pouvoir naître, par une triple métamorphose, à une parole véritable: celle du Livre, dira Mallarmé" (*LV* 325).[34] The "triple métamorphose" by means of which the writer reifies the temporarily arrested murmur is none other than what we spoke of earlier as the "triple existence" of words, the continuous oscillation between presence and absence as (*i*) the word ideally represents the absent thing named; (*ii*) the materiality of the word refuses to fade completely away into this idea; and (*iii*) at the level of the literary text taken as a whole (a set of words), the text is a "rien soutenu par rien."

Blanchot situates the murmur at the origin (and at the end) of the literary work in a manner consistent with his declaration that poetry precedes conventional language. He grants poetry precedence because he sees it as an irreducible inextrication of sound and sense, matter and idea, whereas the use of everyday language requires a suppression of the former of these terms. Their nonpeaceful coexistence precedes the decision to privilege one of them. Expressions like "murmure" and "bruissement anonyme" are metaphors that Blanchot uses to describe this state of perpetual contestation that resides at the heart of language. The murmur is, in Deleuzian terms, an original "disparité de fond" which provides for the possibility of subsequent differentiation; the *parole non-parlante* comes before the *parole* that has something to say. To return to the Judeo-Christian tradition, in the beginning was not the word, the *Fiat lux*, but rather the Spirit (wind, breath) of God as it moved over the surface of the waters. The articulated logos proceeds from the inarticulated *souffle*. The murmur does not communicate any particular piece of knowledge. What does speak is the language of unspecified being: "non plus ce qui parle, mais ce qui est, le langage devenu la profondeur désoeuvrée de l'être, le milieu où le nom se fait être, mais ne signifie ni ne dévoile" (*LV* 305).[35]

The ontology of the *il y a*, of which the murmur and its equivalent expressions are poeticized versions, contests, as does Bataille's unemployable negativity, the closure of the Hegelian model of history. In the beginning *and* in the end, which is to say all the time, is the *il y a*, an uneliminable remainder of negativity that will not be assimilated at the end of history. According to Blanchot, the history of language mirrors this movement toward incompletion. It may even be responsible for the failure of history to achieve totalization by failing itself to do so. In linguistic terms, totalization would be the realization by humanity of its task to "proférer tout et tout réduire au silence, même le silence" (*PF* 47),[36] a limit that can be approached but never reached because

> Il y a donc en lui [le langage], à tous niveaux, un rapport de contestation et d'inquiétude dont il ne peut s'affranchir. Dès que quelque chose est dit, quelque chose d'autre a besoin d'être dit. Puis, à nouveau quelque chose de différent doit encore se dire pour rattraper la tendance de tout ce qu'on dit à devenir définitif, à glisser dans le monde imperturbable des choses. Il n'y a pas de repos, il n'y en a ni au stade de la phrase, ni à celui de l'oeuvre. (*PF* 30)[37]

The contestation and lack of repose that exist at the heart of language render vain the attempt to reduce silence itself to silence. We can adapt what Levinas said about the *il y a* to the perspective of totalization as absolute silence: even if there were nothing but silence, the fact that "there is" is undeniable; the scene of being is opened: there is (silence). The murmur constitutes from a linguistic standpoint what the *il y a* does from the ontological point of view: excess negativity in which only the pure passivity of being speaks, and nothing else.

Language is in a continual state of restlessness because "le langage de la littérature est la recherche de ce moment qui la précède" (*PF* 316).[38] Literary language seeks to recover that which it had to destroy in order to come into existence: "il reste que ce qui 'est' a précisément disparu: quelque chose était là, qui n'y est plus; comment le retrouver, comment ressaisir, en ma parole, cette présence antérieure qu'il me faut exclure pour parler, pour la parler?" (*EI* 50)[39] The literary object par excellence, the poem, is written in language that calls attention to itself, unlike conventional language, which fades into the result that it brings about. The physical characteristics of words contribute to the materiality of the artifact which, for Blanchot, signifies language's attempt to supplement an originary lack, the destruction of the thing. The poem-object tries to replace the object proper that was previously eliminated. In "Poésie et pensée abstraite," Paul Valéry compares poetic language to the oscillating movement of a pendulum as it swings back and forth between sound and sense. Blanchot subscribes to this view of poetry as well; this movement makes poetry possible. While Valéry stresses the poetic effect or state that is produced in the mind of the reader of a poem, however, Blanchot takes a different tack when he suggests that this oscillating movement that renders poetry possible tends toward the impossible, the vain attempt to be simultaneously and wholly sound and sense, transparent ideal absence and opaque material presence. He explains the dialectical path that language must follow on its way toward totalization:

> Le langage veut s'accomplir. . . . Il prétend à un véritable absolu. Il y prétend de la manière la plus complète, et non seulement pour lui-même, dans son ensemble, mais pour chacune de ses parties, exigeant d'être entièrement mots, entièrement sens et entièrement sens et mots, dans une même et constante affirmation qui ne supporte que les parts qui se heurtent s'accordent, ni que le désaccord gêne l'entente, ni que l'entente soit l'harmonie d'un conflit. (*PF* 56–57)[40]

Francis Ponge's *Le Parti pris de choses* has been read as an attempt to overcome this dilemma by putting ideality and materiality on equal footing "in a single, constant affirmation." Ponge's book evokes a golden age of adequation between language and the world, a time when instead of being the murdered victims of words, things could speak as well: "Les descriptions de Ponge commencent au moment où, le monde étant accompli, l'histoire achevée, la nature presque rendue humaine, la parole vient au-devant de la chose et la chose apprend à parler" (*PF* 323).[41] Another avid reader of Ponge, Jean-Paul Sartre, also situates this moment at the beginning of the end of history. Sartre characterizes the longing for totalization that he senses in the poems as "une sorte de rapport avec la terre, un certain sens de la fusion, . . . un rapport du tout avec la mort" (*Situations I* 356).[42] Ponge's attempt to reconcile words and things constitutes another effort to render death possible, just as Bataille sought to do in his meditations on sacrifice. In Sartrean terms, the happy death, the victory of constructive negativity over the *mourir*, would occur with the fusion of the *en-soi* and the *pour-soi*, and it is precisely this problem that, for Sartre, occupies the center of Ponge's enterprise:

> il semble qu'il ait choisi un moyen rapide de réaliser symboliquement notre désir commun d'exister enfin sur le type de l'en-soi. Ce qui le fascine dans la chose, c'est son mode d'existence, sa totale adhésion à soi, son repos. Plus de fuite anxieuse, ni de colère, ni d'angoisse: l'imperturbabilité insensible du galet. J'ai noté ailleurs que le désir de chacun de nous est d'exister *avec sa conscience entière* sur le mode d'être de la chose. Etre tout entier conscience et à la fois tout entier pierre. (351)[43]

This desire to exist simultaneously as conscious subjectivity and unconscious objectivity recalls Bataille's dilemma of how to achieve complete consciousness of death. Sartre admits that such a condition is a limit that cannot be reached: "faute d'une fusion réelle de la conscience et de la chose, Ponge nous fait osciller de l'une à l'autre avec une très grande vitesse, espérant réaliser la fusion à la limite supérieure de cette vitesse. Mais cela n'est pas possible" (351).[44] The perpetual movement of this oscillation cannot be arrested because of the permanent state of contestation that is at work at the center of language itself. The literary *parole* is a hybrid creature of transparent idea and opaque materiality. Language is at war with itself, and it is futile, therefore, to hope to find in it a mediating force that could bring about a fusion of consciousness and matter. Literary language is marked by a tension between a projection into the future and a return to the moment that precedes it. When thought of as a vehicle for transmitting ideas, language seems to have its gaze focused directly on the horizon of future progress as a tool of constructive negativity. At the same time, however, language casts guilty (Orphic) glimpses over its shoulder as it attempts, in vain, to recover the presence of the object it excludes by naming thanks to its materialistic qualities. The irresolvable tension between these two components of language precludes the closure promised by historical totalization. We now see that the condition of language is analogous to the human condition at the end of history as Bataille portrayed it. "La cruauté du langage vient de ce que sans cesse il évoque sa mort sans pouvoir mourir jamais" (*PF* 30).[45] Language tends to the absolute silence of totalization—"proférer tout et tout réduire au silence, même le silence," to say everything once and for all, after which nothing more need be said—an unattainable limit, as is the human desire to have complete consciousness of death.

THREE

BLANCHOT'S SUICIDAL ARTIST

WRITING AND THE (IM)POSSIBILITY

OF DEATH

LANGUAGE and human beings share the same destiny of incompletion. Death as an approach, a passivity that cannot be rendered
present or personal, worklessness and failure: these exigencies
that Bataille posits as the basis of both sacrifice and his *expérience* are also
categories that serve to organize Blanchot's account of the experience of
the writer's approach to the space of literature. Literature's involvement
with death is central to Blanchot's thinking, and it is a theme that I would
like to explore in this chapter on three fronts: first, in connection with
his comparison of writing and suicide; second, by examining a particular
kind of writing, autobiography; and, finally, by reflecting on why literature is more concerned with the loss of our right to death than with its
affirmation.

Kafka serves as the exemplary writer in the section of *L'Espace littéraire*
entitled "La mort possible," where Blanchot draws a parallel between suicide and artistic activity. There is a sentence from Kafka's *Diaries* that he
finds particularly intriguing: "Le meilleur de ce que j'ai écrit se fonde sur
cette aptitude à pouvoir mourir content" (*EL* 107).[1] Blanchot wonders
what Kafka means by the expression "this capacity to die content," and he
offers this tentative response: "il faut être capable de se satisfaire de la
mort" (*EL* 108).[2] He then proceeds to question this answer: how is this
possible?

The two cases that Blanchot analyzes in which one often associates satisfaction with death are stoicism and suicide. Of the first, Blanchot states
that the stoic attitude of indifference in the face of death, although noble
and impressive, is nothing more than an expression of the desire to die
with grace and dignity out of respect for the living. For the stoic, Blanchot states, "Bien mourir signifie mourir dans la convenance . . . et cette
bonne mort indique plus de politesse pour le monde que d'égards pour
la profondeur de l'abîme" (*EL* 121).[3] He then concludes that this tasteful
death could not be what Kafka was referring to. Perhaps he who takes his
own life has the aptitude to die content—provided that one considers
self-destruction as supreme self-affirmation. Blanchot's analysis of suicide

revolves around the question of whether complete consciousness of death can be achieved. If it can, says Blanchot, the victim "aura été conscience de disparaître et non pas conscience disparaissante, il aura entièrement annexé à sa conscience la disparition de celle-ci, il sera donc totalité réalisée, la réalisation du tout, l'absolu" (*EL* 119).[4] Unfortunately it does not, for the victim is inevitably on the side of "conscience disparaissante." The error to which suicide victims succumb is, as Blanchot says, like a bizarre play on words: they take one death for another. Their attempt to domesticate death by taking their own life constitutes an act of power. Constructive negativity, however, is a restricted instance of *le mourir*, which falls outside the aims of any project. All efforts to have mastery over *le mourir*, to personalize it and render it present are futile. Suicide is an

Acte inespéré (sans espoir) d'unifier la duplicité de la mort et de réunir en une seule fois, par une décision d'impatience, les répétitions éternelles de ce qui, mourant, ne meurt pas. Puis la tentation de nommer, c'est-à-dire de personnaliser, en se l'attribuant, l'anonymat, cela qui ne se dit qu'en troisième personne et au neutre. Ou encore le pouvoir d'élargir, comme à sa mesure, en le localisant et en le datant, l'infiniment petit, et qui toujours échappe, de la mort. (*PAD* 135)[5]

Writers fall into the same trap as do suicide victims except that instead of taking one death for another, "la mort contente" for "le mourir," they mistake the book for the work, "le livre" for "l'oeuvre."[6] Both tend to a point by taking the initiative and exercising skill and know-how, but this point escapes any such determinations. The perpetrator of suicide sets out with great determination to conquer and possess death, to make it his or her own, but, suggests Blanchot, it is just the opposite that occurs: "Même là où je décide d'aller à elle [la mort], par une résolution virile et idéale, n'est-ce pas elle qui me saisit, qui me dessaisit, me livre à l'insaisissable?" (*EL* 118).[7] In a similar way writers, although they may initially feel confident in their ability to have control over the raw materials of their craft, undergo the same kind of dispossession. The more they write and the farther they advance into the literary space, the less clear their original project becomes. Writing involves a pact made with the night and cannot be equated with any mundane task to be accomplished in the realm of the day. Writers are, therefore, not related to what they have written in the same way that they are to anything else they have done through an act of power. In the cases of both suicide and writing, what begins as a concerted act of the will is transformed into fascination, indecision, and passivity. The English phrase "suicide victim" aptly describes this transformation from active to passive: whoever resolves to kill himor-herself ultimately becomes one who submits passively to death and awaits its approach.

The contradictory pair of terms, active and passive, organizes Blanchot's interpretation of Kafka's enigmatic statement that writing was somehow linked to the aptitude of knowing how to die. This is, however, only half the story, for Kafka completes this statement with its complementary other, which allows Blanchot to elaborate a theory that he calls the "exigence circulaire" and that he considers to be the essence of writing.[8] The first statement, to die in order to be able to write, indicates that a close rapport with death is a prerequisite for writing and suggests the writer's attitude of passive patience as he approaches the origin of the work.

The second statement, to write in order to be able to die, says that writing is a prerequisite for death and seems to treat death more in terms of negativity, active impatience which intervenes, the "healthy hand" that removes the pen from the "sick hand," thereby putting an end to the interminable. The word "negativity" must, however, be used with caution. It would be incorrect to view patience engaged with impatience in a dialectical struggle in which mastery and power win out. There is no victory here; as Valéry said, no work of art is ever fully realized, and writing remains an incomplete, repetitive endeavor. Blanchot relegates the role of power to a status secondary in importance to that of worklessness. The fact that he considers the active impatience of beginnings as a limited rather than the determining factor is evident in this statement about short cuts: "Le raccourci ne permet pas de parvenir plus directement (plus vite) à un lieu, mais plutôt de perdre le chemin qui devrait y conduire" (*ED* 174).[9] The suicide victim's attempt to shortchange death and to experience it on *his* or *her* terms leads to failure and perpetual wandering. Yet if anything in Blanchot's universe can be said to be authentic (a word that he mistrusts), it is *errance*. The only authority or source of authenticity in the writer's experience is the experience itself as an approach.

The literary activity *per se* that Blanchot sees as the most telling demonstration of the metamorphosis from active initiative to passive indecision that the writer undergoes is autobiography. The motivations for autobiographical forms of writing are numerous. Writers might engage in this activity to justify publicly their actions, to explain why they lived their lives the way that they did. A more disinterested motive might be to offer themselves up as an example to others so that the latter might not make the same mistakes. Or perhaps the reasons might be of a more personal or intimate nature, such as indulging in the sheer pleasure of reminiscing, conferring a retrospective aesthetic unity on a chaotic life, or leaving behind a monumental image of oneself that will endure for posterity.

Blanchot does not deny that such considerations may induce writers to record their activities, memories, dreams, and reflections on a regular basis, as would be the case for a journal. But he does see something more ominous at work; the desire to know oneself by means of a recourse to writing is symptomatic of a deeper, less obvious malaise. If writing is, as Blanchot claims, to enter into a rapport with passivity, indecision, and the fascination of the image and the absence of time, the journal would seem to represent a safe form of writing with built-in defense mechanisms that hold the impending threat of the loss of personalized consciousness at bay. He designates the journal as "un garde-fou contre le danger de l'écriture" (*LV* 274).[10] The danger that Blanchot is referring to is that

> l'écrivain éprouve toujours davantage le besoin de garder un rapport avec soi. C'est qu'il éprouve une extrême répugnance à se dessaisir de lui-même au profit de cette puissance neutre, sans forme et sans destin, qui est derrière tout ce qui s'écrit. (*EL* 20)[11]

The journal is perfectly suited to allow a writer to write without falling prey to the two principal menaces implicit as one approaches the literary space, the loss of both individual subjectivity and linear time. The presupposed identity of the writer of the journal and its subject seems to guarantee protection against the threat of the loss of individualized consciousness, and the danger of the absence of time is eliminated thanks to the assurance of the calendar: "Ici, qui parle garde un nom et parle en son nom, et la date qu'on inscrit est celle d'un temps commun où ce qui arrive arrive vraiment" (*EL* 21).[12]

The question remains, however, whether these two safeguards are foolproof. To what extent do the apparent laws of this genre enable the writer to approach the point at which the metamorphosis from the personal to the impersonal occurs without going beyond it? Blanchot often characterizes writing as "le passage du *Je* au *Il*," another expression that he takes over from Kafka's *Diaries*. Autobiographical writing would appear to enable the writer to make this transition while at the same time remaining *I*, that is, while retaining the powers of the individual subject to witness the transition objectively and impassively without being overcome by it. The subject's desire to be itself and the Other simultaneously recalls the dilemma that sacrifice and suicide attempt to resolve: how to maintain consciousness during and after death. In a move analogous to his analysis of suicide as being powerless in its effort to have mastery over death, Blanchot exposes what he calls "le piège du journal" (*LV* 274): not surprisingly, the keeper of the journal falls into the trap of taking the happy, optative death for the incessant, noneventful *mourir*. The apparent laws that govern the journal, the calendar and the identity of the writer with the subject of the entries of the journal, would seem to ensure an economy grounded in power, initiative, and decision; but Blanchot asserts that there is a secret law that governs this kind of writing that, although usually overlooked, belongs to a general economy of powerlessness, passivity, and indecision. Both of these laws are in force, as we see once again with respect to Kafka's *Diaries,* in which

> Kafka a écrit tout ce qui lui importait, événements, descriptions des personnes et des lieux, descriptions de ses rêves, récits commencés, interrompus, recommencés. Ce n'est donc pas seulement un "Journal" comme on l'entend aujourd'hui, mais *le mouvement même de l'expérience d'écrire,* au plus proche de son commencement et au sens essentiel que Kafka a été amené à donner à ce mot. C'est sous cette perspective que le *Journal* doit être lu et interrogé. (*EL* 59, my italics)[13]

The fundamental theme of modern art, according to Blanchot, is its preoccupation with itself, its Narcissistic search for its own origins. In the particular domain of literature, the texts that Blanchot examines in his critical writings are for the most part pretexts which serve as stepping-stones on the way to larger questions such as what it means to write and how literature is possible at all. The fact that he has a predilection for journals or other autobiographical writings that deal not only with the author's life but also represent "le mouvement même de l'expérience d'écrire" is, therefore, consistent with his views on art.[14] Kafka's journal, with the fragmentary sketches of stories that never came to fruition, reveals something about the experience of writing and, more precisely, about beginnings, that is, how books come into being. It is not a journal of the work in progress; for Blanchot, who insists on the incapacity of the author to read his own works, such a book cannot exist, or if it does, it is not a journal in the usual sense of the word; it tends rather to the world of fiction: "ce journal ne peut s'écrire qu'en devenant imaginaire et en s'immergeant, comme celui qui l'écrit, dans l'irréalité de la fiction" (*LV* 277).[15] Besides Kafka's *Diaries,* Blanchot mentions some other examples of this "genre" which approach the unattainable limit of being histories of their own origins: Bataille's *L'Expérience intérieure* and *Le Coupable,* Rilke's *The Notebooks of Malte Laurids Brigge,* Joubert's *Carnets,* and even *Les Chants de Maldoror,* which Blanchot reads as a *mise en scène* of Isidore Ducasse's transformation into le comte de Lautréamont, the metamorphosis from the personal *Je* to the impersonal *Il* of writing. This seemingly disparate collection of books finds its unity in that each adheres to the same "secret law": "Une des lois secrètes de ces ouvrages, c'est que plus le mouvement s'approfondit, plus il tend à se rapprocher de l'impersonnalité de l'abstraction" (*LV* 278).[16] The law that apparently governs autobiographical projects—that writing can lead to self-presence and self-knowledge—is eventually subverted by the "secret law," that writing will lead to nothing else except more writing.

The tension between these two laws that Blanchot observes in many autobiographical writings has been examined systematically by Michel Beaujour in his admirable book *Miroirs d'encre*. Beaujour proposes two genres: autobiography, written in accordance with the apparent law, and *autoportrait*, which testifies to the subversion of the apparent law by the secret law. The task that autobiographers set out to accomplish is to answer the questions of what they have done and why, and they do so by setting down chronologically the facts of their lives. Self-portraitists, on the other hand, wish to arrive at the essence of their *moi*, to answer the question of who they are. Beaujour argues that this question is inevitably displaced and that problems concerning language and writing get the upper hand:

> Il n'y a pas d'autoportrait qui ne soit celui d'un écrivain en tant qu'écrivain, et sa culpabilité est celle de l'écriture au sein d'une culture où la rhétorique ne tourne pas rond, où l'écriture utilitaire ou intransitive confère tour à tour pouvoir et impuissance, où le sujet se cherche des semblables tout en affirmant sa différence absolue. Voilà pourquoi l'autoportrait n'a pour vrais lecteurs que des écrivains en mal d'autoportrait. (15)[17]

The autoportrait is a genre practiced by the "writer's writer," for personal problems tend to be replaced by literary ones. The title of Beaujour's book evokes the paradox that is responsible for this: writing is not a transparent medium that enables writers to attain a rapport of immediacy with their *moi*. On the contrary, it clouds the issue.

What is responsible for this undermining of the best autobiographical intentions? How is it that problems concerning writing supplant the writer's quest for self-knowledge and come to occupy center stage? The answers to these questions are to be found in Blanchot's reflections on the nature of language which, as we have seen, is composed of words, "two-faced monsters," combinations of transparent ideas and obscure materiality. The major impropriety of language is that words can "changer indifféremment et de sens et de signe" (*PF* 329).[18] That the valence of a word can change from positive to negative, as its binary nature causes it to oscillate incessantly between the clarity of an idea and the impenetrability of an object, indicates that the dual status of death dwells at the heart of language: language as a purveyor of ideas constitutes a form of constructive negativity, whereas the swinging of the pendulum back toward the materiality of language which obstructs them betrays the presence of an irreducible excess of negativity. *Le mourir*—this surplus of unemployable negativity—is responsible for the failure of suicide to have mastery over death, and in the same way, it is responsible for the subversion of the apparent law of autobiography by the secret law, or in Beaujour's terminology, for the emergence of the *autoportrait* over (and sometimes in spite of) autobiographical intentions. The writer shares the same destiny of incompleteness that language does because "celui qui parle poétiquement s'expose à cette sorte de mort qui est nécessairement à l'oeuvre dans la parole véritable" (*LV* 334).[19] Literature is a privileged form of human endeavor because nowhere else is the duplicity of death more striking, and writing is the activity that best portrays the futile search for the "capacity to die content":

> La littérature est cette expérience par laquelle la conscience découvre son être dans son impuissance à perdre conscience, dans le mouvement où, disparaissant, s'arrachant à la ponctualité d'un moi, elle se reconstitue, par delà l'inconscience, en une spontanéité impersonnelle. (*PF* 320)[20]

Writing as exposing oneself to the eternal torments of the *mourir* and as the transformation from "the well-delineated confines of a self" into "an impersonal spontaneity" recalls what Philippe Sollers says, in *Writing and the Experience of Limits*, about literature and suicide: "genuine suicide can only be literary. It implies the *sacrifice* of he who writes, a sacrifice 'in relation to personality' unique in its kind" (68). Michel Beaujour says much the same thing about the author of the *autoportrait*: "l'auto-portraitiste est toujours déjà un *Autre*, 'mort comme un tel', 'omission de soi', selon les formules mallarméennes. Ce qui pourrait aussi s'écrire 'mort comme Untel', absent du texte, comme le corps du Christ ressuscité du tombeau" (276).[21] The author ends up by being absent from his own portrait just as the resurrected Christ vacated his tomb. If Beaujour speaks of death and resurrection in connection with the *autoportrait*, it is because he considers them to be recurring structural and archetypal images: "les figures les plus fréquentes dans l'autoportrait sont . . . celles du Christ et de Socrate au moment de leur mort. L'autoportrait est hanté par la passion et le récit du *Phédon*" (26).[22] Elsewhere he states that "L'auto-portraitiste doit se faire l'artisan de sa propre résurrection" (348).[23] Blanchot's discussion of Michel Leiris's *L'Age d'homme* dovetails nicely with the thesis proposed by Beaujour (for whom Leiris represents the major contemporary practitioner of the *autoportrait*). The passage from *L'Age d'homme* that Blanchot finds most interesting and that he quotes in his article "Regards d'outre-tombe" is the following:

> Je ne puis dire à proprement parler que *je meurs*, puisque—mourant de mort violente ou non—je n'assiste qu'à une partie de l'événement. Et une grande partie de l'effroi que j'éprouve à l'idée de la mort tient peut-être à ceci: vertige de rester suspendu en plein milieu d'une crise dont ma disparition m'empêchera, au grand jamais, de connaître le dénouement. Cette espèce d'irréalité, *d'absurdité* de la mort est . . . son élément radicalement terrible. (*PF* 245–46)[24]

Leiris casts the anguish that precedes and accompanies us in our confrontation with death in the same terms as do Bataille and Blanchot: the fear of being unable to die completely, of being a "disappearing consciousness" rather than "complete consciousness of disappearing." As Blanchot states in his commentary of this passage, "nous voulons être sûrs de la mort comme achevée . . . nous désirons pouvoir nous regarder morts, nous assurer de notre mort en dirigeant sur notre néant, d'un point situé au-delà de la mort, un véritable regard d'outre-tombe" (*PF* 246).[25] If, as Beaujour suggests, the *autoportrait* is animated by the desire to reenact the passion play, if the author is interested in fashioning his own resurrection, does that mean that autobiographical writing succeeds where suicide fails, that is, in providing a view into the grave from beyond it? That would mean that the literary suicide of the writer would have a reward: the resurrection, recuperation, and reincarnation of the self in the text. Beaujour tells us, however, that what survives is a text that is impersonal in nature. Once again the attempt of personalized consciousness to go through death and survive it is foiled:

> Le mythe du ressuscité (Lazare, le Christ) souligne le paradoxe de l'autoportrait qui assure une survie à *personne*, de telle sorte que personne ne s'y représente jamais, du moins dans la particularité d'un corps unique, et irremplaçable. Et pourtant le corps propre cherche à y prendre sa revanche contre l'impersonnalité du logos philosophique. (303)[26]

The subject of the self-portrait cannot pronounce his own *Lazare, veni foras*; only a future reader can. And there are as many Lazaruses summoned up by reading as there are readers. The book is a monument, but an empty one. It is not a resting place from which surges forth an integral, inviolate self. This has been dispersed; no one in particular is there. *Homo absconditus.*

The other figure that haunts the writing of self-portraits, the episode of Socrates' death, places the meditation on the question of death as a possibility within a philosophical rather than a theological framework. Although Mallarmé's *Igitur* cannot properly be classified as an autobiographical piece of writing, Georges Poulet, in *La Distance intérieure*, equates it with an act of philosophical suicide. Blanchot agrees with this assessment up to a point—that the *conte* depends, for Mallarmé, on a profound rapport with death—but he disagrees with Poulet as to the nature of this rapport. The latter insists that this philosophical suicide is an act of power:

> La mort est le seul acte possible. Pressés que nous sommes entre un monde matériel vrai dont les combinaisons fortuites se produisent en nous sans nous, et un monde idéal faux dont le mensonge nous paralyse et nous en-

sorcelle, nous n'avons qu'un moyen de ne plus être livrés ni au néant ni au hasard. Ce moyen unique, cet acte unique, c'est la mort. La mort volontaire. Par lui, nous nous abolissons, mais par lui aussi nous nous fondons . . . C'est cet acte de mort volontaire que Mallarmé a commis. Il l'a commis dans *Igitur*. (Quoted in *EL* 41)[27]

We have already seen that Blanchot rejects the notion of suicide conceived in dialectical terms ("nous nous abolissons mais . . . nous nous fondons"), for to die, whether by one's own hand or not, is inevitably to await death's approach. According to Blanchot's reading of the *conte*, Poulet also seems to fall into the trap of mistaking one death for another. The confrontation of *la mort heureuse* with *le mourir* is indeed the dilemma posed by *Igitur*:

Déjà Nietzsche s'était heurté à la même contradiction, lorsqu'il disait: "Meurs au moment juste." Ce moment juste qui seul équilibrera notre vie par une mort souverainement équilibrée, nous ne pouvons le saisir que comme le secret inconnaissable, ce qui ne pourrait s'éclairer que si nous pouvions, déjà morts, nous regarder d'un point d'où il nous serait donné d'embrasser comme un tout et notre vie et notre mort, ce point qui est peut-être la vérité de la nuit d'où Igitur voudrait précisément partir pour rendre son départ possible et juste, mais qu'il réduit à la pauvreté d'un reflet. (*EL* 146)[28]

This vantage point from beyond the grave and from which death could be viewed in its entirety is not accessible by means of the thoughtfully committed suicidal act. It is an illusion that has been "reduced to the poverty of a reflection" in the course of the *conte* because, as Blanchot sees it, "*Igitur* ne cherche pas à se dépasser, ni à découvrir, par ce dépassement volontaire, un point de vue nouveau de l'autre côté de la vie" (*EL* 138).[29] This point is a mirage. It ultimately eludes Igitur and everyone else because of the incessant pressure of the *mourir*, which allows for the possibility of the idea of a content death while at the same time canceling it out. There is no other side of life; there is only an encounter with the *other* night—not the restful dialectical opposite of the day—but the ontological domain characterized by loss of self, the abyss of the present, passivity, and worklessness.

The surplus of the *mourir* in relation to the negativity of power guarantees the failure of suicide and writing, even of the autobiographical sort, to have mastery over death. When Sollers states that true suicide could only be literary in nature, he does not mean that the writing and publishing of a book or journal will make death lose its sting by ensuring a miraculous afterlife for its author. Blanchot explains the paradoxical position of the writer caught in limbo between two negativities the only way he can: by evoking another paradox: "Ecrire son autobiographie soit pour s'avouer, soit pour s'analyser, soit pour s'exposer aux yeux de tous à la façon d'une oeuvre d'art, c'est peut-être chercher à survivre, mais par un suicide perpétuel—mort totale en tant que fragmentaire" (*ED* 105).[30] Suicide is not the apotheosis of the instant during which the victim exists (however fleetingly) in a state of perfect equilibrium between life and death. Its essence is the patient waiting for a moment that never comes, and if writing can be compared to suicide at all, it is only in terms of the self-contradictory notion of a perpetual suicide, which leads to the equally contradictory notion of a death which is complete because fragmentary. To write is to enter into a rapport with the *mourir*, therefore, to produce fragments, because there is no "last word." The literary history of Blanchot's narrative works seems to confirm this on two points. He ironically entitled his first *récit*, written in 1935, "Le dernier mot," thereby inaugurating his literary career by uttering the last word. And he subsequently abandoned the novel and the *récit* in favor of fragmentary works such as *L'Attente l'oubli*, *Le Pas au-delà*, and *L'Ecriture du désastre*.

Suicide and writing both have something in common: on the surface each of these activities purports to accomplish something, and yet each must ultimately be considered as failing to do so. Each activity represents an extreme situation, an experience of limits, the crossing of which implies entering a domain where power is not of prime importance. The subjects of these experiences, according to Blanchot, have traditionally overlooked or ignored this; each usually falls into the trap of taking one thing for another, in the case of suicide, "la mort heureuse" for "le mourir," and in the case of writing, the book for the work. Each of these experiences exceeds an ontology based on power and is, therefore, considered by Blanchot to be a transgressive act. He defines transgression as "l'accomplissement inévitable de ce qu'il est *impossible* d'accomplir, et ce serait le mourir même" (*PAD* 147).[31] Both actions are attempts to render death humanly possible, but the inescapable truth is its impossibility. "Mourir ne se décline pas" (*PAD* 147).[32] It is a defective verb that cannot be conjugated, for it has no forms in the present tense, nor can any personal pronoun serve as its subject. Culture (in general) and suicide and writing (in particular) try unsuccessfully to force this impersonal infinitive into a personal paradigm.

It is on the question of survival that the destiny of language and that of the being endowed with language part company. The book is the survivor, on two different occasions. There is, first, the figurative death of the author, who is expelled from the work once it is written, and, second, the definitive disappearance of the deceased author. In both cases, the book exists all by itself: "il a lieu tout seul: fait, étant." During their lifetimes, writers can, thanks to literature, perform continual acts of suicide by approaching and letting themselves be approached by the *mourir* in its impossibility. After their disappearance, however, the language of their books continues this experience all by itself. This is what separates people from literature. People do die—*forcément*—and in this sense the impossibility of death is inevitably accomplished. But books survive. They linger on to prolong indefinitely the irresolvable tension between *la mort heureuse* and *le mourir*. It is as if language were infinitely endowed with a capability that human beings possess only briefly: "Mais la parole moribonde (parole, non pas mourante, mais du mourir même) a peut-être toujours déjà passé la limite que la vie ne passe pas, passant à son insu par le chemin qu'a frayé l'écriture en le marquant comme infrayable" (*PAD* 128).[33] The very condition of literary language is that it can do indefinitely what people can do only for a definite period of time. It always already has the capacity to go beyond the limit that the living cannot.

Language's function resembles that of Charon. Whereas mortals are obliged to take one final trip across the Styx, Charon's work is never done. Like the self-contestation that is present at the origin of language, Charon continually conveys passengers to the other side and returns alone. Like language, he can go to the other side of death *and* come back. Writers, by accepting the conditions of the approach of the literary space, participate for a time in this movement, but in the end, their books carry on without them.

FOUR

MYTHICAL PORTRAYALS OF

WRITING AND READING

T HE PREMISE of an excessive, nonrecuperable negativity that causes the closure of Hegel's model of history to crack wide open has served both as our point of departure in our analysis of Bataille's theory of sacrifice and transgression and as a *fil conducteur* in the successive chapters in which we turned our attention to Blanchot, specifically his elaborations on the nature of literary language and literature's involvement with death in his comparison of suicide and writing. The articulation of the literary practices of writing and reading and the two negativities is crucial to our understanding of Blanchot. Having established that literature and death are intimately connected, I propose to pursue this line of thinking in this chapter by concentrating on the myths that Blanchot makes use of in his presentation of the economical relationships that exist between author, text, and reader. Generally speaking, the Orphic myth illuminates the writer's plight, whereas the miracles of two resurrections, of Jesus and Lazarus, are the vehicles for his analysis of reading. All three myths, nevertheless, tell of close encounters with death.

Blanchot considers modern art to be the third great epoch in the history of art, the first two being religious and humanistic art, respectively. What separates this last period from the first two is that instead of being in the service of someone or something exterior to it—God or humankind, for example—modern art is self-reflexive, concerned with the search for its own origins, and the artist and his work are irresistibly attracted to an originary point without, however, being able to reach it: "Le point central de l'oeuvre est l'oeuvre comme origine, celui que l'on ne peut atteindre, le seul pourtant qu'il vaille la peine d'atteindre" (*EL* 56).[1] Blanchot dramatizes this dilemma by casting it in terms of the descent of Orpheus into the underworld.

For Orpheus, Eurydice is "l'extrême que l'art puisse atteindre" (*EL* 227).[2] The task that Orpheus sets out to accomplish is to encounter Eurydice in the *other* night of Hades and to make manifest this encounter in the realm of the day by giving to it "forme, figure et réalité" (*EL* 227). He must respect, however, a precondition imposed by the gods: he is not to look directly at Eurydice. The only rapport that he can have with her is an indirect one. He can know her only in a relationship of proximity, for the possibility of the mutual presence of one to the other, which would be fulfilled by the fusion of their gazes, is ruled out from the start. He must be content to hear the sound of her footsteps as she follows him, and the interval between the two must be maintained if Orpheus is to succeed. He knows this, and yet he is unable to resist the temptation to turn around to see whether she is, in fact, behind him. Of prime importance to Blanchot's interpretation of the myth is Orpheus's decision to look at Eurydice, thereby transgressing divine law: "Regarder Eurydice, sans souci du chant, dans l'impatience et l'imprudence du désir qui oublie la loi, c'est cela même, *l'inspiration*" (*EL* 231).[3] Orpheus's decision to look over his shoulder marks the point at which power and mastery cease to be his overriding concerns and are replaced by the dispossession of fascination. Orpheus's transgression occurs as a result of the conjunction of impatience and desire: "Le désir . . . qui porte Orphée . . . n'est pas l'élan capable de franchir l'intervalle. . . Le désir est la séparation elle-même qui se fait attirante, est l'intervalle qui devient *sensible*" (*EI* 280).[4] Desire is not the power that enables Orpheus to establish contact with Eurydice. Instead, Blanchot situates the motivating force behind his gaze in the interval that lies between them. Eurydice's presence is not what becomes irresistibly attractive to the point of becoming almost palpable; it is rather the distance that separates them. In contrast to traditional interpretations of the myth, Blanchot's shift of emphasis from Eurydice herself to the interval indicates that the only positivity in Orpheus's experience is the experience as an approach, an approach to an ever-receding horizon that remains perpetually out of reach. This approach is what Orpheus must maintain if he is to bring his task to a successful conclusion. Such an approach cannot be endured indefinitely, and he succumbs to the temptation of impatience: "Son erreur est de vouloir épuiser l'infini, de mettre un terme à l'interminable" (*EL* 230).[5] From the point of view of the day, he desires to leap across the necessary interval, to eliminate the distance that separates them, by establishing direct visual contact which would confirm the success or failure of his endeavor. What his gaze encounters in the *other* night, however, is not the revelation of something. The only manifestation of Eurydice is her disappearance.

Far from criticizing Orpheus's impatience, which is responsible for the loss of Eurydice a second time (this time for good), Blanchot makes of this failure the essential feature of artistic activity: "tout se passe comme si, en désobéissant à la loi, en regardant Eurydice, Orphee n'avait fait qu'obéir à l'exigence profonde de l'oeuvre" (*EL* 230).[6] Orpheus's betrayal of Eurydice is performed in accordance with the profound exigency of the work, impossibility. "For Blanchot, inspiration is Orpheus's adventure: a mobilization of possibility which, when Eurydice has been lost, realizes too late its essential rapport with impossibility, and realizes that its unwavering trajectory toward failure is its only 'authenticity'" (Libertson 146). Seen from the perspective of the day, Orpheus's project is to lead Eurydice back to the land of the living, and in this context the myth is one of power that describes the ability of poetry and music to act as a mediating force between the two realms.

Blanchot, on the other hand, views Orpheus's original project as a necessary prelude to what he considers the essential moment of the myth to be, the impossibility of seeing Eurydice in her nocturnal element: "Orphée . . . oublie l'oeuvre qu'il doit accomplir, et il l'oublie nécessairement, parce que l'exigence ultime de son mouvement, ce n'est pas qu'il y ait oeuvre, mais que quelqu'un se tienne en face de ce 'point'" (*EL* 227–28).[7] Thus, although Orpheus betrays Eurydice by forgetting the conditions that had to be respected in order for his project to succeed, he remains faithful in so doing to the "ultimate exigency of his movement":

> ne pas se tourner vers Eurydice, ce ne serait pas moins trahir, être infidèle à la force sans mesure et sans prudence de son mouvement, qui ne veut pas Eurydice dans sa vérité diurne et dans son agrément quotidien, qui la veut dans son obscurité nocturne, dans son éloignement, avec son corps fermé et son visage scellé, qui veut la voir, non quand elle est visible, mais quand elle est invisible. (*EL* 228)[8]

The fact that Blanchot interprets Orpheus's betrayal of Eurydice as a gesture of fidelity coincides with Bataille's schema of transgression, in which the *interdit* and its violation are linked in a relationship of concealed solidarity. The same inextrication of the law and its infraction forms the crux of Blanchot's interpretation of the Orphic myth. To illustrate this, we must once again turn our attention to the "circular exigency of writing," this time as it is presented in terms of the myth:

> Ecrire commence avec le regard d'Orphée . . . Mais pour descendre vers cet instant, il a fallu à Orphée déjà la puissance de l'art. Cela veut dire: l'on n'écrit que si l'on atteint cet instant vers lequel l'on ne peut toutefois se porter que dans l'espace ouvert par le mouvement d'écrire. Pour écrire, il faut déjà écrire. (*EL* 234)[9]

From the vantage point of the day which recognizes the limits within which one must work in order to have a smoothly functioning and productive world, Orpheus sins twice. He not only transgresses the law by attempting to see whether Eurydice is really behind him; he has also already done so by being there in the first place, since a living mortal is not ordinarily entitled to have access to the realm of the dead. Moreover, the technique that he employs to gain access to this forbidden (and forbidding) realm is "la puissance de l'art": his music is what enables him to reach the point at which he has the opportunity to try to look at Eurydice.

Creative activity, therefore, seems to begin at a stage in which artists feel confident in their ability to have control over the raw materials of their craft. This initial confidence tends to waver, however, as they make further advances, and it is eventually replaced by impersonality, passivity, and fascination. In order to write—to have the ultimate Orphic encounter of experiencing the presence of absence—it is necessary to write already as a prelude to this moment, *as if* writing were the exercise of a power.

This situation plays a major role in determining the importance that the myth has for Blanchot insofar as temporality is concerned. The adverb "déjà" in the statement "pour écrire, il faut déjà écrire" as well as the sequence of events recounted by the myth in which Orpheus first plays his music in order to enter Hades and at some later moment interrupts it when he turns to look at Eurydice is potentially misleading. It is really too simple to say (as we just did) that an initial stage of confidence is subsequently overwhelmed by fascination and loss of power. These two forms of singing (and writing) are not related to each other in the same way that two events in linear, chronological succession would be, for the writing of passivity and the writing of power are in a relationship of mutual contamination from the start. To say that worklessness follows an earlier exercise of power is only half right. There is no such *sens unique* in Blanchot's exigency that he describes as "circular," which is to say that it is a reversible situation: passive writing not only "follows" active writing but "precedes" it as well (as if one could assign precise points on a circle that is in perpetual motion). It is more appropriate to think of temporality in the nocturnal world of artistic activity in terms of repetition and synchronicity than in terms of the unicity and chronological sequence of events. If we do so, we realize that Orpheus's decision to look at Eurydice never takes place a first time; it has always already happened: "Il est inévitable qu'Orphée passe outre à la loi qui lui interdit de 'se retourner', car il l'a violée dès ses premiers pas vers les ombres. Cette remarque nous fait pressentir que, en réalité, Orphée n'a pas cessé d'être tourné vers Eurydice." (*EL* 229).[10] When Orpheus turns around again to look at Eurydice ("se *re*tourne"), he is engaged in the repetition of an act that has not ceased occurring ever since his decision to use his music as a ruse that allows him to pursue Eurydice at all. Orpheus's failure to see Eurydice in her nocturnal element indicates that he can have power over her only in the measured limits of his songs, but these are dissimulations, imperfect renderings of the fatal moment in which Eurydice is always already lost: "dans le chant seulement, Orphée a pouvoir sur Eurydice, mais, dans le chant aussi, Eurydice est déjà perdue et Orphée lui-même est l'Orphée dispersé, l'infiniment mort' que la force du chant fait dès maintenant de lui" (*EL* 229–30).[11]

Blanchot cherishes the myth of Orpheus, "le mythe inépuisable" (*EI* 280) that he never tires of alluding to, because it tells the story of an event that always already has had to have taken place in order to occur. This paradox at the level of temporality—the impossibility of situating the events of the myth at particular moments in a chronological sequence—points to a more fundamental paradox: that of the impossibility of clearly situating the law in relation to the transgression that violates it. The law and its transgression share the exigencies of impossibility and failure: the law, because it contains an inherent weakness that temporarily authorizes violations of it, and transgression, because it fails to do away with the law once and for all; limits are always eventually restored. This schema in which the law is put forth as possessing from within the (suicidal) provision that allows for its own undoing applies to Orpheus. As Libertson correctly notes, Orpheus's decision to look at Eurydice is a perfect example of Bataillian transgression, for "it is unfaithful to the putative limits of prohibition, and correlatively unfaithful to the explosive negativity which would destroy limits" (140). Orpheus goes against the edict of the gods when he turns around, but this inspired gesture does not constitute an act of power that does away with it. The law goads Orpheus into the transgression by making his anxiety unbearable, and at the same time it remains triumphantly in force since Orpheus does not succeed in seeing Eurydice "in the flesh"; what he does see is Eurydice receding into her own image.

The interdependence of taboo and transgression finds its expression in Blanchot's version of the myth when he speaks of Orpheus's impatience. Blanchot's discussion of the relationship between patience and impatience is perhaps the most problematic moment of his reading of the Orphic myth, and efforts to pin down what he means by assigning to them a permanent, definite meaning encounter resistance. Such obscurity may very well be intended. If so, Blanchot's text would be playing Eurydice's role by leading us, as we blindly follow, to the unstable point of origin where the language of literature "peut changer indifféremment et de sens et de signe" (*PF* 329).[12] Such would seem to be the case if we examine for a moment the coefficients that he places before these words at different moments of his discussion. At first, he equates patience with the music that he mobilizes as an instrument of power that gives him access to the underworld: "La patience est la ruse qui cherche à maîtriser cette absence de temps en faisant d'elle un autre temps, autrement mesuré" (*EL* 230).[13] Patience is clearly identified here with power, mastery, and a willingness to act in accordance with divine law. Things become less clear, however, in the sentence that follows the one just quoted, in which he says that "la vraie patience n'exclut pas l'impatience, elle en est l'intimité, elle est l'impatience soufferte et endurée sans fin" (*EL* 230).[14] The fact that patience does not exclude impatience takes us back to the collaboration of the law and its violation. In other words, Orpheus's respect for the law does not rule out his transgression. Moreover, we are told that patience is the intimate, secret side of impatience. At this point, Blanchot seems to set up an opposition in which patience is associated with the restricted economy of power, and impatience, of which patience is a part ("l'intimité" [de l'impatience]), is consequently identified with the general economy of loss of power. A few pages farther on, however, Blanchot writes that "l'impatience doit être le coeur de la profonde patience" (*EL* 234),[15] and this statement seems to fly in the face of the earlier one by making *impatience* a restricted moment of a general economy of patience: impatience is "the heart" or a part of patience. The association of patience with the general economy of repetition and failure indicates that language and poetry have a dual status. The identification of Orpheus's music and patience as the ruse that gives him the power to have mastery over the realm of the dead involves only one aspect of language, the "good version" of the imaginary in which language functions as a tool of constructive negativity. Orpheus's music serves as a means to reach the end he desires so much, to be reunited with Eurydice.

This utilitarian conception of language reflects the point of view of the day toward the events recounted by the myth, but it does not take into account the "second version" of language, the "parole essentielle," intransitive language which is more an instrument of dispersion and separation than of unification. What the myth recounts is the definitive disappearance of Eurydice and the dismemberment of Orpheus at the hands of the bacchantes. These are the "end" results. The dual status of Orpheus's music both offers him the possibility of bringing his project to a successful conclusion and at the same time assures his failure to do so. His failure is prefigured from the outset, and the beginning of his adventure is already the end. When Orpheus heroically undertakes to tame the underworld with his lyre, Eurydice is already lost and he has left behind the land of the living for good. The music that enables Orpheus to go ahead with his plan already tells of his plan's undoing.

The ambivalent nature of Orpheus's songs is the cause of our problem of how to interpret patience and impatience. Impatience as the abdication of power belongs to the general economy as long as patience is identified with Orpheus's courage, genius, and the maintenance of limits. This situation, however, is easily reversible, as is the case when Blanchot ceases to identify patience with power. Patience, in this context, is the equivalent of enduring the repetitious, incessant, interminable approach of Eurydice, and his impatience takes on the characteristics of an act of power. While transgressing one limit, Orpheus establishes another one of his own by arresting the never-ending approach. Unable to be satisfied with the sound of Eurydice's footsteps, the murmur of language that had been previously dissimulated by the sounds of his music, he opts for unmediated vision. He decides to "instituer une limite, prononcer l'inaugural, briser le mouvement de la répétition et de l'incessant" (Préli, 66).[16] The problem is whether or not we are to interpret Orpheus's impatient decision as an act of power. In the following characterization of writing, which parallels the description of Orpheus's descent, impatience certainly seems to take on the attributes of power, mastery, and authority:

> celui qui écrit est . . . celui qui a "entendu" l'interminable et l'incessant, qui l'a entendu comme parole, est entré dans son entente, . . . s'est perdu en elle et toutefois, pour l'avoir soutenue comme il faut, l'a fait cesser, . . . l'a proférée en la rapportant fermement à cette limite, l'a maîtrisée en la mesurant. (*EL* 32)[17]

There appear to be two ways in which we can view patience and impatience and the values that Blanchot assigns to these words. According to the first, Orpheus's initial patient confidence in the power of his music is followed by impatience as he abdicates his power by interrupting his singing to look at Eurydice. Or, instead of associating impatience with the loss of power, we can read it as a decisive action on Orpheus's part which "masters" the endless ascent by "making it cease" and "measuring it," and here it is patience that is identified with lack of initiative and powerlessness. The natural tendency of the reader of Blanchot is to view patience and impatience engaged in a dialectical struggle in which Orpheus's impatient gaze wins out. The temptation to do so is quite understandable, but to succumb to it would be to fall into a trap that may or may not have been deliberately set by Blanchot. In the same way that *l'autre nuit* of the underworld is not the dialectical opposite of the day, and just as the events of the myth do not really take place within a dialectical temporal framework, patience does not stand in simple, logical opposition to impatience. At times, Blanchot's text invites us to identify patience with power and impatience with the abdication of that power. At others, it resists such an interpretation by seeming to propose just the opposite. In this sense, his text, as an invitation and an obstacle, imitates the very movement of transgression that it describes. The circular structure of the myth of Orpheus prevents us from identifying patience and impatience with either power or passivity, respectively. Each term has the attributes of the other. What is indispensable is to recognize (1) that Blanchot subordinates patience as power to another kind of patience, which he variously calls "la vraie patience" (*EL* 230), "la plus haute patience" (*EL* 230), and "la profonde patience" (*EL* 234); and (2) that these generalized forms of patience include momentary lapses of impatience. Moreover, these lapses of impatience do not constitute acts of power, although they sometimes seem to, notably when Blanchot uses words such as "mesure" and "maîtriser" to describe them. Instead they are transgressive acts, in which Orpheus's *oeuvre*, originally thought to be his project to lead Eurydice back to life, is suddenly sacrificed in favor of another *oeuvre* and its most fundamental exigency of failure. Orpheus's gaze ruins his plan, but at the same time, thanks to this gaze, "l'oeuvre peut se dépasser, s'unir à son origine et se consacrer dans l'impossibilité" (*EL* 232).[18] Libertson comments on the reversal of the potentially successful enterprise into irremediable failure in the following way: "The name for the event in which the *oeuvre*, Eurydice, the night, and Orpheus himself are lost is the *oeuvre*. The pertinence of the myth of Orpheus, for Blanchot, is the definition of the *oeuvre* as impossibility" (140).

Blanchot's affinity with Bataille reaches its highest degree of intensity when he equates Orpheus's transgression with an act of sacrifice. Orpheus sacrifices Eurydice, his project, and the night of the underworld that his music succeeds in taming in favor of the *other* night: "Toute la gloire de son oeuvre, toute la puissance de son art et le désir même d'une vie heureuse sous la belle clarté du jour sont sacrifiés à cet unique souci: regarder dans la nuit ce que dissimule la nuit, *l'autre* nuit, la dissimulation qui apparaît" (*EL* 228–29).[19]

Both Blanchot's Orpheus and Bataille's last man are beings endowed with a surplus of negativity that is irrecoverable at the end of history. The last man's comportment is determined by a different set of priorities, once he becomes conscious of the excess negativity within him. According to Blanchot, "s'il en vient à pressentir ce surplus de néant, . . . alors il lui faut répondre à une autre exigence, celle non plus de produire, mais de dépenser, non plus de réussir mais d'échouer, non plus de faire oeuvre, . . . mais . . . de se désoeuvrer" (*EI* 305–6).[20] Orpheus acts in accordance with these very same exigencies. His sacrifice of Eurydice in favor of *l'autre nuit* is a useless expenditure that guarantees the failure of his mission. Blanchot speaks of Orpheus's gaze as "le don ultime d'Orphée à l'oeuvre" thanks to which the work "peut se dépasser, s'unir à son origine et se consacrer dans l'impossibilité" (*EL* 232). The portrayal of the myth in terms of "gift," "sacrifice," and "failure" gives it a particularly Bataillian flavor, and the following statement by Blanchot on the important role that the notion of the gift plays in Bataille's thought applies just as well to his own version of the myth of Orpheus:

> La recherche de *l'autre*—sous le terme d'hétérologie—précède chez Bataille, ce que voudrait nommer le "don" ou dépense—dérangement de l'ordre, transgression, restitution d'une économie plus générale que ne dominerait pas la gestion des choses (l'utilité); mais la perte impossible, liée à l'idée de sacrifice et à l'expérience de moments souverains, ne laisse pas se

figer en un système les tensions qui déchirent la pensée et que soutient l'âpreté d'un langage sans repos. (*ED* 168–69)[21]

A close examination of this fragment of a fragment will reveal just how similar Blanchot's myth and his characterization of Bataille's *expérience* are. There is, first, their commonly held belief concerning the rapport with alterity: the Other remains radically other, unable to be reduced to a symmetrical, mirrorlike reflection of the Same. In the myth, the reduction of the Other to the Same would have occurred had Orpheus been content to lead Eurydice all the way out of Hades, but we have noted that for Blanchot, this scenario is not even hypothetically possible. Orpheus responds to a greater, more fundamental exigency when he gives up on this project in favor of seeing Eurydice "dans son obscurité nocturne."

Another important concept common to both thinkers is that any attempt at reduction is inevitably transformed into transgression, which is not an act "dont . . . la puissance de certains hommes et leur maîtrise se montreraient encore capables . . . Elle [la transgression] s'ouvre à l'homme lorqu'en celui-ci le pouvoir cesse d'être la dimension ultime" (*EI* 308).[22] In terms of the myth, Blanchot designates Orpheus's transgression as the performance of a sacrifice "qui a la légèreté, l'insouciance, l'innocence pour substance" (*EL* 233).[23] The concepts that Blanchot habitually uses in connection with power—mastery, decisiveness, initiative—are absent, and instead he insists on the "lightness" and irresponsibility of Orpheus's gesture. Moreover, the transgression is situated as taking place within a general economy which has been *re*instated ("*resti*tution"), and the prefix of these two words indicates that this "économie plus générale que ne dominerait pas la gestion des choses" is anterior to and forms the undifferentiated, neutral space upon which the regional economy of power can appear. Orpheus's progress is actually regression: the deeper he penetrates into the underworld and the closer he gets to Eurydice, the more he regresses as he approaches the general economy that has precedence over the regional economy.

Two further points remain to be made concerning the affinities between Bataille's *expérience* and Blanchot's myth. Blanchot notes that Bataille's meditations on expenditure, sacrifice, and transgression do not lend themselves to easy systematization, no doubt something desired by Bataille, who was well aware of the impossible, self-contradictory logic of his *expérience*, which is to "sortir par un projet du domaine du projet" (*Oeuvres complètes* V: 60).[24] The question of whether or not the *expérience* is a project is insurmountable. He claims that it is "le contraire de l'action," action being "tout entière dans la dépendance du projet," and that "la pensée discursive est elle-même engagée dans le mode d'existence du projet."[25] Such thinking would seem to (but does not) exclude the declaration that "L'expérience intérieure est conduite par la raison discursive" (60–61).[26] A meditation that sets out to attain "l'extrême du possible" and which involves participation in such marginal activities as laughter, madness, and eroticism could only produce a text fissured by the incompatibility and unresolvability of these tensions. Although the tone of Blanchot's analysis of the Orphic myth is miles apart from Bataille's in *L'Expérience intérieure*, a close reading of his text encounters the same tension, the same resistance to synthesis and comprehension, which we encountered specifically in connection with chronology and in his discussion of the interrelatedness of patience, impatience, and "la vraie patience."

The lack of the texts' internal coherence, however, is *our* problem as readers, and this is the final point that I would like to make regarding the affinities between Blanchot's discussion of sacrifice as it appears in Orpheus's case and in his comment on expenditure and its importance for Bataille. This unreadability is certainly not a state of affairs bemoaned by Blanchot. On the contrary, literature's reason for being is its capacity to maintain these tensions as such without making them fit into place in a well-designed, grand scheme. Literature owes its ability to keep the question open and the tensions unresolved to its medium, language that is "sans repos." The state of perpetual contestation that resides at the heart of language makes it the most suitable vehicle for Bataille's *expérience*, which is also an endless activity of self-contestation, "supplication sans espoir" (*L'Expérience intérieure*, 47). And Blanchot's interpretation of the Orphic myth rests on the very same conception of language as fundamentally and uncontrollably ambivalent, Orpheus's music which supposedly helps him in his quest but which also foretells its failure. Just as Eurydice irresistibly attracts Orpheus to a point where she is revealed to him by disappearing, there is a major impropriety at the origin of language "dont l'étrange effet est d'attirer la littérature en un point instable où elle peut changer indifféremment et de sens et de signe" (*PF* 329).[27] The instability of literature is represented in the myth by the reversal of the status of Orpheus's music from a source of power to the loss of it. Orpheus was bound to fail once he decided to use music as the arm with which he would defend himself from the perils of death. A strange choice of weapon indeed! Even though he did not heed this call written by Blanchot in *L'Ecriture de désastre*, "Que les mots cessent d'être des armes, des moyens d'action, des possibilités de salut. S'en remettre au désarroi" (25),[28] he might as well have done so, for he ended up in a state of disarray anyway, at the hands of the bacchantes. He was so blinded by his Apollonian confidence in the power of his art that he overlooked its other, dark side: its capacity to lead him into a Dionysian state of power-lessness, fascination, and passivity, which culminates in the sacrifice of Eurydice.

.   .   .   .   .

Although Blanchot uses the myth of Orpheus primarily to describe the path of writers as they approach the space of literature while writing, there is yet another application of the myth which addresses the problem of the relationship of writers to their work once they cease writing it. In this context, instead of signifying an author's inevitable failure to capture completely the experience of seeing the nocturnal Eurydice by transpos-ing it into a diurnal literary form, the gaze of Orpheus represents the in-ability of an author to retrace the steps made while writing by means of a retrospective reading:

> Si l'écrit, toujours impersonnel, altère, congédie, abolit l'écrivain en tant que tel, . . . alors comment pourra-t-il se retourner (ah, le coupable Orphée) vers cela qu'il pense conduire au jour, l'apprécier, le considérer, s'y re-connaître et, pour finir, s'en faire le lecteur privilégié, le commentateur prin-cipal ou simplement l'auxiliaire zélé qui donne ou impose sa version, résout l'énigme, délivre le secret et interrompt autoritairement (c'est bien de l'au-teur qu'il s'agit) la chaîne herméneutique, puisqu'il se prétend l'interprète suffisant, premier ou dernier? (AC 88)[29]

The notion that the writer is not in a privileged position of authority, as the creator of the work, to explain the mysteries of creation after the fact of the work's completion is more frequently referred to in Blanchot's text by the Latin phrase *noli me legere*, a parody of the warning not to touch him (*noli me tangere*) that Jesus issued to Mary Magdalene just after the resurrection. The negative imperative "don't read me" is uttered to the author by the work and indicates that the only rapport that writers can have with their work is to write it. Once the work is written, however, they are expelled from it, unable to regain the same access to it as a reader that they had as its author. The incapability of authors to read their own works signifies that once finished, the works have a life of their own inde-pendent from and oblivious to that of their creators. They do not need them anymore. In the words of Mallarmé, who is clearly Blanchot's au-thority on the subject, "[le volume] a lieu tout seul: fait, étant" (372).[30] In describing the definitive separation of the impersonal text from the personal author, Mallarmé speaks of the latter as "mort comme un tel" (370)[31] and of the "sacrifice, relativement à sa personnalité" (370)[32] which is performed in the writing of the book.

Blanchot situates the origin of reading at the very moment that the author is dismissed from the work: "Le moment où ce qui se glorifie en l'oeuvre, c'est l'oeuvre, où celle-ci cesse en quelque sorte d'avoir été faite, de se rapporter à quelqu'un qui l'ait faite, . . . ce moment qui annule l'auteur est aussi celui où . . . la lecture prend origine" (*EL* 268).[33] And yet in the passage just alluded to, Mallarmé says that "Impersonnifié, le volume ne réclame approche de lecteur" (372).[34] These two declarations, however, are at odds with each other in appearance only, for Blanchot takes Mallarmé to mean that the first moment of reading does not consist in the approach of a particular reader but exists rather as an impersonal, anonymous activity. Reading is thus the disappearance of both a personal author *and* a personal reader. The former has been dismissed and the latter has no place here (yet). At this stage, any reader at all will do, and Blanchot emphasizes the aspect of interchangeability: one reader is as good as the next. Other words he uses to describe reading are "légèreté," "innocence," "insouciance," and "irresponsabilité," the same words he uses to describe Orpheus's decision to look at Eurydice, which suggests that the same attitude on the part of the reader is what allows the work to affirm itself in its incompletion. Blanchot speaks of the "lightness" of reading because he says that it adds nothing to the work; it is not an act of comprehension that seeks to weigh the work down with interpretations. "La lecture est ignorante. . . . Elle est accueil et entente, non pas pouvoir de déchiffrer et d'analyser . . . elle ne comprend pas (à proprement parler), elle entend. Merveilleuse innocence" (*EI* 468).[35] In a Heideggerian inspiration, once again Blanchot gives priority to the verb *entendre* over other verbs such as *comprendre* and *voir*. Functions of constructive negativity, the latter activities participate in the reduction of the Other to the Same. *Entendre*, on the contrary, implies a role for language that is not limited to the useful exchange of information and maintains the interval that lies between the Other and the Same. Just as the only authenticity in Orpheus's experience is the sound of Eurydice's approaching footsteps, the authenticity that links a writer and a reader to the literary language of the book is their vigilant attentiveness to the *murmure*.

This is, of course, only one moment in the activity of reading, for the existence of both empirical readers and their interpretations is obviously undeniable. Blanchot uses the story of another resurrection, that of Lazarus, to describe the rapport of the reader (as opposed to the impersonal activity of reading) with the work. He likens the reader's situation with respect to a text to that of Jesus before Lazarus's tomb when he says, "Lazarus, come forth." Whereas the rapport between authors and their work is expressed in terms of a negative imperative uttered to them by their work, the readers' rapport is expressed by means of a positive imperative uttered by them to the works: "Le livre est donc là, mais l'oeuvre est encore cachée, absente peut-être radicalement, dissimulée en tout cas, offusquée par l'évidence du livre, derrière laquelle elle attend la décision libératrice, le *Lazare, veni foras*" (*EL* 259).[36] Reading would thus seem to involve the miraculous retrieval and resuscitation of something or someone that has been buried beneath the tombstone of the book. It is important to note a subtle distinction in Blanchot's critical vocabulary (one that recalls Heidegger's regarding world and earth) that we only briefly touched on in our discussion of suicide and writing: the book and the work do not refer to the same thing. The book, the artifact produced by Paulhan's Terrorist, describes the manifest aspect of the work, that which is available to comprehension: "le Livre indique toujours un ordre soumis à *l'unité*, un système de notions où s'affirme le primat de la parole sur l'écriture, de la pensée sur le langage et la promesse d'une communication un jour immédiate ou transparente" (*EI* vii).[37] The work, on the other hand, escapes comprehension. It contains an inexhaustible reserve that can never be completely explained away, accounted for, or summed up by interpretation. The "evidence of the book" seems to be a solid structure, but it is an edifice built on the ever-shifting sands of the work. The lack of a solid foundation accounts for the inadequation of the work with itself, which Blanchot calls "the absence of the book." The *oeuvre* is "toujours en divergence, toujours sans rapport de présence avec elle-même" (*EI* 626).[38] The work is and is not there. Its constant movement is an oscillation between apparition and disappearance, like Eurydice at the moment of Orpheus's fleeting glance, like Christ's appearance on earth before ascending to heaven, and like Lazarus, who is brought back to life only to be sentenced to death immediately afterward by the chief priests so as to quell all the publicity generated by the working of the miracle. Since the work does not coincide with itself, no rapport of presence between the writing and the reading of it is possible: ce qui fut écrit au passé sera lu à l'avenir, sans qu'aucun rapport de présence puisse s'établir *entre* écriture et lecture (*PAD* 45–46).[39] Thus the *noli me legere*, which Blanchot consistently invokes to describe writers' incapability of authoritatively reading their own works, actually applies to all readers. No one can read the work. It is the book that lends itself to understanding, and it can be read by both author and reader.

Given the double status of the negative and the two versions of the *parole* and of the imaginary that stem from this duality, it follows that there are two ways to interpret the *Lazare, veni foras,* and the shift of meaning depends on whether it is given to the book or the work. The book is the target if it is spoken by a Hegelian reader, one who is capable of "enduring death and maintaining himself in it," celui qui, sans s'abîmer dans la réalité cadavérique, est capable, tout en la fixant, de la nommer, de l'"entendre" et, en cette entente, de prononcer le *Lazare veni foras*, par lequel la mort deviendra principe, la terrible puissance en laquelle la vie qui porte la mort doit se maintenir pour la maîtriser et y trouver l'accomplissement de sa maîtrise. (*EI* 49–50)[40]

The fully resuscitated Lazarus who comes forth into the light of day intact and untouched by the ravages of death is Blanchot's image of the book as a vehicle for transmitting knowledge which can be received and interpreted by an act of reading conceived as an exercise of power. The *noli me legere* is always violated by a *Lazare, veni foras* that seeks to exhume the exquisitely preserved cadaver, to bring him back to the world of truth, and to interpret his resurrection as proof of the human possibility of death. And yet, this Lazarus, "qu'a-t-il à voir avec ce qui est là et vous fait reculer, l'anonyme corruption du tombeau, celui qui sent déjà mauvais, le Lazare perdu, et non le Lazare rendu au jour . . . ?" (*EI* 50).[41] Not just one but two Lazaruses are summoned forth. The first Lazarus who emerges is the one held together by clean, white, tightly wound bandages, and the other much less palatable Lazarus is the one whose partially decomposed body would be revealed were the bandages to come undone. The parallel that Blanchot draws in this grisly comparison of the two Lazaruses (which recalls his discussion of the image and of *la ressemblance cadavérique*) is that the book is a dissimulation of the work in the same way that the whole Lazarus is a dissimulation of the rotting one.

The book is a receptacle of dormant knowledge which is awakened thanks to the participation of readers, who endow the lifeless ideas of the closed book with "la vie de l'esprit" as they open the book and beckon these ideas forth with their *Lazare, veni foras*. In both the language of the book and the world, words are subordinated to ideas which are, in turn, mobilized in the historical process of becoming. The writing and reading of a book can, therefore, have as much impact in and on the world as any other activity which might be deemed more concrete and immediate: "Le livre, chose écrite, entre dans le monde où il accomplit son oeuvre de transformation et de négation. Lui aussi est l'avenir de beaucoup d'autres choses, et non seulement de livres . . . il est source infinie de réalites nouvelles, à partir de quoi l'existence sera ce qu'elle n'était pas" (*PF* 305).[42]

The work, on the other hand, embodies the persistence of unemployable negativity which lingers on after the constructive negativity of the book has run its course. The work is the *part maudite* of the book, an excessive remainder over and beyond the closure of the book. The rapport of inadequation between the work and the book is a consequence of the dual nature of language and reflects the disproportion between the two negativities. Thus the internal dynamics of a literary text, the interaction of the tension between the work and the book, play out in the microcosmic confines of the text the forces that are at work in history in general. Just as unemployable negativity is irreducible to constructive negativity, so is the work irreducible to the book, for between the work and the book there is "une rupture violente, le passage du monde où tout a plus ou moins de sens, où il y a obscurité et clarté, à un espace où, à proprement parler, rien n'a encore de sens, vers quoi cependant tout ce qui a sens remonte comme vers son origine" (*EL* 260).[43]

The gap between the work and the book is never completely closed, although the coincidence of the work with the book (with all the books about a work) would represent the crowning achievement of literary history. The book belongs to the regional economy where everything has varying degrees of meaning. This is, however, a dissimulation of the general economy of the work which points the way to a realm where "nothing has meaning *yet*." The work opens up onto that which is "quand il n'y a plus de monde, quand il n'y a pas encore de monde" (*EL* 28),[44] a neutral space "où sans cesse être se perpétue sous l'espèce du néant" (*EL* 330)[45] which both precedes and outlasts the regional economy of being, governed by such established categories as "obscurité" and "clarté" and where the power of the negative holds sway.

The *noli me legere* is a weak interdiction that invites the reader to violate it by pronouncing the *Lazare, veni foras*. The neutrality of the work inevitably becomes charged with positive or negative values of some sort. In other words, the self-willed destiny of every work is to become a book. In order for a work to proclaim its sovereignty, it needs to be confined—unsuccessfully—within the limits of some interpretative scheme. The sovereignty of the work can be measured only in terms of its ability to exceed such limits. The betrayal of the *noli me legere* is thus part of a higher fidelity to the principle of the irreducibility of the work, and, once again, the law and its transgression exist in a relationship of hidden collaboration: "L'oeuvre, fût-elle sans auteur et toujours en devenir par rapport à elle-même, délimite un espace qui attire les noms, une possibilité chaque fois déterminée de lecture, un système de références, une théorie qui l'approprie, un sens qui l'éclaire" (*PAD* 53).[46]

A work would not be a work if it did not participate in this movement of cultural appropriation. A work relegated to the dusty shelves of some library that has never been read or commented on is not somehow purer or more intact because preserved from necessarily incomplete interpretations that alter it. The transformation of the work into a book by a reader's active interpretation constitutes a violation of the *noli me legere* which has the same characteristics as Orpheus's transgression. The reader who succumbs to the need to interpret a work casts an Orphic gaze on it that arrests for a time the state of perpetual contestation that resides at its center. When this occurs, the work, instead of being nothing more than "l'affirmation impersonnelle qu'elle est,"[47] becomes the "communication de quelque chose"(*EL* 276)[48] which one might read "pour s'instruire, pour mieux se connaître ou pour se cultiver" (*EL* 276).[49] Every work contains a book, an index of the work's power. The duplicity of language, however, prevents us from equating the work with the book. This very duplicity is responsible for Orpheus's failure in that he mistakes his music for an instrument of power. And as we noted in the preceding chapter, suicide victims encounter the same problem as they realize too late that death must come to them and that they are powerless in their attempts to have complete control over death and to experience it on their terms: they mistake one death for another. Similarly, the reader mistakes the book for the work. All three give in to impatience provoked by anguish. Orpheus's anguish grows with every step he takes as he becomes increasingly unsure of whether or not Eurydice is really following him. And just as death inspires anguish because of our fear of being unable to die completely, the dilemma that suicide purports to resolve, there is an anguish of reading which arises because of our incapacity to read works completely: "L'angoisse de lire: c'est que tout texte, si important, si plaisant et si intéressant qu'il soit (et plus il donne l'impression de l'être), est vide—il n'existe pas dans le fond; il faut franchir un abîme, et si l'on ne saute pas, on ne comprend pas" (*ED* 23).[50]

Of the *saltus mortalis* which forms an integral part of the experience of Orpheus, the suicidal artist, and the reader, Blanchot reminds us that "Il faut un espace libre pour sauter, il faut un sol ferme, il faut un pouvoir qui, à partir de l'immobilité sûre, change le mouvement en bond" (*EI* 25).[51] All three protagonists take great flying leaps, only to discover, much to their horror, the lack of both a solid jumping-off point and a firm landing area. Whether we are speaking of the underworld, death, or a literary work, there is no "immobilité sûre," no reliable foundation to support the leaps. To endow any of these entities with such a foundation would be an act of faith, in Blanchot's opinion, a misplaced trust in power and a willingness to close one's eyes to the general economy of the *mourir*. *Le neutre* does not describe a confined region that is bounded on all sides by the *terra firma* of the negative; on the contrary, it is constructive negativity which possesses a regional, insular status surrounded by the murky waters of the *dehors*, where "il n'y a rien de sûr, rien de ferme" (*EI* 25).[52]

We find these remarks on the leap of faith in the second chapter of *L'Entretien infini*, entitled "La question la plus profonde." Blanchot makes a distinction in this essay between two types of questions, one which he calls "la question d'ensemble," the question of the whole, and the other "la question la plus profonde," the most profound question. Françoise Collin summarizes Blanchot's presentation of the question of the whole by calling it "la question de la totalité au sens propre, la question métaphysique par excellence, celle qui se situe dans l'ordre de la vérité, là où le symbole est gage de savoir" (*Maurice Blanchot et la question de l'écriture*, 167).[53] The chief characteristics that make up the question of the whole, "totalité," "vérité," et "savoir" clearly indicate that Blanchot situates it within the regional economy of manifestation and power. It is of the order of knowledge, the kind of question to which the Hegelian power of the understanding can provide answers in a dialectical process toward totalization. The most profound question, however, is what the question of the whole becomes when the latter type of question approaches the unreachable limit of being the final question, the ultimate question that would lay to rest all further questioning. The most profound question is what the question of the whole has in reserve. There is more to the question of the whole than meets the eye of understanding, and Blanchot calls this unknowable surplus "the most profound question."

The belief that the eye of understanding can see all and know all constitutes itself an attitude of blindness, a refusal or an inability to see things as they really are. The risk of mistaking one thing for another has been an important element in our discussion in this chapter of the myths that Blanchot adapts in his portrayals of writing and reading, as it was in the previous chapter on the comparison of suicide to writing. Orpheus views his music solely as an instrument of power, incapable of realizing that in his music Eurydice is already lost. Jesus performs the miracle of Lazarus's resurrection as a dazzling display of what awaits those who invest their faith blindly in the belief of eternal life after death. Suicide victims aspire to a similar but misguided ideal: that of having mastery over their own death and of experiencing it on their terms alone. And the reader mistakes the book for the work. We may add one more mythic hero to our list of protagonists whose failures are brought about by their inability to see through a blind spot: Oedipus at the moment of his encounter with the Sphinx, which Blanchot portrays as a "mémorable confrontation de la question profonde et de la question d'ensemble" (*EI* 22).[54] Oedipus, too, falls into the trap of taking one thing for another, in his case, "la question la plus profonde," the riddle put forth to him by the Sphinx, for a "question d'ensemble," a problem that can be solved by the intellect. He is praiseworthy in his courageous act of standing up to the Sphinx at the risk of losing his life. He embodies the Hegelian life of the spirit which is capable of "enduring death and maintaining itself in it." And he seems to come out of the encounter unscathed: thanks to his superior intelligence, he answers the riddle, restores order to Thebes, and reduces the Sphinx to silence. Or does he? "Certes, il a *su* répondre, mais ce savoir n'a fait qu'affirmer son ignorance de lui-même et n'a même été possible qu'à cause de cette profonde ignorance" (*EI* 22–23).[55] Oedipus's solution to the riddle does not succeed in pacifying the Sphinx's capacity to question; on the contrary, his answer ("man") is itself a riddle that will draw him into the depths of his own personal "question la plus profonde," his ignorance of his origins and his painful recognition of them. The fact that Oedipus's cunning furnishes only a partial answer to the riddle, while at the same time giving rise to other more pertinent and profound questions, demonstrates reason's persistent tendency to misinterpret powerlessness as power. Since Oedipus had successfully delivered Thebes from the ravages of the plague, it was only natural for him to assume the duty of eradicating the other curse that hung heavy over the city: to arrest and punish the murderer of Laius. He had no choice but to shoulder this burden, and he did so willingly, ignorant that the consequences of his investigation would involve another encounter with "la question la plus profonde." In the end, he is obliged to see this question for what it is—by blinding himself and assuming a nomadic existence, exiled to the *dehors*.

Whereas the myth of Orpheus, the *noli me legere*, and, to a lesser degree, the *Lazare veni foras* occur as integral and widespread elements in Blanchot's theory of literature, the story of Oedipus occupies a much more limited place—to the best of my knowledge, this is the only essay in which he speaks of it. It is, nevertheless, relevant to our discussion of the myths of reading, for the predicament of a reader before a text is analogous to Oedipus's confrontation with the Sphinx. The *noli me legere* pronounced by a work to its reader gives to the work a quality that is every bit as enigmatic as the puzzle that confronts Oedipus. The literary work and the riddle are texts that demand to be deciphered, and at the same time defy any attempts to do so. Both also seem to be of easy access: the riddle is couched in deceptively simple, even frivolous language and resembles a game more than anything else. And reading is first and foremost for Blanchot "un bonheur qui demande plus d'innocence et de liberté que de considération" (*LV* 133).[56] The threat of failure, however, taints the pleasurable, playful aspects of the decoding process. Oedipus's and the reader's anguish are the same. The former turns "la question la plus profonde" into a "question d'ensemble," and the latter the work into a book. Both realize too late that their efforts have come up short of their desired aims when they understand that the language of their interpretations cannot do justice to the original language of the riddle/work. What it does do is dissimulate the profound question, to make it seem like it has been taken care of and dispensed with.

Oedipus misreads the riddle, and we can apply the example of his failure to interpret the enigma correctly to the problem of reading. Oedipus performs a symbolic reading of the riddle which is complete. Blanchot does not reproach him for doing so, but he does criticize a method of reading based on such an approach. "La lecture symbolique," he writes, "est probablement la pire façon de lire un texte littéraire" (*LV* 125).[57] Those who would incur Blanchot's wrath by reading a text in "the worst possible way" would be guilty, like Oedipus, of seeing only part of the problem, of opening their eyes to see only the "good" version of the imaginary, logocentrism, at the expense of casting the other version of the imaginary, *ressemblance*, into oblivion. Given such a harsh characterization of symbolic reading, we would expect Blanchot to stay as far away as possible from engaging in it. This is, however, not always necessarily the case. After all, Orpheus's impatient gaze, by means of which he attempts to leap across the interval separating him from Eurydice, is responsible for his losing her. For someone acting in accordance with the exigencies of the day, Orpheus betrays Eurydice. For the artist who has left behind this domain by entering the space of literature, however, this so-called betrayal is actually an act of fidelity which permits the work (the disappearing Eurydice) to affirm itself as an impossibility, as something that will not let itself be dominated by the gaze of its author or its reader, a gaze which the latter mistakes for an act of power but which is, in truth, a transgression predicated on failure. To give in to impatience is inevitable, for impatience is a part of "true patience." It should not come as a surprise, therefore, that Blanchot succumbs to the same temptation, that he, too, has momentary lapses of impatience during which he comes dangerously close to engaging in a style of reading that he elsewhere deplores. A particularly salient example of practical criticism which reproduces this same transgressive movement that he describes in his theoretical texts can be found in an essay on Kafka's *The Castle*, entitled "Le pont de bois."

Like Oedipus's meeting with the Sphinx, Blanchot's encounter with Kafka's novel has all the trappings of a "mémorable confrontation de la question profonde et de la question d'ensemble." As a work of art, the novel (and this is Blanchot's superiority over Oedipus: he knows this) asks the most profound question, and yet Blanchot very nearly treats it as a "question d'ensemble." The riddle of the book concerns how we are to interpret the castle and Kafka's relationship to it. In other words, Blanchot would like to know what the castle symbolizes, although he does not do so blindly: he is fully aware that he is transgressing the law of the inviolable work, and he wants us to know that he knows this. He does so by half-heartedly proposing the most banal interpretations of the castle that he can think of:

C'est étrange: on a beau aller chercher les désignations suprêmes, celles que depuis des millénaires l'humanité a mises au point pour caractériser l'Unique, on a beau dire: "Mais le Château, c'est la Grâce; le *Graf* (le comte), c'est *Gott*, comme l'identité des majuscules le prouve; ou bien c'est la Transcendance de l'Etre ou la Transdescendance du Néant, ou c'est l'Olympe, ou la gestion bureaucratique de l'univers. Oui, on a beau dire tout cela, . . . il n'en reste pas moins que toutes ces profondes indications . . . ne manquent pas de nous décevoir encore: comme si le Château, c'était toujours infiniment plus que cela, infiniment plus, c'est-à-dire aussi infiniment moins. (*EI* 579–80)[58]

At this point in his interpretation, Blanchot is mimicking a symbolic reading; he proposes these interpretations while at the same time rejecting them on the grounds of insufficiency. The locutions "On a beau aller" and "on a beau dire" signal to us that he is familiar with such attempts of exegesis and that he just does not buy them. Thus far he seems to be adopting a symbolic approach in order to subvert it by pointing out its inadequacies. He has not, therefore, transgressed his law—not yet, anyway. But we do not have to wait very long. In the sentence following the ones just cited, he rephrases the central question posed by the book: "Qu'y a-t-il donc au-dessus de la Transcendance, qu'y a-t-il au-dessous de la Transdescendance?" (*EI* 580).[59] How is it that no one, single designation for the castle seems to fit? This is the moment at which Blanchot takes the plunge. We now arrive at the fatal moment of his transgression (of the law of the work, of the interdiction against symbolic reading proclaimed in his own critical corpus) when he proposes to answer this most profound of questions by saying: "Eh bien (répondons hâtivement, seule la hâte autorise la réponse)." (*EI* 580).[60] One senses the diffidence that Blanchot must have felt in undertaking this explanation; the fact that he states his intentions to do so in parentheses betrays his reservations. They almost play the role of framing a disclaimer: he knows deep down that what he is about to do is wrong, so he hopes to get it over with as quickly as possible, preferably without the reader's taking too much notice. He is guilty of Orphic impatience. He is going to jump to a conclusion ("seule la hâte autorise la réponse") which, like Oedipus, he will regret, namely, that the castle represents "cela au regard de quoi toute évaluation déroge" (*EI* 580),[61] *le neutre*. It is not a triumphant declaration, however, as was Oedipus's, for he hesitatingly puts his explanation in the interrogative mode: "avons-nous le droit de suggérer que le Château, la résidence comtale, ce ne serait rien d'autre que la souveraineté du neutre et le lieu de cette étrange souveraineté?" (*EI* 580).[62] This is as close as Blanchot ever gets to assigning a concept to a particular symbol. He practically comes right out and says that the castle is the *neutre*, but this will not be his last word on the subject. Having momentarily transgressed the limits of the *noli me legere*, he quickly pulls back in retreat, which allows the *noli* to reassert itself, for, lest we forget, the law always survives the infraction. By identifying the castle with neutrality, Blanchot, like Oedipus, has treated the most profound question of the work as the general question of the book. He, too, briefly mistakes one thing for another, which he wastes no time, however, in setting aright by immediately answering his own question ("avons-nous le droit de suggérer que . . ."): "On ne peut malheureusement pas le dire aussi simplement." (*EI* 581).[63] To designate the castle as the seat of neutrality is an oversimplification. The neutral is everywhere and nowhere; it cannot be situated in relation to one particular image or symbol:

> le neutre ne saurait être représenté ni symbolisé ni même signifié et . . . s'il est porté par l'indifférence infinie de tout le récit, il est partout en lui . . . comme s'il était le point de fuite à l'infini à partir duquel la parole du récit et, en elle, tous les récits et toute parole sur tout récit recevraient et perdraient leur perspective, l'infinie distance des rapports, leur perpétuel renversement, leur abolition. Mais, arrêtons-nous là de crainte de nous engager à notre tour dans un mouvement infini. (*EI* 581)[64]

Having gone too far in suggesting that the castle represented the *neutre*, Blanchot withdraws from this overextended position with dizzying speed. First, he reiterates his "first law," the unrepresentability of the neuter, after which he changes scope completely, zooming out, as it were, from the particular problem posed by Kafka's novel in order to embrace the general concerns of all of literature. We move from "la parole du récit" (Kafka's) to "tous les récits" (fiction in general) and, finally, we arrive at "toute parole sur tout récit" (literary criticism as a whole). All too aware of the haste with which he is beating his retreat and of the proportions it has suddenly assumed, he is obliged to curb his enthusiasm in a somewhat arbitrary fashion ("arrêtons-nous là") thereby instituting a temporary limit to his "entretien infini" with and about literary texts. Thus, although he temporarily transgresses the law of the *noli* by engaging in a brand of reading that borders on the symbolic, he ultimately abandons this position in favor of a method of reading according to which "Lire, ce serait lire dans le livre l'absence de livre, en conséquence la produire" (*EI* 626).[65] For a brief moment, he filled the void at the center of the work with the proposition: the castle = *le neutre*. At the end of the article, however, he refutes his own thesis, calling to the fore the absence of the book by invoking the *neutre* as the unlocatable source of not only *The Castle* but of all literature, both fictional and critical. In the end, the only answer that he gives to the riddle of the castle is to leave the question open.

In fact, the article closes with a question. The final sentence, "Pourquoi ce nom?" (*EI* 581) enunciates what is perhaps the most fundamental question posed by Blanchot's *oeuvre*, that is, what the consequences of giving a voice to the ineffable neuter are. We have just witnessed an immediate consequence of this: his unwillingness to equate it with the castle in Kafka's novel. Blanchot does not fault Kafka (or any other writer, for that matter) for failing to measure up to the neutral and to do it justice by creating a more effective literary expression of it. It is not that the castle was a poor choice of symbol, whereas some other image would have been better. The problem can be stated in a much more radically concise way: how is it that the *word* "le neutre" itself can exist, let alone a symbolic representation of it?

Le neutre is a perfect example of what Bataille calls, in *L'Expérience intérieure*, a *mot glissant*. The word that he uses to illustrate this phenomenon is "silence." A *mot glissant* is a word that establishes a limit that it cannot hold itself to. Libertson explains: "The enunciation of the word is a strangely excessive, violent alteration of the silence it would inscribe in the discourse. The function of the word as expression is essentially compromised by the paradox of its reference" (120). As a sound, the word abolishes the concept it is supposed to represent; the phonetic dimension of the word transgresses the semantic limit that it pretends to set up. "Silence" is a word that, paradoxically, renders impossible its own existence, or in the words of Bataille, "il est lui-même gage de sa mort" (*Oeuvres complètes* V: 28).[66] *Le neutre*, too, is a *mot glissant* which undermines its own pretension to signify a concept. It, too, is responsible for its own undoing and is, therefore, "the pledge of its death." In the following fragment from *Le Pas au-delà*, Blanchot explains what is involved when we use the word *le neutre*. It thus provides us with a response to the question "Pourquoi ce nom?" that leaves us hanging at the end of "Le pont de bois":

> Le neutre peut être nommé, puisqu'il est (même si ce n'est pas une preuve). Mais qu'est-ce qui est alors désigné par le nom? Le désir de maîtriser le neutre, désir auquel aussitôt se prête le neutre, d'autant plus qu'il est étranger à toute maîtrise et qu'il a toujours déjà marqué, de son insistence passive, le désir qui ainsi infecte son objet et tout objet. (116)[67]

To attribute a name to designate the neuter is to succumb to the impatient desire to have mastery over it within the well-established bounds of the concept. Moreover, we are told that it lends itself to this desire (as in "la vraie patience n'exclut pas l'impatience"). And yet the *neutre* has always already left its imprint on desire, thereby contaminating any rapport between a desiring subject and a desired object which would be based on the appropriation of the latter by the former through an act of power, in this case of the concept that the person who writes the word *neutre* hopes to work with in so doing. For Blanchot, desire is always indicative of a rapport of impossibility, incompleteness, and inadequation (cf. Orpheus's desire to see Eurydice in the underworld, the work's unfulfilled desire to become a book, etc.). The word as an instrument used in the service of the transmission of conceptual knowledge is transgressed by the very phenomenon it seeks to express, which is of the order of *non-savior*. *Le neutre* is the paradoxical nonconcept Blanchot invokes to designate in one fell swoop something that denies such a categorization: the ever-restless state of contestation that exists at the heart of language, a condition responsible more for the dispossession of human beings by language than for the possession by human beings of themselves and the world thanks to language.

.   .   .   .   .

As a manner of concluding my discussion of Blanchot's theoretical texts, I would like to reflect on the circularity of the laws that govern the general economies of the production and reception of a work of literature. We have already had occasion to refer to one of the laws, the circular exigency of writing, which concerns the rapport of authors with their work. Although Blanchot never explicitly does so, it is possible to complement this law by proposing an additional one that would take into account the point of view of the reader. Such a theory might be entitled "the circular exigency of reading," and it will reveal the reader's rapport with the work to be a doubling of the author's rapport with it. Blanchot defines the essential circularity of the law that we will apply to both positions as follows: "Le cercle de la loi est celui-ci: il faut qu'il y ait franchissement pour qu'il y ait limite, mais seule la limite, en tant qu'infranchissable, appelle à franchir, affirme le désir (le faux pas) qui a toujours déjà, par le mouvement imprévisible, franchi la ligne" (*PAD* 38).[68]

The first half of the circular exigency of the law states that there must be some sort of transgression in order for a limit to be established. Orpheus's adventure bears this out: he crosses the threshold of the underworld, just as Eurydice had before him, thereby setting up the possibility of the *expérience-limite*, his nocturnal encounter with Eurydice. According to the second half of the exigency, however, this limit that becomes recognizable thanks to the transgression is not itself immune from transgression. On one hand, it resists transgression: Orpheus willingly complies with the interdiction not to look at Eurydice during his mission, for it is the only way he has to arrive at the point where the *expérience-limite* can take place. On the other hand, Orpheus ceases to comply with this condition once he arrives at that point, a betrayal that is really an act of fidelity, since it allows Eurydice to affirm her sovereignty through her disappearance. Desire, moreover, predetermines the encounter as a failure. Orpheus's choice of weapon to satisfy his desire, his music, is a two-edged sword: what he uses to achieve his unification with Eurydice always already tells the story of their ultimate separation. The fact that "le désir a toujours déjà franchi la ligne" signifies that Orpheus has never stopped looking at Eurydice, even before taking his first steps into Hades. Writers follow the same path traced out by Orpheus, which takes them from an initial stage of (misplaced) confidence in their power to have mastery over language to a second stage characterized by indecision and loss of personal identity. The transgressive decision to put an end to this stage results in the autonomous existence of the work, which eludes any authority they might claim to have over it, just as Eurydice eludes Orpheus's gaze.

We can now make the parallel case for a circular exigency of reading, illustrated mythically by Lazarus's resurrection. Lazarus had committed the ultimate transgression by dying, and Jesus, the son of God who is always already mortal *and* immortal, most certainly violates the law of the everyday by undertaking to raise a person from the dead. These transgressions, Lazarus's necessary death and Jesus' command that he should come forth, establish a limit: the mummified Lazarus does indeed appear as if to confirm that death *is* within the realm of human possibility. And yet there is a "cursed," unthinkable part that exceeds this version of Lazarus, the part that had to be excluded, "le Lazare du tombeau et non le Lazare rendu au jour, celui qui sent mauvais, qui est le mal, le Lazare perdu et non le Lazare sauvé et ressuscité" (*PF* 316),[69] so that the Lazarus who represents the life of the spirit and the power of the negative could appear. To perform a resurrection is to transgress the limits of what power can normally accomplish. A limit does result, living proof that death is humanly possible, which, however, is exceeded by the cadaveric reality that is sublimated in the act of calling forth (naming) Lazarus.

To put Blanchot's interpretation of the story bluntly, Jesus got more than he bargained for: two Lazaruses emerged from the tomb instead of just one. Readers, too, get more than they bargain for. The decision to start reading a book constitutes a transgression—the reader quits the real world for the world of fiction. The limit which is thus established is that of the work. The work needs reading to affirm itself as a thing with an existence independent of that of any particular author or reader. Reading not only lets the book be; it lets it be written: "Lire, ce serait donc, non pas écrire à nouveau le livre, mais faire que le livre s'écrive ou *soit* écrit— cette fois sans l'intermédiare de l'écrivain, sans personne qui l'écrive" (*EL*

256).[70] As Ann Smock aptly puts it in *Double Dealing*: "The reader's situation is peculiar in that he wants to read a book that isn't written yet . . . Something strange, it would seem, happens to the normal sequence of events in the neighborhood of a work of literature; something strange happens to time" (5). We encountered some of this strangeness with respect to the Orphic myth: Orpheus's adventure was over before it started. Similarly, and contrary to our habitual way of thinking which says that first a writer writes, then a reader reads what has been written, the writing of a book is over before it starts. One writing is over (that done by the author) before another writing can begin (that to which authors have sacrificed themselves, the writing of works *by themselves* under the indifferent gaze of the reader).

The "limite infranchissable" of the work needs and encourages transgression, Orphic gazes by the reader that arrest its perpetual movement by turning it into a book. The impersonal attitude of passive indifference and acceptance is inevitably replaced by the individual reader's anxiety when confronted by the "horreur du vide" (EL 270), the impulse to analyze and to understand that must be satisfied. Like Orpheus's betrayal of Eurydice, the reader's betrayal of the work is necessary, and the destiny of every work is to become a book, even while remaining irreducible to this dimension that lends itself to conceptualization. The work always remains outside the scheme of things, aloof and impervious to the reader's attempts to explain its secrets. To begin to read a book is to become mindful of the *noli me legere* it proclaims, an interdiction that is inevitably violated, but never completely. The reader fails in his quest to read the work completely to the same degree that Orpheus fails in his mission. Moreover, the sacrifice that Orpheus performs in the course of his mission—of himself, of Eurydice, of his project—is ordained from the start. Reading, too, involves a sacrifice, that of the work to the book while the ban governing the work's inviolability is temporarily lifted. (We might mention in passing that the titles of Blanchot's first two books of critical essays, *Faux Pas* and *La Part du feu*, suggest that his reading the books of others constitutes transgressive and sacrificial activities, respectively.)

Nor is this sacrifice, which is nonutilitarian, a pure expenditure on the part of the reader which culminates in the loss of the work—paradoxically, the only way in which the work can affirm itself, by being absent—merely something that occurs during or after the reading of the work. It, too, is ordained from the very start, as soon as the book is in the process of being opened. Mallarmé speaks of the deadly violence inherent in the act of reading in *Quant au Livre*: "Le reploiement vierge du livre, encore, prête à un sacrifice dont saigna la tranche rouge des anciens tomes; l'introduction d'une arme, ou coupe papier, pour établir la prise de possession" (381).[71] Like Orpheus's songs, which are responsible for his getting as far as he does *and* for his undoing, readers' letter openers are sharpened on both sides. They have two blades, one that seems to give them the power to appropriate the work for their own uses, and another one that they might cut themselves on when they realize that, in fact, they possess nothing.

FIVE

WRITING THE DISASTER

HENRI SORGE'S JOURNAL

> ... le désastre entendu, sous-entendu non pas comme un
> événement du passé, mais comme le passé immémorial (*Le
> Très-Haut*) qui revient en dispersant par le retour le temps
> présent où il serait vécu comme revenant.
> *L'Ecriture du désastre* 34[1]

Silencing the Critics of the State

BLANCHOT'S third novel, *Le Très-Haut* (1948), recounts the events of a few days in the life of Henri Sorge,[2] a loyal employee in the bureaucracy of a totalitarian state, a model citizen, and a member of a politically influential family. At the beginning of the novel, Sorge, who had previously been on sick leave, resumes his duties in the administration with seemingly renewed vigor, only to find himself strangely overcome by a lack of enthusiasm for his work. In need of more time to recuperate from his illness, he once again vacates his post. In the meantime, an epidemic has broken out in the capital. His apartment building is transformed into a clinic, and the rest of the novel is centered around the efforts of the authorities to control the spread of the epidemic and those of a revolutionary movement whose strategy is to overthrow the all-powerful regime by taking advantage of the chaotic conditions created by the epidemic. During his quarantine, Sorge learns that his building is a hub of subversive activity when he is befriended by Pierre Bouxx, the leader of the movement, and Dorte, one of the latter's closest allies. Thanks to Bouxx's capabilities as organizer and tactician, he and his followers ascend to positions of power in the State, at which point disillusionment sets in as they realize that they have been absorbed by the very system they had hoped to eliminate. The novel then concludes on a most perplexing note: the death of Sorge at the hands of his nurse. Allan Stoekl comments on this unforeseeable turn of events and provides us with a clue as to how we might proceed in responding to this enigmatic conclusion:

> [Sorge's] transformation seems most unexpected: to go from being a perfect
> representative of the State to being the only individual capable of a radical

enough revolt to defy the appropriating powers of the State is quite a leap
... What is most interesting is that here the radical negativity of death is
explicitly connected with the possibility of use of language. (*Politics, Writing, Mutilation*, 27)

I propose to investigate the questions of how Sorge's death is connected to language and why his death is more transgressive than Bouxx's
revolutionary project. To do so, I will treat the novel as a journal written
by Sorge. He is not only the protagonist of the book but its narrator as
well. Moreover, at the end of the first chapter, he expresses the desire to
keep a diary:

> J'aurais aimé rédiger un rapport sur cette journée, comme du reste sur l'ensemble de ma vie: un rapport, c'est-à-dire un simple journal . . . J'eus alors
> la certitude qu'il me suffirait d'écrire heure par heure un commentaire de
> mes actions pour y retrouver l'épanouissement d'une vérité suprême, celle
> même qui circulait activement entre nous tous et que la vie publique
> relançait sans cesse, surveillait, réabsorbait, rejetait dans un jeu obsédant et
> réfléchi. (26)[3]

Although it has never been approached from this angle, *Le Très-Haut*
is just such a book. Its subject matter is nothing if not a meticulous commentary of Sorge's activities during his period of confinement, and writing is a logical choice of activity to pass all the free time he has at his
disposal as a patient. His room, like those of all of Blanchot's other protagonists in his other fictional works, is sparsely furnished. The basic elements of the *décor* of "la solitude essentielle" are present: a bed, a chair,
a table covered with sheets of paper, and there are frequent allusions scattered throughout the text that indicate that Sorge spends much of his
time writing. The composition of the first chapter, however, presents us
with the most striking evidence in support of the theory that the book we
are reading is a journal. Although they are not dated, there are what we
might call six "entries" which can be loosely situated chronologically.
Sorge writes brief passages about an altercation in the subway, a visit by
his mother and sister while he was in the clinic (before his *quartier* was
condemned), a luncheon discussion at his habitual restaurant near the
Hôtel de Ville where he works, making Bouxx's acquaintance, an outing
with his sister Louise to a café on Saturday, and his activities while he
stayed home the following day. The second chapter picks up Sorge's actions on Monday morning. From then on, as Sorge settles into the monotony of convalescence, he loses interest in noting the precise days of his
activities.

The new conditions of Sorge's existence certainly contribute to his decision to keep a diary, but his newfound free time is not the determining factor in his decision. Although filling up empty hours is one reason to write, something much more important is at stake behind this apparently innocuous occupation. He is convinced that by keeping a diary, he will come into contact with "l'épanouissement d'une vérité suprême." He seems to know exactly what he is referring to in this phrase, but for us as readers it is not at all clear. What exactly is the nature of this "supreme truth" that will be revealed to Sorge as he writes? I would like to suggest that this truth is related to Sorge's death at the end of the novel and that as a result, the explanation of his death is closely tied to his decision to write his journal. We may, therefore, find the key to understanding Sorge's declaration at the moment of his death, when he discovers the possibility of the use of language, "Maintenant, c'est maintenant que je parle" (243), by examining the experience that Sorge undergoes while writing and the form that his book takes.

I will read his book in a manner consistent with Blanchot's statements on journal writing that we studied in chapter 3. His main point that concerns us here is that the "apparent law" of this genre is always subverted by a "secret law." Although the journal's point of departure is rooted in the concrete and the everyday, its author is inevitably drawn away from recording the details of daily occurrences of his life as his original intentions are replaced by abstract questions concerning the nature of language and writing. The themes of law, writing, and subversion will, therefore, occupy a major place in my reading of Le Très-Haut. The problematical relationship between the law and writing—at times complementary, at others antagonistic—creates dramas that are played out simultaneously on two levels. On the very public level of the political arena, Sorge's diary documents the subversion that takes place in the capital by charting the progress made by Bouxx's movement. In addition, many pages of the book are devoted to debates on the goals, tactics, and even the legitimacy of this movement, of which Sorge is mercilessly critical. On a much more private level, we witness the story of a second kind of subversion, this one purely literary, which occurs within the confines of the book that Sorge writes: the subversion of the apparent law of his journal by its secret law because of a language which refuses to adhere to the original intentions which fueled his desire to write in the first place.

By its very nature, the structure of a journal is fragmentary. This fragmentary structure which is in evidence in chapter 1 is maintained throughout the rest of the book in a less explicit way by means of a number of anecdotes that the characters tell each other. The major, continuous narrative of Sorge's diary, his account of a city under the siege of an epidemic and the effects it has on his life, is punctuated by stories which are nearly always told by someone other than Sorge. Rarely the "author" of these stories, he contents himself with listening to them, after which he almost invariably provides us with a commentary of them. Several stories deal with the role that the State plays in the lives of its citizens, and the "readings" that these episodes elicit from Sorge are consistently oriented in favor of the State. On a few occasions, however, stories which he has just heard provoke no such response, and Sorge the loyal functionary remains uncharacteristically silent as he refrains from interpreting them from the point of view of the State. The moments at which the secret law of Sorge's writing encroaches on the apparent law that governs his book, that it is a diary written in praise of the State by one of its most faithful representatives, occur in his silent refusals to comment on the stories. Before turning our attention to the stories that have the effect of subverting Sorge's readings in support of the State, a brief consideration of some examples of these readings is in order.

The source of the first such incident is, curiously enough, a *journal*, more precisely a newspaper article that Sorge reads during his lunch break about a woman who had plunged five stories to her death. The circumstances surrounding the tragedy are unclear, and he ponders the question of whether it was a suicide or an accident, although he is quick to point out to his uninterested interlocutor, the man with whom he is sharing a table at the restaurant, that a suicide *is* an accident which, as we have seen, coincides with Blanchot's reflections on the subject. The article does not specify whether she jumped or fell, but it does insinuate that the woman's doctor was at fault for not having her admitted to the hospital (like Sorge, she had been granted sick leave). The fact that the article concludes by pointing an incriminating finger at a member of the medical establishment induces Sorge to pose the question of the validity of criticizing the regime. Two attitudes toward criticism are possible: it either contributes to civil disorder and a weakening of the State, or it is part of a constructive dialectical process which leads to reforms that strengthen the State, the opinion personally held by Sorge. Thus, in his first commentary, Sorge raises the issue of the possibility of dissent and gives us a hint as to what will be the underlying tenet of all the pro-State readings that will follow: that there is no negativity which cannot be appropriated by the State and turned to its advantage.

Sorge has the opportunity to expound on his philosophy when he tells his neighbor Marie Scadran the story of a purse snatching incident that he had witnessed in the metro. Although the incident holds no great interest for Marie, Sorge is fascinated by it. The unsettling question of why someone would deliberately go against the law had kept him awake all night, and he cannot wait to share the lesson of this story with her. He reaches the conclusion that the man stole from the woman "non parce qu'il est en dehors de la justice, mais parce que l'Etat a besoin de cet exemple" (34).[4] There is no such thing as an outlaw, and a person who commits an infraction is actually doing his part to reinforce the law which has need of these infractions in order to assert itself.

We find a variation on this theme in Sorge's interpretation of a story that Bouxx tells him about a cashier with whom he had worked in a hospital. This employee, after an impeccable record of fifteen years of service, was accused of theft. Suspecting that his friend was perhaps the victim of a frame-up, Bouxx made some inquiries into the matter. When he read the official report on the case, he learned to his surprise that his friend had actually been charged with plotting to sabotage the State. He does not understand why the original charge of theft had been changed to sabotage, but Sorge has no trouble explaining it to him. No matter what the specific nature of any criminal act may be, it is carried out with one purpose in mind, to contest the power of the State. Any particular disregard for the law, therefore, amounts to one crime and one crime alone: treason. And it fails to do any lasting damage: "à travers le vol c'est un crime infiniment plus grave que l'on commet, le plus terrible de tous, et d'ailleurs un crime qui ne se réalise pas, qui échoue" (47).[5] It no longer matters what particular statute is violated. The only crime that has any real status is sabotage, and it does not succeed in doing what it sets out to do, in seriously shaking the legitimacy of the foundations of the State.

Bouxx is an idealist who believes that human intervention can alter the shape of things and change them for the better. He sums up his philosophy of praxis best when he says to Sorge: "j'ai vu clairement que, même si je réussissais, en rassemblant toutes mes forces, à ne changer qu'une seule chose, à ne remuer qu'un fétu, cela ne serait pas inutile. Et peut-être aussi ferais-je beaucoup plus" (20).[6] Thus, he cannot accept Sorge's position that all criminal activities are really performed with the blessings of the State, and his efforts and those of his cohorts are dedicated to proving Sorge wrong. The stories that Dorte tells Sorge about the time he and Bouxx spent in prison provide us with a most striking example, in its irony, of these irreconcilable differences of opinion. According to Dorte, Bouxx urged his fellow prisoners to do everything they could to extend their prison sentences. His reasoning goes something like this: a perfect society would have no bad elements, and, as a result, no prisons would be needed to lock these elements up. Therefore, if Bouxx and his followers work hard at staying in prison, they create a thorn in the State's side by making an institution which testifies to the imperfections of the system flourish. A refusal to be rehabilitated by the department of corrections constitutes a revolutionary stance. Sorge denies, on the contrary, that voluntary incarceration can be construed as anything other than playing into the State's hands:

> Vous avez cru habile de vous enfouir dans vos cellules, mais qu'avez-vous fait? Rien que de vous conformer au désir de l'Etat, car son voeu le plus cher

était de vous garder en prison, parce que vous aviez commis une faute, et de vous y faire rester librement, parce que cette conquête de la liberté était le vrai but de votre détention. (167)[7]

The irony of the situation is that Sorge's position turns out to be the right one and that when in power later on, Bouxx is forced into issuing the self-contradictory order to evacuate the prison in order to turn it into a dispensary. This action goes against one of the platforms of his own revolutionary program and is an indication that Bouxx is a part of the establishment rather than its most dangerous opponent.

Although well versed in the ways of the law, as he tirelessly demonstrates in his exegeses of Bouxx's and Dorte's stories, Sorge derives no great pleasure in this activity. In fact, on several occasions he makes it quite clear that he has an aversion to stories in general. He abruptly dismisses a story that Marie tells him about a child whose death marks what is perhaps the first fatality caused by the epidemic as a "récit insignifiant, simple bavardage" (41).[8] Before commenting on the case of the cashier, his initial reaction had been: "ce sont des histoires inventées . . . Je déteste cette manière de s'exprimer" (46).[9] He sounds the first note of suspicion concerning the validity of stories when Bouxx relates to him how he originally became interested in making Sorge's acquaintance. Bouxx's interest in Sorge was aroused when he saw Sorge give some money to a beggar. Does the fact that Sorge opted for a personal gesture of compassion over following the official channels that the situation would have normally required mean that he is disillusioned with the system that he serves and is, therefore, a good candidate to become a mole for Bouxx's cause? Bouxx thinks so and follows him home. The significance of this episode, however, is entirely different as far as Sorge is concerned. He does not give much thought to the motivations that prompted him to act as he did. He focuses instead on the beggar, and he doubts whether it was a person who was truly in need. Beggars, he claims, are characters of "histoires . . . montées de toutes pièces" (16),[10] and their role is to "donner l'impression que les choses ne vont pas parfaitement bien, que le système, malgré ses mailles de plus en plus serrées, laisse toujours passer une poussière de cas misérables et affligeants" (17).[11]

If Sorge is suspicious of people who tell stories, it is because he associates stories with transgressive behavior. This mistrust reappears in his reaction to a recurring dream that Bouxx recounts to him. In the dream, Bouxx presents himself before a magistrate in order to be judged. Instead of rendering a verdict on him, however, the judge waits on him hand and foot and treats him like royalty. When the moment arrives for the ball to begin, Bouxx understands what he has vainly been searching for: a woman. A widower, he believes that the interminable waiting for a verdict of acquittal that never comes has something to do with the absence of women in the carceral environment he inhabits in the dream: "L'acquittement ne pouvait signifier que la présence d'une femme, mais je ne pouvais chercher l'acquittement que dans les prisons où il n'y a pas de femme. C'était là le châtiment" (51).[12] Sorge is quick in handing down his own verdict on the worth of Bouxx's dream: "Votre rêve prouve vos pensées malsaines et débauchées . . . Je comprends vox allusions. Mais ce bavardage à demi-mot dure trop. Si c'est ma voisine et ma promenade de ce soir avec elle qui se tiennent derrière vos rébus, n'insistez pas" (52).[13] Sorge thinks he sees right through Bouxx's "dream." The woman who holds the key to Bouxx's salvation is none other than Marie Scadran, their neighbor, a photographer whose talent at manufacturing fake ID cards could be quite useful to Bouxx's cause. The magistrate who stands in the way of this salvation is Sorge himself, a friend of Marie. A good word from him on Bouxx's behalf might be enough to persuade Marie to help, but Sorge is incredulous that Bouxx would even consider asking such a favor of him, a loyal functionary, and he will have no part of it.

Professing a distaste for story-telling, which he puts on a par with idle gossip, he nevertheless displays a talent in adapting the circumstances of each incident in order to illuminate a facet of the law. His readings have the effect of converting useless banter into something practical that can be of service to the State. A link, therefore, exists between his profession and the way in which he interprets the episodes recounted to him by his neighbors. Describing the task of a bureaucrat, Sorge states: "de l'huissier au plus haut commissaire, nous étions tous ainsi, indulgents, comprenant, clarifiant tout, transformant en actes normaux, par un déchiffrage à l'envers, les pires manquements à la règle" (101).[14] This characterization also applies to his method of reading, in which the transgressions committed not only in the events recounted by the stories but in the very telling of the stories as well are transformed into acts that adhere to the norms of the State. He decodes the stories only to reencode them, in the code of the law.

Sorge is indulgent in his debates with Bouxx and Dorte. He always gives them a chance to state their views before refuting them. Once in a while, however, we get the impression that his patience is wearing thin. He is dogmatic in his approach. After all, there is only one way to interpret the stories they tell him, and Bouxx's refusal to open his eyes to this fact exasperates Sorge. There are no outlaws. All citizens are not just subjects of the law but its representatives as well, and Bouxx appears ridiculously misled as he adamantly refuses to accept this. He should know better. Sorge chides Bouxx on this point when he curtly ends the discussion on the case of the hospital cashier by saying: "vous ne m'apprenez rien, vous ne faites qu'exprimer ce que je pense, et quand vous parlez, ce n'est pas vous, c'est moi qui parle" (47).[15] Bouxx cannot do or tell him anything that he [Sorge] cannot recuperate on behalf of the State.

Along with this stubborn attitude not to see things as they really are, another reason that contributes to Sorge's dislike for stories is that he considers them to be obsolete means of expression. Having listened to Bouxx paint a picture of their society as "une poignée d'hommes contre une masse d'hommes" (47),[16] Sorge responds in a fit of pique: "Vous ne m'étonnez pas. Vous ne me scandalisez pas non plus. Vous n'êtes qu'un livre périmé et sans date, rien d'autre" (47).[17] At the end of the same discussion, Sorge states that Bouxx's political tracts also emanate from the law and do not, therefore, constitute attacks on it made from the outside: "La vérité, c'est que toutes vos critiques vous sont soufflées par la loi elle-même: elle en a besoin, elle vous en est reconnaissante" (53).[18] Bouxx tries to counter this by saying: "Et les hors-la-loi?"[19] Upon hearing this, Sorge explodes (although on the inside, perhaps preferring to keep it to himself rather than to let it fall once again on Bouxx's deaf ears): "Mais vous êtes fou. C'est une histoire d'autrefois, une réminiscence. Vous êtes un livre, vous n'existez pas" (54).[20] Evelyne Londyn astutely notes the resemblance between Bouxx's name and the English word "books" (183). As the author of stories, political tracts, and laws which are all in service of his philosophy of praxis, Bouxx utilizes language as an instrument of power, and his very name, Pierre Bouxx, evokes the "pierre tombale du livre" which, as we saw in the preceding chapter, is the dimension of a work that lends itself to constructive negativity, the work being the surplus which escapes any such utilization. It is an appropriate name for someone who operates within the regional economy of power.

Sorge faults Bouxx on two counts: first, for believing the negativity of his subversive movement to be radically other, outside the system it intends to destroy rather than one of its moments; second, for his outmoded conception of language. In the second half of the novel as Bouxx's influence spreads within the bureaucracy, Sorge no longer has the opportunity to see and talk to him in person. They keep in touch by writing letters to each other. In his first letter to Bouxx, Sorge plays the role of literary critic when he appraises Bouxx's style as it is manifested in one of his political tracts:

> J'ai lu vos papiers. Vous ne m'avez pas demandé de conseil, mais depuis plusieurs jours, je voudrais donner celui-ci: vous écrivez trop. Vouz avez la superstition de ce qui est écrit. Vous vous préoccupez excessivement des commentaires, des consignes, des rapports. En outre, il manque à vos formules je ne sais quelle exactitude. Ce sont des copies ignorantes, un langage appris qui tend à ressusciter d'anciens exemples s'appliquant mal à ce qui se passe, de sorte que le passé paraît bien revenir, mais c'est comme une prophétie caricaturale qui rend illusoire tout ce qu'on entreprend. (149–50)[21]

Sorge makes his critique of Bouxx's writing on the grounds that not only his message is passé but also the way in which it is transmitted. Sorge's claim that Bouxx's program and the language in which it is couched are out of step with the times can be made from one perspective alone: that which maintains that history has run its course and that totalization is at hand. Sorge's stepfather, whose tranquil respiration while taking a nap is described as "un récit, complet et achevé, de tous les événements d'une journée interminable" (64),[22] is the most powerful political figure in the novel and the most eloquent spokesman for the closure of history. He is worried neither by Bouxx's group nor by the epidemic. These are mere ripples that will fail to have any lasting impact that would prove damaging to the State. All that matters to him is, as he says, that "à chacun de mes pas je puisse me remémorer, du commencement à la fin, le mouvement plein de malheurs et de triomphes qui à nous tous permet de dire le dernier mot en justifiant le premier" (132–33).[23] There *is* a beginning and an end, a first word and a last according to the official version of history, which explains why he does not feel threatened by the revolutionaries. He need not fear a future that would bring reprisals crashing down on his head, for the future is now. He explains to Sorge his attitude of peaceful indifference in the face of the ominous events taking place around him by saying: "Les régimes des temps passés pouvaient craindre les mesures nouvelles parce que le mouvement vers l'avenir les menaçait. Mais nous, nous n'avons rien à redouter de semblable: nous sommes cet avenir, l'avenir se fait, et c'est notre existence qui l'éclaire" (131).[24] He is smugly confident in what for him is the unshakeable certainty that the society he has helped shape is a utopia. No one can improve on a system in which "il n'y a plus de condamnation, parce qu'il n'y a plus de manquement. L'intérieur et l'extérieur se répondent, les plus intimes décisions sont tout de suite intégrées dans les formes d'utilité publique dont elles sont inséparables" (133).[25] Perfect equilibrium exists between the law, the State, its agent and representative, and the people, its beneficiary. Earlier regimes had good reason to fear what the future held in store for them because these conditions had not yet been met. Now that they have, there is no turning back the clock. Bouxx and his followers mistakenly think that they can turn back the clock or, more accurately, that they can build a new future by creating a new state and writing new laws.

Sorge's position concerning history is problematic. It falls somewhere in between those espoused by Bouxx and his stepfather. In his arguments with Bouxx and Dorte, he sounds like his stepfather. In his confrontation with his stepfather in chapter 6, on the other hand, he sounds very much like Bouxx in his questions regarding the State's official position toward the epidemic and subversive activity. Sorge should take his stepfather's version of history as an article of faith, but he does not. In fact, in the same scene, he is unmoved by his stepfather's overtures to bring him back into the fold and refuses to sign the "profession de foi" which would reaffirm his status as a loyal employee of the State. Although he does not take sides in this matter, he does state in no uncertain terms to Bouxx his conviction that a critical juncture in history has been reached:

> tous les événements de toute l'histoire sont là autour de nous, exactement comme des morts. Depuis le fin fond des temps, ils refluent sur aujourd'hui; ils ont existé, certes, mais pas complètement: lorsqu'ils se sont produits, ce n'étaient que des ébauches incompréhensibles et absurdes, des rêves atroces, une prophétie. On les a vécus sans les comprendre. Mais maintenant? Maintenant, ils vont exister pour de bon, c'est le moment, tout réapparaît, tout se révèle dans la clarté et la vérité. (88–89)[26]

Sorge sees a (final?) revelation on the horizon in this prophetic-sounding statement that calls to mind the one we quoted earlier in which he associated his desire to keep a journal with the "épanouissement d'une vérité suprême." Moreover, he believes that the direction that history will take is closely related to his own destiny: "Je sens parfaitement que, si je changeais ou si je perdais la tête, l'histoire s'écroulerait" (30).[27] Sorge does not literally "lose his head" at the end of the novel. As a sacrificial victim, he does, nevertheless, become an Acephalic figure. Sorge seems to represent two opposing attitudes toward history. At times, it appears that the glorious end of history has been reached, as in this enthusiastic statement made on his first day back at work: "j'étais emporté par un sentiment de triomphe, la certitude à jamais aperçue que le ciel aussi nous appartenait, que nous avions la charge de l'administrer avec tout le reste, qu'à chaque instant je le touchais et le survolais" (40).[28] Sorge's confidence in the State knows no limits, and as he walks the city streets, he is exhilarated to see the imprint of the law on the face of each passerby he meets. And yet this sensation of exaltation disappears into thin air when he reaches the banks of the river that traverses the capital, overcome by the sinking feeling that the so-called triumphant end of history is a sham:

> le fleuve, lui aussi, semblait avoir coulé à travers le temps, affirmant avec sa vaste tranquillité qu'il n'y avait ni commencement ni terme, que l'histoire ne construisait rien, que l'homme n'existait toujours pas, que sais-je? De cette assurance montait comme une tromperie suffocante, le rappel d'un mensonge, d'une duperie sans fin, une insinuation faite pour dégrader des sentiments nobles. (40)[29]

Has history finally succeeded in constructing the ideal world, as Sorge's stepfather would have us believe? Is there one more chapter to be written by Bouxx before this goal is achieved? Or will the truth of what Sorge senses to be a turning point in history be more in line with the impression he had while gazing at the river, that the end of history will really involve a crumbling under the weight of old myths that fail to keep pace with the human condition? We will approach these questions from the perspective of language because for each version of history, there is a corresponding philosophy of language. Sorge criticizes Bouxx on the basis of language and style, claiming that his project is cast in terms that are no longer applicable for the situation at hand. Blanchot makes the same objection in an article written sixteen years later entitled "L'Apocalypse déçoit" in which he discusses the new era that mankind has entered since acquiring the power to destroy itself thanks to the discovery and proliferation of nuclear weapons. The disappointment that Blanchot feels as he reflects on the end of the world results either from the unwillingness of intellectuals or, more likely, from the inadequacy of their language to render a satisfactory account of what the significance of this new epoch is. This radical change in the human condition demands an equally radical change in the language that will write its story. What disappoints Blanchot is the lack of initiative shown on the part of writers and thinkers in developing this new language:

> pourquoi une question aussi sérieuse puisqu'elle détient l'avenir de l'humanité, question telle qu'y répondre supposerait une pensée radicalement nouvelle, ne renouvelle-t-elle pas le langage qui la porte et ne donne-t-elle lieu qu'à des remarques, soit partiales et, en tout cas, partielles lorsqu'elles sont d'ordre politique, soit émouvantes et pressantes lorsqu'elles sont d'ordre spirituel, mais identiques à celles qu'on entend en vain depuis deux mille ans? (*L'Amitié*, 120)[30]

Although Blanchot's *oeuvre* taken as a whole constitutes a relentless effort to get out of this "rut," it is in his third and final novel that he specifically confronts head-on the question of the apocalyptic end of history in his portrayal of a capital city under siege, not at the hands of an enemy equipped with nuclear firepower which would bring about instant destruction, but rather at the mercy of a plague that promises a slow, agonizing death. Sorge's transformation from functionary to sacrificial victim which he undergoes thanks to his decision to keep a journal is the vehicle Blanchot chose to dramatize the approach of this new language.

The type of language in use in the State bureaucracy which is charged, as Sorge said, with administering everything, even the heavens, has the principal function of organizing things. Blanchot's characterization of classical language by way of Foucault's *L'Ordre du discours* corresponds to a linguistic ideal that, although not attained in the seventeenth century, would have purportedly been achieved in Sorge's utopia:

Le langage classique (Foucault l'énonce par la formule la plus nette) "n'existe pas, mais fonctionne". Il représente identiquement la pensée, et la pensée se représente en lui (qui n'est pas) selon l'identité, l'égalité et la simultanéité. . . . Le projet d'une langue universelle, de la *mathesis universalis*, le
discours où se disposera, dans la simultanéité de l'espace, l'ordre, c'est-à-
dire l'égalité hiérarchisée de tout ce qui est représentable, enfin la vocation
analytique de ce langage fonctionnel qui ne parle pas mais classe, organise et
met de l'ordre, constituent la réponse au défi de Pascal. (*EI* 380)[31]

Bouxx's tracts lack these qualities according to Sorge, and his conviction that such a perfectly transparent language which classifies and orders
things with respect to the law exists is what enables him to say to Bouxx,
"quand vous parlez, ce n'est pas vous, c'est moi qui parle" (47).[32] The
history of language has been a progressive process of refinement which
has culminated in a mode of communication that is almost telepathic.
Sorge knows everything that Bouxx can possibly say before he says it, and
he also knows how to interpret everything that Bouxx says in terms of the
law. His readings reduce Bouxx's and Dorte's variations on revolutionary
activity to the common theme of the law which absorbs all. Stories and
story-telling—"récits," "bavardage," "rébus," "allusions," "vieilles histoires" are among the denigrating expressions Sorge uses to designate
them—are vestiges of a form of communication that dies hard. They are
dangerous in that they give rise to different interpretations and misunder-
standings, which rarely happens thanks to Sorge's readings which reveal
their true meaning. His role as faithful apologist for the State, however,
has its limits. He is not always so forthcoming in his commentaries in
defense of the law, and on several occasions he remains conspicuously
silent. I would now like to discuss in detail one such occasion and to
examine the consequences of Sorge's decision to remain silent.

An Awkward Silence

The story in question is told to Sorge by his stepfather, who had gone to
see him for three reasons: to ask him about his so-called "letter of resignation," to get him to sign a new oath of allegiance to the State, and to
persuade him to move to the country away from his plague-infested
neighborhood. Obliged to look into the rumors that were floating
around concerning Sorge's recent behavior at the ministry, his stepfather
arranged for a meeting with Marie Scadran: perhaps she could give him
some fresh insight into the matter. He began the interview with Marie by
telling her a story, and he repeats all of this to Sorge. We are thus dealing

with the story that Sorge's stepfather tells him about telling a story to Marie. This story within a story provides us with the most complex narrative structure of any of the anecdotes in *Le Très-Haut*.

He first tells Sorge why he recounted Marie an episode from his youth. He did it for two reasons: "pour mieux entrer en rapport avec elle," to break the ice, so to speak, and "[pour] vérifier notre commune valeur des mots" (128), to make sure they would be "speaking the same language." He then proceeds to tell the story. At the age of twenty, he worked as a supervisor in a print shop that turned out textbooks, brochures, and disciplinary signs used in schools. During his tenure there, he became quite close to one of the employees who was older than he and whose opinions he valued and respected. This employee was an excellent worker until the day he was struck by a car. After that, he could no longer perform his functions in a satisfactory manner, and Sorge's stepfather was forced to relieve him of his duties, much to his dismay. Thus ends the story within the story. The story that contains this story continues, however, as we listen to a series of reactions to it: Marie's reaction, the stepfather's reaction to her reaction, both of which he relates to Sorge, and Sorge's reaction, which closes out the episode in which, as we have already mentioned, he makes no attempt to use the story as a pretext for a discourse on the State.

The comments that the telling of the story gives rise to occupy a more important place than do the details of the story itself. The stepfather asked Marie what she thought of the story, but the manner in which he did so must have taken her by surprise: "cette histoire vous plaît-elle? Vous a-t-elle touchée, sentez-vous bien les intentions narratives que j'y ai mises?" (129).[33] Summoned to the office of such a high-ranking government official, she could hardly have expected to discuss his talents at telling stories. In spite of the potentially intimidating situation, she fields his question with ease and is direct in her response: "C'est vous qui sabotiez la machine, parce que son travail n'était déjà plus satisfaisant et parce qu'il parlait trop" (129).[34] She believes that the stepfather framed the worker so as to be able to force him to resign, a reading consistent with those done by Sorge. The law creates its own saboteurs, its own opportunities that will make it possible for it to assert itself. This story repeats the one told earlier by Bouxx about the hospital cashier, and it also has echoes as far as Sorge is concerned, a good employee who suspects that some sort of surreptitious plotting was involved in the arrival of his treasonous letter of resignation, hastily scribbled on a scrap of paper, at the desk of his superior. It must have been an "inside job." One would think that the stepfather would have been pleased by such an interpretation, proof that Marie is a well-indoctrinated student of the law. On the contrary, he is disappointed and frustrated by what Marie has said in her answer which, unfortunately, is all too typical of those he hears everyday:

> Voilà leur tour d'esprit. Ils ne peuvent plus prendre une histoire au sérieux, ils la transposent, ils la dissèquent, ils en tirent une leçon. Sans doute était-ce moi le saboteur, mais qu'importe! l'anecdote n'en existait pas moins, quelque chose dont je lui avais fait don, sans arrière-pensée, parce que je suis un être comme elle et qu'en la voyant j'avais reçu à nouveau ma jeunesse et mes années d'apprentissage. . . . Je ne la blâme pas, c'est elle qui a raison, et si elle n'avait apprécié de mon récit que le côté purement historique, sa valeur décorative, je me serais dit: petite sotte, petite oie sentimentale. (129)[35]

He concedes that Marie's interpretation is the correct one; his disappointment does not spring from her failure to "get the right answer." It results from her failure to receive the story in the spirit in which he intended, as a pure, narrative gift to a pretty young girl who brought back pleasant memories of his youth. She missed the point by reducing his lyrical offering to yet another allegory of the law. It is ironic that he should reproach those who treat stories in this way (and Sorge, of course, falls into this category) of no longer knowing how to take stories seriously. What he really means—if we interpret this remark in light of Blanchot's critical vocabulary—is that people no longer have the ability to take stories "à la légère." Marie weighed the story down with talk of sabotage, and he would have preferred that she accept his gift, welcome it, say "Yes" to it, and let it be at that. This conflict of lyric intention and political reception is a consequence of Blanchot's theory of the *noli me legere*: the stepfather cannot read his own story. Although he is its author, he is unable to impose his own interpretation on Marie. He is obliged to accept her version, which he does half-heartedly, as valid even if it is incomplete.

His disappointment at Marie's reaction to his story seems misplaced and ill-founded; after all, he did not call her into his office to reminisce about "the good old days." His story was not a purely disinterested gift, as he had earlier claimed it to be, and he confesses to Sorge what his ulterior motive was: "mon intention était de la faire parler contre vous, il le fallait, c'était mon devoir de m'approcher par leur plus grande vraisemblance de tous ces bruits répandus sur votre compte" (129).[36] He is a masterful interrogator, capable of painlessly extracting the information he wants from Marie by seducing her with his words, by fascinating her and leading her into a false sense of security, at which point she will divulge whatever incriminating knowledge she may have concerning Sorge's recent conduct without giving it a second thought. He explains his technique to Sorge and outlines the direction these sessions usually take:

Mes insipides paroles se mettent à jeter de l'écume et comme à fermenter, elle découvre là-dedans quelque chose, elle est fascinée. Ce tournoiement, je puis dire que je sais le reconnaître de loin, j'en suis les phases, c'est toute une crise dont le dénouement ne m'est pas moins connu: mille aveux de négligences, de complicités, une inconscience qui brusquement se découvre et se dénonce par des preuves infinies, trop de preuves. (129)[37]

Just when he thought that he had Marie in the palm of his hand—she had finally gotten around to mentioning Sorge's name, and he readied himself to take down all the details of what she had to say on Sorge's account—his plan backfired:

Au lieu de vous accabler, la malheureuse, du fond de sa détresse, fait tout le contraire: elle ne voit plus dans votre nom qu'un moyen de se recommander à moi, un appui, une chance. Vous n'êtes plus le suspect qu'elle doit perdre, vous devenez le seul qui la rendra innocente. (130)[38]

The mere mention of Sorge's name caused his stepfather's plans to go awry. Rather than coming forth with incriminating evidence of Sorge's behavior, she uses his name to ingratiate herself with the State. What was supposed to be a condemnation of Sorge ends up by being a glowing recommendation. The stepfather's final remark on the incident is that "Après de tels mécomptes, on apprend à être patient et l'on découvre comme l'histoire, même terminée est longue, comme elle passe lentement" (130).[39] For his part, Sorge makes no attempt whatsoever to come to his stepfather's aid by transforming the episode into one that would reflect the omnipotence of the law. His only reaction, which he keeps to himself, is one of disgust at someone who would try to manipulate someone else the way his stepfather did Marie by feigning an attitude of honesty and openness in order to induce her to inform against Sorge. It is surprising that Sorge is offended by his stepfather's methods; after all, had he not warned Bouxx not to trust him or to recruit him as a member of his organization for the very same reason? "Je suis un piège pour vous," he advised Bouxx. "J'aurai beau tout vous dire; plus je serai loyal, plus je vous tromperai: c'est ma franchise qui vous attrapera" (84).[40] Sorge is well aware of the duplicitous nature of the law, and it is odd that he should take umbrage at his stepfather's treatment of Marie.

This incident raises some perplexing questions: why does Sorge distance himself from the State—if only temporarily, for he will remain true to his role as its faithful representative in his rapport with Bouxx and Dorte after this episode has taken place—and why does his stepfather resort to the use of a language that we have been told belongs to a bygone era? Stories that nostalgically hark back to a period before the institution of the State of totalization belong in the revolutionary camp, and the

State's function is to dismiss them as old, worn-out myths and to convert their subversive intentions into patriotic ones: this is how the dialectic is supposed to work. In this case, however, the stories originate from within the State, and its two principal representatives are at a loss as to what to make of them. The binary structure of this episode accounts for two failures. There is, first, the story within the story, which shows how far apart Marie and the stepfather were in their interpretations of the anecdote from his youth. He said that he wanted to "measure the common value of their words." What he discovers instead is that they are not speaking the same language at all. The larger narrative that envelops this story also tells of a failure, that of the stepfather to make any significant headway into Sorge's alleged betrayal of his government. His meeting with Marie got him nowhere: at the end of the session, the verdict is still out on Sorge. The evidence against him, his letter of resignation, is inconclusive in the face of Marie's surprising testimony on his behalf. He is neither reprimanded by the State, nor does he sign the oath of allegiance, which would set matters straight. His status remains unresolved. His stepfather fails in his efforts to designate Sorge as an enemy or a servant of the State, either of which position could be easily assimilated by it. His stepfather tried to "fight fire with fire" and lost: he sought to deal with one transgression, Sorge's resignation, by committing another, telling a story which was supposed to accomplish something in the service of the State but which instead exceeded his power over it and had an adverse effect on his original plan. This episode is an important one because it illustrates an inherent weakness in the State. It demonstrates that the State does *not* successfuly recuperate all negativity: unlike Bouxx, Sorge will not be completely absorbed by the system. The failure to do so is brought about by a breakdown of the State's language. The fact that the stepfather regularly uses stories in his work points out the insufficiency of the ideal language of classification. His recourse to a discourse based on narration indicates that the transitive language of the State is rotten to the core. His calculated use of rhetoric failed to get Marie to say anything derogatory about Sorge because it is not a healthy *parole*. On the contrary, it is one that "froths at the mouth" and "ferments," expressions which signify language's excessive potential to transgress the limits that its speaking subject would assign to it.

The Crisis of (Mis)Representation

The outbreak of the plague is the most generalized symptom of the frail condition of both Bouxx's and the stepfather's means of expression. Their system of representation betrays them as does the epidemic which each of their factions fails to exploit successfully. When Sorge questions his stepfather about the government's official position on the status of the epidemic, the latter replies: "ce sont plutôt des cas administratifs, une idée pour en finir avec la crasse des vieux quartiers et mettre au pas une région arriérée" (66).[41] Sorge himself repeats the official line later in a conversation with Dorte, in which he describes the plague as "une mise en scène, . . . un plan pour justifier certaines mesures administratives" (111).[42] The official view, which is consistent with the notion that all transgressions originate from within the State because the State needs to create its own opportunities to assert itself, is that the epidemic is a phony excuse that the State concocted to justify razing certain run-down neighborhoods. Since the plague is a "mise en scène," a fiction that the State devised for its own (the common) good, it poses no threat to the State. The opponents of the regime, however, do not take the plague so lightly. They invest all their energies in the hope that it is the most surefire way they have at their disposal to bring down the State. Dorte explains to Sorge that no greater commitment can be made to the revolutionary cause than to come down with the illness and to transmit it to others. The greater the number of cases, the more Bouxx's influence spreads. It is the patients, therefore, who possess the real power to change the course of events, and Dorte views their very existence as a grave threat to the power of the State. They are suspects, "des gens contre lesquels l'Etat se protège par des barrages, des coups de force, qui lui échappent, qu'il ne reconnaît plus, qu'il ne peut plus traiter comme tout le monde. Nous sommes hors la loi" (112).[43] Sorge wryly notes that such a philosophy could be summarized by this maxim: "La maladie contamine la loi quand la loi prend soin du malade" (165).[44] Each side wishes to lay claim to the epidemic as a weapon which serves its respective cause, but neither can do so completely. It is not an efficient weapon as far as the State is concerned because the entire medical establishment is in the hands of the subversives. It is not effective from Bouxx's point of view, either, for he knows that the more success he has in dealing with the epidemic, the more his influence wanes. Thus, neither side can take credit for the plague. It escapes the intentions of both sides which attempt to harness it in order to reach their respective goals.

As was the case with varying conceptions of history, Sorge's attitude toward the plague must be construed as corresponding to neither that of his stepfather nor to that of Bouxx. He does align himself with the epidemic but in a way that differs from the State's and Bouxx's attempts to appropriate it. He neglects to receive the inoculations that he should have under law, he does not accept his stepfather's offer to move to the country away from the infested areas, and he refuses to sign his pledge of allegiance to the State.

Bouxx and his followers are not the outlaws in the novel; Sorge is. His existence constitutes a breach in the closed system of the State. He sees the epidemic for what it is, whereas his stepfather and Bouxx mistake it for something it is not: an instrument of power. According to Sorge, it exceeds the efforts of either side to mobilize it as a catalyst for change and belongs to the general economy of powerlessness, worklessness, and passivity. Its eruption signifies the release of a surplus of negativity in a world in which the power of the negative has run its course, and its principal consequence is to stand the system of representation that is embodied by Bouxx's group and the State on its head. As for Sorge, the epidemic contaminates or corrupts the healthy rapport that normally exists between the law and the citizens of the State. When one is sick, he tells Marie, based on his own experience, "on ne saisit plus la loi, on la contemple, c'est mauvais" (37).[45] Rather than "seizing" the law in a rapport of immediacy, one begins to "contemplate" it. The illness introduces an element of distance between the law and its subjects that should not be there under normal circumstances. Healthy citizens instinctively know that the whole State is the sum of its parts and that each part individually embodies the whole State; they do not have to think about it. Patients, however, do just that, and the more they contemplate, the less evident the fusion of the individual with the group under the benevolent gaze of the law becomes. Bouxx recognizes that Sorge is not on healthy terms with the law when he remarks: "vous en parlez trop, vous réfléchissez trop, cela n'est pas naturel" (45),[46] which explains to a certain extent why he was attracted to Sorge in the first place and why he thought Sorge could be converted to his way of thinking. In a subsequent meeting with Bouxx, Sorge concurs with this diagnosis when he admits: "mes idées sentent la maladie" (86).[47] Ill health leads to too much reflection, and too much reflection induces one to be fascinated by the law rather than to embody it and to exemplify it as if to do so were a reflex action.

Georges Préli has noted that the outbreak of the plague is symptomatic of the breakdown of a system of representation which is temporarily transformed into *ressemblance*; the "bad" version of the imaginary replaces the "good" version which has proved itself incapable and rendering an account of the end of history. Transposing the dilemma portrayed by the novel in terms of Platonic mimesis, Préli sees the epidemic as standing outside the usual hierarchical order of things. In *Le Très-Haut*, to the *eidos*, the good copy, and the bad copy correspond the law (the original, the ideology of the State), the State (the good copy which faithfully reifies the ideology as it writes and executes laws), and Bouxx's subversive group (the bad, illegitimate copy which tries to usurp the place held by the good copy by redefining the original). To this triad must be added a fourth term, the epidemic, an agent that is more radical than the revolutionary faction:

> il n'y a pas à privilégier dans *Le Très-Haut* la subversion par rapport à l'état ou le simulacre par rapport à la bonne copie de la loi, dont le modèle régnerait à l'abri de toute corruption dans le monde inaccessible des idées. Ce qu'il faut privilégier—le quatrième terme dans *Le Très-Haut*, c'est la maladie elle-même, comme subversion radicale du monde de la représentation sur toute l'étendue de l'échelle—depuis l'eidos, représenté dans le monde par la copie jusqu'au simulacre qui la reproduit. (*La Force du dehors*, 100–101)[48]

The appearance at the end of history of surplus negativity in the form of a plague contaminates the normal rapport between original and copy as the fate of representation is to give way to *ressemblance*. At its most virulent stage, the epidemic has the effect of calling into question the very notion of an original law which could be represented by a smoothly functioning state. Usual methods of classification and differentiation break down. Informers run rampant, and members of the same families turn each other in to the authorities. Given the extremity of the situation, the police is granted special powers of such latitude that it is impossible to distinguish them from the criminals. And Bouxx's measures become so severe that it is deemed safer to be sick and cared for by the hospitals than to be healthy and out in the streets. It is not possible to speak of a copy that represents an original, for in the context of the capital besieged by the plague, these terms have no meaning. They do only in the regional economy of power, once limits have been restored. Sorge's infected quarter describes a locale that precedes the institution of such limits in which differentiation can take place, a "disparité de fond," to borrow Deleuze's expression. It is important to note that in the well-ordered world of the everyday, the potential for reverting to a preoriginary moment of nondifferentiation exists, if only latently: criminals are lawful citizens, functionaries are saboteurs, etc. The epidemic disrupts the delicate balance that enables the State to have control as it converts one into the other in a continual process of appropriation.

Although Bouxx disagrees with Sorge's stepfather on the question of whether or not the ultimate, optimal society has been attained, they are in agreement on one fundamental point: both believe that a state can effectively embody an ideology. For them, the source of any form of government is a set of ideals, values, and principles, and its task is to uphold these values by exemplifying them in its day-to-day functioning. Sorge contests the idea that a state can faithfully reincarnate an original spirit of the law, and it is on the point concerning representation that he distances himself the most from the State and the subversives. He sees examples almost daily of unhealthy situations that come about as a result of the contaminated rapport between intact original and good copy which, according to him, is anything but stable. One such incident is recounted to him by his stepfather. He describes to Sorge an odd occurrence that took place during an official inspection tour of a burned-out building in the infected area of the city. While proceeding down the street, his motorcade came upon a small fair. When the throng of musicians, wrestlers, and dancers saw the approaching limousines, it immediately broke out into patriotic song. Their fervor became so intense that the once happy group of revellers turned into an angry mob that had to be controlled by the police. Sorge does not remain silent after hearing this story. He proposes a reading that is related to the law, but contrary to his other readings, the conception of the law that emerges here points to a collapse of the system that supposedly absorbs all negativity. Moreover, this collapse is closely associated with the representative role of the State. Sorge explains the intervention of the police in the following way:

> Vous avez dû disperser la foule, chasser les gens, faire le vide: personne n'a le droit d'assister à vos cérémonies, et pourtant elles sont faites pour tout le monde. C'est bizarre, mais justement c'est là qu'apparaît la profondeur de la loi: il faut que chacun s'efface, il ne faut pas être là, en personne, mais en général, d'une manière invisible, comme au cinéma par exemple. Et vous-mêmes, vous venez, mais pour quoi faire? C'est un geste officiel, une simple allégorie, c'est honorifique. Avant vous, n'importe qui, en venant examiner les décombres, avait déjà commencé un nouvel édifice, avait fait de ces restes effondrés des matériaux de reconstruction. Et même les incendiaires, rien que pour avoir regardé l'immeuble brûler, avaient déjà éteint le feu et restauré la maison. (68–69)[49]

Sorge's analysis of this political spectacle revolves around three entities: the public, or the spectators for whom the performance is given; the law, the *raison d'être* of the spectacle, the text, what is represented; and the officials of the State, the actors who give the performance. Under normal circumstances, prior to the outbreak of the plague, for example, this ceremony, which amounts to nothing more than what is known today in journalistic parlance as a "photo opportunity," would have come off without a hitch: the functionaries would have appeared at the scene of a burned-out building, and before the appreciative gazes of their fellow citizens, they would have said a few appropriate words to make it known to the people that everything was under control. Then everyone would have returned home peacefully, the politicians reassured of the support of the people, and the people secure in the knowledge that their government was taking good care of things.

Sorge senses, on the other hand, that the circumstances in which this incident occurs are not at all normal, and he raises two points in this episode that are at variance with the way in which this ceremony should normally have taken place. First, one of the entities is excluded from participating: the crowd is dispersed before the ceremony can begin. It is strange, Sorge notes, that the people, for whose benefit these spectacles are usually held, should be forbidden to be present at this one. He wonders what the sense is of giving a performance without an audience. A rehearsal? Has this formerly important communal ritual been reduced to an empty *répétition*? Perhaps we can interpret the State's decision to render absent the presence of the people in light of Blanchot's remarks in *La Communauté inavouable* on where the true power of the people resides. The source of this power is to be found in its refusal to be identified with any particular political ideology, "dans son refus instinctif d'assumer aucun pouvoir, dans sa méfiance absolue à se confondre avec un pouvoir auquel il se déléguerait, donc dans sa *déclaration d'impuissance*" (54).[50] The impersonal collectivity, as far as the State is concerned, is ambivalent in nature. From this formless mass devoid of any particular political exigency, the State derives its authority. At the same time, it poses a threat to this authority which is essentially powerless in the face of the anonymous being that the crowd represents.

Blanchot's statements about the people and authority reiterate in a political mode what he says about the work of literature and reading: the collectivity and the work share the same absence of exigency. Just as the sovereignty of the crowd lies in its fundamental indifference, its lack of interest in such and such a political position, the sovereignty of a literary work is not to communicate such and such a message. It is "l'affirmation impersonnelle, anonyme qu'elle [l'oeuvre] est—et rien de plus" (*EL* 12).[51] To continue the analogy, the authorities of a state and readers who practice the activity of reading as if it were an act of power come up against the same dilemma: the impossibility of making the general and regional economies coincide. A state may be able to mold a cohesive band of loyal supporters, but it will never succeed in completely reducing the collectivity to its ideology. Similarly, a work of literature lends itself to interpretation—the destiny of every work is to become a book—but at the same time the work eludes any determination that would claim to be definitive put forth by such interpretations.

The *noli me legere* uttered by the work to a reader is a weak but resilient defense. It is weak in that it constitutes an invitation to transgress it. It is also resilient, for the law always survives the infraction; in the end, the work remains unread in any exhaustive sort of way. The work seems to surrender itself to reading that would appropriate it and to render the accomplishments of such reading illusory. The collectivity utters a similar kind of negative imperative which possesses the same ambiguity: it offers both an invitation to authorities to have power over it and poses a threat to them by escaping any particular political determinations that they would impose on it. There is an anguish to reading, says Blanchot, which arises when the invitation suddenly, inexplicably changes into the obstacle. Readers' anxiety mounts when they realize that like Orpheus, they lose what they seize. Orpheus sees Eurydice as she disappears, and readers, when they turn a work, "l'absence du livre," into the presence of a book, realize that they have rendered the work absent. "L'angoisse de lire, c'est que tout texte est vide—il n'existe pas dans le fond" (*ED* 23).[52] The anonymous *fond sans fond* of the literary work has its political counterpart in the people, which gives rise to an anguish of governing that runs parallel to that of reading:

> Il [le peuple] est là, il n'est plus là; il ignore les structures qui pourraient le stabiliser. Présence et absence, sinon confondues, du moins s'échangent virtuellement. C'est en cela qu'il est redoutable pour les détenteurs d'un pouvoir qui ne les reconnaît pas: ne se laissant pas saisir, étant aussi bien la dissolution du fait social que la rétive obstination à réinventer celui-ci en une souveraineté que la loi ne peut circonscrire, puisqu'elle la récuse tout en se maintenant comme son fondement. (*CI* 56)[53]

Sorge's commentary of the State's initiative to round up the unruly crowd reflects the State's concern at the threat that the people represent. It had to clear the streets, "faire le vide," create a vacuum around itself as a means of protecting itself by removing the risk of civil disturbance. And yet the ceremony went ahead as planned, played out before no one. The void that the State erected around itself as a protective cushion is transformed from being the result of an oppressive act of power into silent but eloquent testimony that this power is nevertheless precariously founded on the *fond sans fond* of the people, which is present in spite of its absence, in the form of an invisible, indeterminate *personne*.

Sorge sees an additional indication of the breakdown of the State's utilization of representation. He has already shown representation to be unnecessary once the political spectacles are performed without an audience, and he pursues this point as he looks more closely at the role of the players, the functionaries. He believes that these photo sessions are purely symbolic now, empty of the significance that they once had. When he says that *anyone* (from the witnesses of the fire to the arsonists who set it) could have performed the functionaries' office, the dedication of a new building on the ashes of an old one, even before they arrived on the scene, he is suggesting nothing less than that their presence is superfluous. The part of the bureaucracy that engages in the production of civil ceremonies is, for Sorge, a relic. It is no longer needed in a world in which the law has permeated everything. Representation involves having one person or thing take the place of or stand in for someone or something else that is absent. Sorge, however, spends a great deal of time arguing that the law, in this society of totalization, is far from being absent. On the contrary, it has insinuated itself everywhere. It has woven itself into the very fabric of existence. This is the final point that he attempts to make to Bouxx in his last letter to him:

> Vous faites fausse route, vous combattez ce régime comme s'il était semblable aux autres. . . . Il a pénétré si profondément le monde qu'il ne peut plus s'en séparer, il ne consiste pas seulement en une organisation politique, en un système social: les personnes, les choses et, comme les proverbes le disent, le ciel, la terre sont la loi, obéissent à l'Etat parce qu'ils sont l'Etat. Vous attaquez les commissaires d'Etat, les hommes publics, mais il ne serait pas moins utile d'attaquer tous les habitants, toutes les maisons, et puis cette table, ce papier. Vous savez qu'il faudra vous attaquer vous-même. Il n'y a pas un grain de poussière que vous ne deviez regarder comme un obstacle. Contre vous tout est complice de ce que vous voulez renverser. (192)[54]

The State is everywhere. It has penetrated everything. The State *is* everything, and everything has its place in the State. It would be difficult to formulate a simpler, more direct definition of totalization than this. Since its presence can be felt even in every speck of dust, the functionaries' role of representing the law by means of public displays is obsolete and should be recognized as such and abandoned. The law should be seen as something that is contagious and infectious, as something that does not have to be disseminated by the machinery of a bureaucracy. That which is omnipresent does not need to be represented. The strategy of the State, nevertheless, has followed the opposite course. As we already mentioned, in his self-assured characterization of their society, Sorge's stepfather declared that a state of perfect equilibrium had been reached between the law and the world that the law had in its charge to administer. "L'intérieur et l'extérieur se répondent," he proclaimed proudly, "les plus intimes décisions sont tout de suite intégrées dans les formes d'utilité publique dont elles sont inséparables" (133).[55] This rosy picture of things is tempered, however, by his explanation of how the State succeeded in attaining this harmony: by means of a system of representation that has gone as far as it can. He explains to Sorge the plan that the State adopted in view of arriving at this point where "l'intérieur et l'extérieur se répondent":

> Il s'agit de briser définitivement les cadres, de faire disparaître les cloisons qui séparent ceux qui administrent et les choses qu'ils administrent. Déjà, vous savez comme cela se passe: dans tout emploi, il y a un représentant de l'administration; derrière chaque travailleur, il y a un délégué qui incarne en chair et en os la raison de son travail. En principe, le délégué est là pour

apporter une aide technique et morale, mais aussi, ma foi, pour contrôler les
activités et nous permettre de les utiliser au mieux. Tout cela marche cahin-
caha, le système a ses faiblesses. (127)[56]

This approach pushes representation to the highest degree. The ambi-
tious aim of the State's project is to achieve a one-on-one relationship
between the law and those governed by the law. In practical terms, this
project specifies that for every employee there be a representative of the
State. The latter's primary responsibility is to provide moral and technical
support to the former, a noble gesture on the part of the law. A second
perhaps less noble duty of the State's representatives is to keep a close eye
on the activities of their designated employees. One wonders whether
this surveillance involves a gaze that watches benevolently over the employees or one that looks malevolently over their shoulders, especially in
light of the stories we studied that had to do with sabotage, in which the
functionaries were the saboteurs and the employees were the innocent
victims of *coups montés*. This insidious activity on the part of the State in
the name of the perfect society demonstrates the degree of perversity that
has been reached on account of a broken-down system of representation.

Sorge's stepfather is impressed by his subtle interpretation of the significance of the dispersal of the crowd and of the superfluous presence of
the officials and their carrying out of the spectacle before an invisible audience. Furthermore, his remark on what Sorge has said reveals to us
the direction that Sorge takes in his refusal to identify himself with either
the position of the State or with that represented by Bouxx and his
supporters:

Vos observations plairaient à l'un de mes collègues, qui ne manquerait pas
de vous poser sa question favorite, celle qu'il a toujours sur les lèvres: "Et
aujourd'hui, quelle mouche?" La mouche, c'est la réflexion trop forte ou
trop fine, l'esprit de vérité et de profondeur, lorsqu'il prend son essor et
cherche à se séparer du mouvement: elle bourdonne, elle s'entend vibrer.
Vous voyez, c'est encore une allégorie. (69)[57]

In the Socratic tradition, the bee is what appears on the lips of certain
interlocutors. Ideas are the infants that Socrates' maieutic dialogues give
birth to, and the bee symbolizes the verbal formulation of an idea that is
on the verge of taking flight toward the immutable heavens of truth.
Sorge's ideas on the law are characterized by another insect, and the sub-
stitution of a fly for a bee is significant. The fly is an unclean insect, a
transmitter of the epidemic, and the comparison of Sorge's speech, both
oral and written, to a fly indicates that he has allied himself with the epidemic insofar as it stands outside the control that either the State or
Bouxx can have over it. The appearance of the fly on Sorge's lips repre-

sents the birth of an idea, but it's a sick idea, a "réflexion *trop* forte ou *trop* fine," the kind of idea one has when one is ill, when instead of "seizing" the law one "contemplates" it. Sorge is thinking and talking too much for the good of the State. The colleague in question from whom his stepfather borrows this "allegory" happens to be the director of the National Archives, the inner sanctum of a State which prides itself on having achieved the highest level of efficiency possible in the promulgation and execution of decrees. The wheels of the center of documentation ought to turn at a steady pace, as pieces of a well-oiled machine structured in accordance with the blueprints of an ideal language of classification, but they are not at the moment: "son service est l'objet de sévères critiques,"[58] Sorge's stepfather informs him. The director's detractors refer to this branch of government as "le service des mouches," perhaps because of his pet expression, or, more likely, because of the agency's faulty performance. Sometimes it seems to disregard its mandate by creating more disorder than order. At such times, the vast catalogues of information that are housed in the Archives are put to destructive rather than constructive uses: personal dossiers become damaging proof against citizens instead of providing them with helpful credentials. Informers are at work here, *mouchards*, specialists in betrayal, deceit, and misrepresentation, another indication that the ship of State is veering off course.

Sorge's refusal to join Bouxx and to sign his stepfather's pledge of allegiance to the State, along with the pact that he makes with his nurse, Jeanne Galgat, signifies that he becomes a spokesman for the law of *ressemblance*, the law of the general economy and that he abandons his role of apologist for the State, although he seems to retain this role in his debates with the revolutionaries. In fact, he attacks both sides, and the target of his assault is representation. On this point, he does not play favorites. Both factions are guilty of using stories or political performances as means of power to prove or illustrate a particular position. Dorte's prison stories are told to get a point across, and they are representations of an ideology of subversion, the original intent for which they were told. The stepfather's story to Marie was designed to trick her into denouncing Sorge. It represents in a disguised manner the ideology of the State. It is told from a particular point of view in order to produce a particular, desired result. He failed, however, because the language of the story exceeded his original intention. The absurdity of continuing to hold political ceremonies without a crowd of people to appreciate them and the presence of an official supervisor "behind the back" of every worker are other examples Sorge cites as evidence of a crisis of representation.

The subversion of the apparent law by the secret law that governs the activity of journal writing in which he is engaged accounts for his very subtle, almost imperceptible shift from spokesman for the State to partisan of the plague and *ressemblance*. Thus, Sorge's literary and political destinies are intertwined. He deplores stories and story-telling and yet meticulously keeps a journal that is full of them. From the very beginning he identifies stories with transgressive behavior although such behavior is not radical enough to defy the appropriative powers of the State; on the contrary, it strengthens the State's power. This is his apparent motive for undertaking the journal in the first place. His diary might have the same effect as the gesture of a man who steals a woman's purse, that of "un simulacre, une sorte de jeu pour faire circuler la loi" (34).[59] Sorge's dabbling in the illicit activity of writing stories, a minor offense, would actually contribute to consolidating the State he represents. The longer his journal becomes, however, the more time he spends alone in his room writing down the events of the day, recording the stories others tell him and reflecting on them, the more his apparent motive, reinforcing the State, is replaced by a secret motive as it slowly dawns on him that the authority of the State actually rests on an anonymous *fond sans fond*. Sorge becomes the advocate of the law of the general economy as he sees different strategies of representation fail in their attempts to lead humanity into whatever period awaits beyond the end of history.

Sorge attributes Bouxx's failure to his inability to extricate himself from a system of representation that shows itself to be obsolete. He falls headlong into the "piège du signifiant." He cannot help it. "Le dessin de la loi: que les prisonniers construisent eux-mêmes leur prison. C'est le moment du concept, la marque du système" (*ED* 76).[60] He falls into this trap literally when he encourages his men to do everything they can to have their prison sentences extended. He does so in a less obvious way when he fails to realize that the State has a monopoly over totalization; it has "cornered the market" as far as negativity is concerned, and the only way to get outside the market of the limited economy is to embrace the exigencies of contagion: worklessness, expenditure, and failure. Sorge's stepfather is also very much a prisoner of the same system of representation. His inability (or unwillingness) to recognize irrecuperable negativity as such is nowhere more evident than in his gesture of certifying to Sorge in writing that the plague does not exist other than as a pretext that allows the State to go ahead with certain plans for rebuilding the city. Both are "victimes d'un système d'illusion capable de les faire travailler avec enthousiasme à leur propre servitude" (210).[61] Sorge's pact with the epidemic has literary as well as political implications, and as he writes his journal, he is unwittingly engaged in "inventing new references for thought," in creating a new way of looking at language and its place in the world which will respond to the new exigencies. It is to this new form of writing as it is manifested in the structural composition of his journal that we shall now turn.

The Poetics of Writing the Disaster

My reading of the novel thus far has emphasized its fragmentary nature. The structure of the first chapter, taken with Sorge's declaration of his desire to keep a journal at the end of this chapter, lends itself to such an approach, and the anecdotes that crop up constantly throughout the rest of the book reinforce its fragmentary structure. It is my contention that this fragmentary structure foreshadows the "exigence du fragmentaire" that will come to occupy the center of Blanchot's practice of literature in later works. It makes its first fugitive appearance in *Le Dernier Homme* and reaches its culminating point in *L'Attente l'oubli*, *Le Pas au-delà*, and *L'Ecriture du désastre*. Henri Sorge's journal, in my opinion, constitutes an embryonic stage in the development of the fragmentary. The new form of writing that he advocates and with which he experiments in his diary is none other than an early moment of Blanchot's own literary history which will project him toward the writing of fragmentary books. Put another way, Sorge's book about a disaster is an early form of what Blanchot will later call "the writing of the disaster." In the following statement, Blanchot gives us a succinct characterization of fragmentary writing—when it can appear and what devices are involved when it does:

> écrire relève du fragmentaire quand tout a été dit. Il faudrait qu'il y eût épuisement de parole et par la parole, achèvement de tout (de la présence comme tout) comme logos, pour que l'écriture fragmentaire pût se laisser re-marquer. Toutefois, nous ne pouvons pas ainsi, écrivant, nous libérer d'une logique de la totalité en la considérant comme idéalement accomplie, afin de maintenir comme "pur reste" une possibilité d'écriture, hors tout, sans emploi ou sans terme dont une toute autre logique, encore difficile à dégager (celle de la répétition, des limites et du retour) prétendrait nous garantir l'étude. (*PAD* 62)[62]

One aspect of fragmentary writing is that it appears at the end of history as an index of surplus negativity that persists in the wake of totalization. This condition is met in the novel: Sorge views his very existence as convalescent and his written testimonial of it as something that exceeds the aims of the State. Another aspect of fragmentary writing is that it cannot escape "le piège du signifiant." There is no such thing as a kind of fragmentary writing so pure that it would be completely removed from the "logic of totality," a "pure remainder" that would stand outside the totality. Briefly stated, Blanchot's theory of transgression is that "il n'y a pas loi, interdit, puis transgression, mais transgression sans interdit qui finit par se figer en Loi, en Principe du Sens" (*ED* 121).[63] Sorge's transgressive writing is allied with the law of the general economy, a state of transgression with no regard for laws that are normally in force when the regional economy of power dominates. This state is not endless, however, and Sorge's writing, portions of it, anyway, inevitably ends by becoming the communication of something. Every work possesses a dimension that is available to comprehension, and Sorge's diary is no exception. The third aspect of fragmentary writing as it is presented in this passage is that it is organized in accordance with a logic that differs considerably from that of the prefragmentary writing of the totality which is based on continuity. The elements of this new logic mentioned here, repetition, limits, and return, are tropes of discontinuity and interruption. I would now like to show how each of these devices appears in the writing of Blanchot's protagonist/author in *Le Très-Haut*. Reading the fragmentary is risky business: "si écrire, c'est disposer des marques de singularité (fragments) . . . , il y a toujours risque pour que la lecture, au lieu d'animer la multiplicité des parcours transversaux, reconstitue à partir d'eux une totalite nouvelle" (*PAD* 74).[64] One of the consequences of my reading of *Le Très-Haut* is undoubtedly to impose a "totalité nouvelle" on a work that was not the expression of one in the first place. Every reader inevitably commits this transgression. On the other hand, I hope to remain faithful to the exigency of the fragmentary, precisely by "animating the multiplicity" of the transversal rapports that exist between different fragments (anecdotes) rather than by reductively endowing them with a false sense of continuity. After applying the three devices of what we might call "the poetics of the writing of the disaster," repetition, limits, and return to the novel, we shall see that not only is it built on a fragile foundation but that the very notion of foundation is put in serious jeopardy.

Repetition is pervasive in *Le Très-Haut*, and it occurs in two types of series. The first type involves the repetition of a situation, which had originally been told in anecdotal form, in the course of the overall development of Sorge's narration. Some examples include the story about Louise's killing the cat, which prefigures Sorge's death at the hands of Jeanne (63–64), and Bouxx's *récit de rêve*, whose outcome, a verdict of guilty handed down on the basis of his own self-incriminating statements, announces his future position as functionary and failed revolutionary (50–52). Such anecdotes which tell of things that turn out to be true in the course of the book have the effect of creating a fatalistic universe. (We will come back to the notion of predestination very shortly in our discussion of return.) The other type of repetition occurs when an episode recounted in one anecdote is repeated in another anecdote. There are numerous examples of this type of repetition, of which I will now mention just a few. Bouxx tells Sorge the story of how he first became interested in him—he happened to see Sorge give some money to a beggar and followed him home—a version that he later amends by telling him that he had originally been intrigued by Sorge when the latter was in the clinic during his first sick leave (135). Another instance of repetition which occurs from one anecdote to the next are the stories told by Bouxx and Sorge's stepfather about loyal employees who are accused of sabotage, which we have already examined. The most important example of this type of repetition, however, concerns two versions of the same event that are recounted to Sorge, first by Marie (41), and much later on by Dorte (163–64).

Both stories deal with some strange happenings in the lives of the members of a family that lives in their building. According to Marie's version of the story, the eldest daughter of the family fell ill and passed on the disease to the youngest member of the family, who died as a result. Surprisingly, these cases went unreported. No investigation was made by officials from the department of health, supposedly thanks to the connections of the girl's brother: as a member of the police force, he was able to bend the rules and to hush up the affair. Equally surprising is Sorge's reaction upon hearing the story: "Récit insignifiant . . . simple bavardage,"[65] he calls it. Such utter indifference on his part is unusual, and we would have expected him to explain, as a member of the government, why the police and health officials acted the way they did. This story makes no lasting impression on him, which is confirmed later (97) when Marie brings up the incident once again. Sorge denies that she has ever told him the story; he has no recollection of having heard it before.

The story resurfaces a third time (a fourth time, really, since it is a repetition of the newspaper article Sorge read over lunch in the first chapter) when Sorge hears Dorte's version. His account differs considerably from Marie's. The events are altered, and the cast of characters is different. As he tells it, David Roste's (the young policeman in the other version) sister became sick after eating some spoiled food. Their mother panicked and ran madly around their apartment, not knowing what to do. The girl who was renting a room from them, none other than Jeanne Galgat, went out to get help. When she returned, the apartment had been set on fire. We are not told who set the fire, nor do we learn the fates of the sister and mother. What is certain is that Roste achieves the status of a hero for those in the subversive movement, and since arson is identified with one of their tactics, the implication is that Roste himself started the fire. From one version to the next, he goes from being a policeman to being a member of Bouxx's medical organization, a change which is not as radical as it might seem, since we know that the State takes credit for all transgressions and that a subversive serves the State just as well as the most loyal functionary. It makes no difference to the State whether one of its policemen bent the rules by avoiding an investigation or whether a revolutionary set the fire; the end result is the same: the State is better off because of it. One other difference between the two versions of this story is that Sorge does not write it off as a "récit insignifiant." It is after hearing this story that he argues that the epidemic is not a form of employable negativity that can be successfully exploited by either the State or the subversives.

The consequence of the repetitions of the same events is to give precedence to the narration of the event over the event itself. Everything is in the telling of the story. An effect of "cross pollination" is created when different versions of the same event confront each other in our minds as readers; some details vary and some remain the same, but the net result is that the presence of stories that both corroborate and contradict each other ends up by casting doubt on the very existence of an event that supposedly took place at one time and that the story is supposed to represent. If there is a multiplicity of versions of the "same" event, each of which can claim to be as true as the next, it is because there is no event that can qualify as an original occurrence which would exist in a pure, untouched state prior to subsequent representations and interpretations of it. Repetition is thus a function of *ressemblance* by reversing the usual order of things, that first there is an event independent of its being recorded and reported. The telling of the stories has precedence over the event. The event to which they would refer under the traditional system of representation is untraceable, and the stories refer to nothing outside themselves. They exist on their own terms. They recede into the images they create, which is particularly the case when Sorge is speechless after hearing them, incapable of reducing them to allegories of the State's power.

The most glaring example of the lack of an absolute, initial event is the outbreak of the epidemic itself. Because of the importance given to the Roste family's story, we are tempted to see it as the beginning of the plague, the starting point in the *quartier de l'Ouest* from which it will fan out in all directions. Does Roste's sister contract the first case of the plague, which is allowed to spread since the case goes unreported? The epidemic is the original event of which Sorge's diary tells the story, and yet we know nothing of how this situation came about in the first place. And even if Roste's sister did come down with the earliest known case of the plague, the conflicting versions of this event call into question the manner in which this event originally took place. Moreover, we cannot help thinking that the outbreak of the plague is connected in some way to the end that Sorge's father met. The conspicuous absence of references to his father makes him an ever-present figure behind this story. He is mentioned only once, in the following exchange between Bouxx and Sorge: "Vous ne lui en voulez pas du tout?" asks Bouxx. "Il a pourtant pris la place de votre père."[66] To which Sorge replies: "Oui, mon père."

Vous savez, je ne l'ai pas beaucoup connu, je ne me le rappelle presque pas" (88).[67] It is impossible not to ask ourselves what series of events led up to his father's death and the usurpation of the latter's place by his stepfather, and on this score, comparison with the *Oresteia* are inevitable.[68] Sorge's mother is described as a queen ("Louise ne parlait d'elle qu'en l'appelant la reine" [59])[69] who is tormented by relentless feelings of guilt: "Et ma mère: elle ne peut même pas me regarder en face, elle me couve, elle m'épie—mais jamais en face, tant elle a peur que son regard n'appelle derrière moi une figure terrible, une réminiscence qu'elle ne doit pas voir" (89).[70] Is this figure that she is afraid to see lurking behind Sorge the specter of her dead husband whom she had a role in slaying as did Clytemnestra? And in this promise for vengeance that Louise makes to Sorge, "là où il y a eu une mort injuste, il va y avoir une mort juste; là où le sang s'est fait crime dans l'iniquité, le sang va se faire crime dans le châtiment" (74),[71] she sounds very much like Electra. Perhaps Sorge's stepfather owes his rise to power to a heinous crime, the murder of Sorge's father. On the third page of the book, Sorge tells us what his family signifies for him: "La famille, c'était cela. Le rappel des temps antérieurs à la loi, un cri, des paroles brutes venues du passé" (11).[72] The life of Sorge's natural father would thus seem to correspond to a transhistoric period of the rule of the law of the general economy ("transgression sans interdit") prior to the institution of limits rendered possible by one final transgression, the murder-sacrifice of the natural father, by his usurper, a transgression "qui finit par se figer en Loi" in the form of the accession to power of the *beau-père* who is Sorge's father *in law* only. Perhaps Sorge's destiny is to follow in his father's footsteps by repeating the latter's death. Such theories are purely speculative, for we remain in the dark on these questions regarding the original cause of the plague and whether it is linked to the fate of Sorge's father. Blanchot's refusal to supply us with the details that would answer these questions is consistent with his belief that there is no originary source out of which the river of history flows.

Sorge's father is absent in that he is not a character who operates within the regional economy of power, but he is very present as the invisible, undefined figure of anonymous being of the general economy. The absence of references made to Sorge's father endows him with a haunting presence. He is there without being there, lurking over Sorge's shoulder or fading in and out of photographs, portraits, and mirror images. Sorge's first experience of being plunged into the space of *ressemblance* occurs during his first visit to Marie's studio. While waiting for her to finish for the day, he spends a few minutes shuffling through a stack of pictures she had taken. He describes the effects the pictures had on him in this way:

Toutes ces photographies se ressemblaient, comme c'est le cas chez les photographes professionnels: l'attitude était la même; les habits, toujours des habits de fête, passaient d'une personne à l'autre; la différence des traits s'effaçait sous l'identité des expressions; bref, la plus grande monotonie. Pourtant, je ne me lassais pas de les regarder, il me'en fallait toujours plus. C'étaient les mêmes, mais les mêmes en nombre infini. J'y enfonçais les doigts, je les palpais, j'en étais ivre. (43)[73]

This scene takes place in the middle of chapter 2, immediately after he had hastily scribbled his letter of resignation and left the office, perhaps an early indication that Sorge is not a representative of the regional economy of the law embodied by the State and that he is, in fact, already allied with the general economy, given the amount of pleasure he receives at looking at the photos. The two-hundred-odd photos contain the same expression. They resemble each other, which is to say that they refer to no original models which exist prior to and outside them. What appears, and what transports Sorge, is the monotonous repetition of the same, no one in particular, nothing but an incessant pulse of anonymous being. Interestingly, the apparition of this anonymous being is associated with the notion of *fête*, which suggests that it manifests itself only when one has removed oneself from the regional economy of the everyday, as Sorge has done by retreating into the "essential solitude" of his room during his leave of absence. This scene about a repetitious series of photographs constitutes a doubling of the repetitious series of anecdotes which, according to Sorge, tell of the same event in spite of changes in detail. The "event" in question, of course, is the impossible existence of an event in pristine form, anterior to and independent of accounts of it. Similarly, these pictures point to the same figure in spite of minor differences in clothes and physical traits, this figure being the absence of an original, grounding figure which would be the guarantor of the copies.

Sorge undergoes the same kind of experience at the beginning of the following chapter, while contemplating a portrait in Louise's room. The atmosphere is funereal. Her room is likened to "une caisse," and the picture itself rests on a pedestal. It seems to hold an important place for Louise and to possess the qualities of a sacred relic. Sorge characterizes it as "un vrai monument" and "une véritable icône." As he gazes at this painting whose frame reminds him of a slab of granite, once again *la ressemblance cadavérique* surges forth:

Je regardais ce visage long et osseux, peu expressif, mais les yeux avaient une fixité farouche, frappante dans cette figure qui n'avait pas d'air. Un homme de devoir, certes; il paraissait quarante ans. Louise soutenait le cadre par derrière et, en même temps que le portrait, je voyais sa figure à elle, ses regards également froids et vifs qui, du haut du cadre, avec une hâte jalouse, glissaient vers l'image comme pour en vérifier l'identité matérielle. Je me rappelai alors toutes ces autres photographies, derrière lesquelles il y avait aussi quelque chose à chercher, toutes semblaient aujourd'hui me renvoyer à cette figure aux regards farouches, dont seuls les yeux perçaient. (56)[74]

If we take into account the special status that this portrait has for Louise in comparison to her other possessions and the veneration that it inspires in her, it is not unlikely that it is a portrait of her late father. She is described as "having her father's eyes"—the same "regard farouche," the only distinctive traits that can be made out. It is another portrait of no particular person; it is a face "qui n'avait pas d'air." While looking at the painting, Sorge has a flashback: he recalls having had the same sensation in Marie's studio, but with one big difference: this time he feels that the person in the painting is the invisible model that he sensed behind all the other photos. He has found the original, the guarantor, the absolute first version of which all future reproductions would refer. It is not a flawless, integral original, however. It, too, remains ultimately invisible. It escapes Sorge's appropriating gaze by taking flight, by receding inwardly into its own image. No absolute origin is revealed to Sorge; on the contrary, dissimulation appears.

The same phenomenon occurs immediately afterward in the same scene as Sorge studies another of Louise's cherished possessions, an ancient, moth-eaten tapestry. It depicts a horse rearing up on its hind legs, its head thrust high toward the heavens in an extraordinary pose of anger, suffering, and hate. This magnificent head occupies the foreground of the picture. Sorge is incapable, however, of making out what is portrayed in the background, another example of an image's excess over its own closure. Sorge is fascinated as he tries to give chase to the receding image which ends up turning the tables on him by contemplating him:

> dans le fond, il y avait certainement beaucoup de détails, mais là l'usure avait eu raison des couleurs, des lignes et de l'empreinte même sur la trame. En reculant, on n'apercevait rien de plus; en me rapprochant, je brouillais tout. A rester tout à fait immobile, je sentais un léger reflet passer derrière ce chaos en loques, l'effleurer; de toute évidence, quelque chose bougeait; l'image se tenait par derrière, elle m'épiait, et moi aussi je l'épiais. Qu'était-ce donc? Un escalier en ruine? Des colonnes? Peut-être un corps couché sur les marches? Ah! image fausse, image perfide, disparue, indestructible. (58)[75]

The physical condition of the tapestry is revolting—"une ordure," Sorge calls it, that is in the process of an infinitely slow decomposition thanks to the efforts of the "milliers de vers, de mites, de bêtes de tout genre qui foisonnaient là dedans" (57–58).[76] This decomposition is responsible for Sorge's inability to see what lies behind the painting, the original event that it represents. The only specificity that can be accorded to an origin is that it is the life of a death that is repetitious, that knows no beginning or end, the presence of an absence, an incessant pulse of impersonal being, symbolized here by the gnawing worms, moths, and other insects. This tapestry has always already been in the process of being devoured by moths just as the State has by a sickness that has been in a temporary state of remission. The conflicting versions of what went on in the Roste family remove us farther from pinpointing the origin of the plague. Similarly, Sorge's fascination, his inability to relate what is depicted in the tapestry to the original event and to see an original patriarchal/paternal figure behind Louise's portrait and the hundreds of photos in Marie's studio which would endow history with meaning points to the lack of such origins. *Ressemblance* contests the ordering of an original which precedes a less perfect copy, and the absence of references to Sorge's father's death, an absence so notable that it finishes by becoming an ever-present concern for the reader, makes of his father a perfect figure of *ressemblance*. Both the end of his father and its relationship to the origin of the plague remain invisible, unknowable, and unassignable to a particular point in time.

The second element of what I have called "the poetics of the writing of the disaster," *limites*, also concerns repetition. Each version of a story sets up limits. When the same story is repeated, one version or limit is established only to be transgressed by a later version which puts the veracity of the earlier version into question. Bouxx tells one version of his life's story, and Sorge learns later, much to his surprise, that Bouxx had served time in prison. Sorge is told one version of what happened to the Roste family, then another. This procedure has an unsettling effect on readers who, after drawing one conclusion, are forced to reassess and perhaps to modify their earlier view of things. It requires a constant process of reevaluation by readers of what they thought they knew to be true. Nothing is certain in this universe where truth sometimes no longer seems to be a valid category for thought. The setting up and subsequent tearing down of limits is most insistent in the person of Sorge himself. One never quite really knows where he stands. His desire to return to his job and his exhilaration at serving the State are the initial limits within which we form an impression of his character, but these limits do not always remain firmly in place. The difficulty we encounter in assigning limits to Sorge results from his refusal to align himself definitively with either the political position of the State or that of the subversive movement, which is itself a consequence of the fundamental ambiguity of the word "loi" and whether we read it as (*a*) the lawless condition of the general economy or as (*b*) the existence of institutionalized laws of the State in the regional economy.

Return, the third and final compositional element of the poetics of fragmentary writing that I wish to consider, contributes to the same movement of calling into question the possibility of an absolute, fully self-present origin that would serve as an authenticating starting point of a historical process of becoming culminating in totalization and a knowledge of the absolute. Return obviously plays a role in constructing the path of discontinuity that readers are obliged to follow when they must go back to reevaluate events about which they once felt certain. It also plays a major role in the construction of the novel itself. The circular exigency of writing applies to *Le Très-Haut* because the end of the novel, Sorge's final declaration, "Maintenant, c'est maintenant que je parle,"[77] engenders its beginning. In order to reach the point where he would be able to make such a statement, he had to begin somewhere, by saying, for example, "Je n'étais pas seul, j'étais un homme quelconque" (9).[78] In order to be able to begin, however, he has to have gone through the final moment, after which he can make of it a point of departure.

Sorge follows a course that parallels Orpheus's. The same kind of reversal occurs: what begins as a written apology of the State turns out, in fact, to be the most radical statement possible against it. Sorge's project is subverted from within by his own writing, just as Orpheus's is ruined by his own music. Like Orpheus who falls under his own spell, Sorge has periodic lapses during moments when he falls under the spell of the story he is recording in his journal. In his first conversation with Sorge, Bouxx makes this observation about him: "On dirait que pas une seconde vous ne voulez interrompre le fil des aphorismes et des maximes. Le tour de votre esprit a été solidement façonné par les fonctions publiques" (18).[79] It is true that in his discussions with Bouxx, this flow of maxims on the all-encompassing State is uninterrupted, and he shows himself to be an indefatigable debator. At other times, however, we know that he stops "singing the State's tune." There are moments of fascination that he experiences as he writes during which he suspends his usual political judgments regarding transgressions and the State's ability to appropriate them. Unable to speak up on behalf of the State, he betrays the apparent law of his journal—his original intent—as language betrays him. Sorge and Orpheus both transgress laws which are regulating forces in the regional economy of power, but their betrayals of these laws are actually acts of fidelity that are performed in accordance with the "fond sans fond anonyme" of the law of the general economy.

Although Sorge's alliance with the epidemic and his pact with Jeanne Galgat that is consecrated by his sacrificial death testify to his betrayal of the law of the State, it is not completely accurate to speak of a gradual evolution on Sorge's part which culminates in his death. In one way, we can say that when the novel begins, Sorge is a loyal bureaucrat and that at the end he becomes a sacrificial victim. On one level, *Le Très-Haut* is the story of this metamorphosis. On another level, this transformation has been preordained even before the story can start to be told, and the die is cast the moment that Sorge makes the contaminated (transgressive) decision to write in the first place, mistakenly thinking that he has a trustworthy language at his disposal that he can use to preach the virtues of the State.

The book is, therefore, animated by a tension that pulls the reader back and forth between two possible ways of viewing Sorge's trajectory. On one hand, Sorge seems to be a man who has some degree of control in the direction that his life takes. He seems capable of making his own choices and of accepting the responsibility for these choices. His pact with the epidemic seems to be made of his own free will on the basis of much reflection during his sick leave. On the other hand, given the circular structure of the novel and the latent presence, at the outset, of the radically subversive language at the heart of his transitive language (just as there is a subversive law of journal writing lying in wait to undermine the conscious intentions of the journal writer, and just as the plague has been latently present within the structure of the State from time immemorial), there is an overwhelming feeling that the story is over before it starts, that Sorge's fate is sealed, and that he knows how everything turns out, having been through it before, although it is a knowledge that is immediately forgotten, irreparably lost until the circle is retraced another time. Concomitant with Sorge's dual status as representative of the law, that of the regional economy (as civil servant) and that of the general economy (as convalescing writer) are two views of existence and predetermination. When speaking on behalf of the regional economy, he seems in control of his own destiny, whereas if we consider the fruits of his labor, the repetitious, circular book of fragments that he produces, it is as if he knows and passively accepts in advance what fate has reserved for him. In any case, there is no particular point in the book which we can identify as the specific moment at which Sorge definitively turns his back on the State and becomes a spokesman for the epidemic. Sorge's transition does not have the characteristics of an event, which is why Bouxx's ambiguous prophecy, "Un jour ou l'autre, vous glisserez," (54)[80] is so pertinent and accurate. Whereas Bouxx meant that Sorge would inevitably slide from the government's position to that of the revolutionaries, he actually slides back and forth between the two positions, not "one day or another," as if it were specifiable, but one day *and* the next, again and again.

The return of circularity and repetition, which blurs our attempts to trace linear development and to establish beginning and ending points between which such development would take place, is an important structural element of the first chapter as well as of the entire book. The first scene, when Sorge is attacked in the subway, is a repetition and an extension of the final scene in the book. Jeanne's physical gestures at the end are described in this way: "Mais brusquement son visage se figea, et son bras se détendit avec une telle violence que je sautai contre la cloison en criant:—Maintenant, c'est maintenant que je parle" (243).[81] The same verb is used to describe the action of Sorge's attacker: "Son poing se détendit avec une rapidité fascinate, je m'écroulai à terre" (9).[82] The novel picks up exactly where it leaves off at the end: the unsuccessful putting to death of Sorge. After the initial scene in the metro and the five vignettes which follow, we learn of Sorge's desire to keep a journal, the first six entries of which we have just finished reading. Thus, similar to the book, which needs to end so that it can begin again, the first chapter is over before it starts. The end of the first chapter somehow already had to have taken place before the first words of the chapter could be written by Sorge.

Sorge has no illumination at "the end" which endows his life with some ultimate meaning. Nor does the *parole* with which the novel concludes, "c'est maintenant que je parle," constitute the revelation to Sorge of a new language which would mark a drastic break from the language of totalization. It is not the arrival of the event he had waited so long for. No, it is no different from the one he has been writing all along. Since, in a certain sense, the story is over before it begins, Sorge is already in possession from the very "beginning" of the language of passivity, based on fragmentation, repetition, limits, and return, which takes precedence over the temporarily impotent language of power. In this respect, his situation mirrors that of his creator. Sorge's example shows us that a radically new style of writing is present at the outset of the most banal of literary enterprises, a journal. Blanchot's position is similar in that we can gleen evidence of the direction his writing will take in the years to come, as he pursues "l'exigence du fragmentaire," in his third and final novel, on the surface, at least, one of the most conventional of genres.

Ink-Stained Pages

Sorge's writing is undermined from within by the language he is forced to use. Since the subversion that goes on within the book mimics the subversion taking place in the outside world, it is not surprising that the subversion of the apparent law of the genre by the secret law is expressed in terms of a spreading infection. Sorge's writing is not immune to the phenomenon it describes. Although he is holed up in his room, Sorge cannot insulate himself completely from the epidemic. It worms its way into his room and his writing, and its physical presence makes itself manifest to him in the form of a spot of moisture that appears on the wall that separates his room from Dorte's:

> Cette tache avait ceci de particulier qu'elle n'était qu'une tache. Elle ne représentait rien, n'avait aucune teinte et, sauf l'imprégnation poussiéreuse, rien ne la rendait visible. Etait-elle même visible? Elle n'existait pas sous le papier; elle n'avait aucune forme, mais ressemblait à quelque chose de salissant, de gâté, à quelque chose de propre aussi. (48)[83]

This is the first mention of the spot in Sorge's room, but he is already quite familiar with it, having previously seen it at the home of his parents and on the wall of his room in the clinic during his first sick leave. It possesses contradictory attributes. The use of oxymoron and the linkage of opposites by means of correlatives is a well-known stylistic device that Blanchot exploits in order to verbalize the neutral. The spot has no particular shade or distinctive coloring. The only thing that renders it visible is its "imprégnation poussiéreuse": the moisture is composed of dust. Nor is it certain that the spot is even visible; the formless stain hovers between being and not being there. Moreover, it resembles something that is both impure and clean at the same time. Invisible yet visible, moist yet dusty in appearance, spoiled yet pure: the coexistence of such contradictory aspects designates a dimension prior to "la décision tranchante" of differentiation. The moist spot is merely one member of a network of liquid imagery which pervades the entire book and whose function is to describe recalcitrant negativity that cannot be appropriated. The river, which, in Sorge's eyes, is "le rappel d'un mensonge, d'une duperie sans fin, une insinuation faite pour dégrader des sentiments nobles" and affirms that "il n'y avait ni commencement ni terme, que l'histoire ne construisait rien" (40)[84] is the first appearance of this imagery in the book, and subsequent manifestations of it, chiefly in the form of the spot and in certain physical characteristics of Jeanne Galgat—her voice is likened to "un glouglou" and to "un murmure d'eau" (200),[85] and from her body flows "une eau noire et épaisse . . . semblable à celle qui une fois déjà s'était infiltrée à travers les murs" (216)[86]—add to the development of the theme of excess negativity.

This murky liquid infiltrates Sorge's writing and manages to seep up through the layers of stories, commentaries, and reflections that he makes as a conscientious public servant and defender of the State. At one point, the notes of his journal that litter his desk are portrayed as "les papiers couverts de taches d'encre" (227).[87] The ink that flows from Sorge's pen is just as treacherous as the water that runs in the river of the capital. It simultaneously holds out a promise to him and betrays that promise. It enables him to write something in the first place, an apology of the State, for instance, and it also undermines the foundations on which this original project rests. Sorge's stepfather is unable to see the epidemic for what it is and, consequently, takes Sorge's resignation and the writing that comes out of it for something that can be turned into employable negativity by the State. He does not blame Sorge's writing or his language for being responsible for the betrayal of the State. On the contrary, too much free time away from the office is the culprit responsible for giving him an erroneous view of things:

> Vous avez eu des congés, vous vous êtes cru diminué. Avec vos loisirs, vous avez pu fréquenter celui-ci, celui-là; vous êtes devenu inquiet; vous vous êtes lancé à la recherche de quelque chose comme si tout ne vous avait pas déjà été donné. Et puis, qu'arrive-t-il? A la fin, on est pris par le vertige, on croit que l'histoire vous a quitté, qu'elle continue son chemin sans vous, et l'on se met à juger, à parler, et même à écrire avec la stupeur d'un homme qui court toujours après ses bottes. (123)[88]

Sorge's stepfather thinks that he has all the answers, that he can show Sorge the errors of his ways, and that he can bring him back into the fold. While absent from the ministry, Sorge lost touch with the law and, as a result, lost sight of the fact that "everything had been given" in advance, that the work of the negative had reached its ultimate stage. A marvelous equilibrium between means and ends, negativity and accomplishment had been achieved. He feels out of step not only as far as history is concerned but also with respect to the story (*histoire*) that he is writing. His book proceeds along its own merry way without him, fluctuating indefinitely between encomium and critique of the State. The language of his own writing has led him into the stupor of fascination and has had the effect of erecting a wall within him. No longer a self-assured functionary like his stepfather, Sorge has been split into two beings, and the more he writes, the more distance his conformable self must cover in order to catch up with and overtake his subversive self.

His stepfather's use of the verb *écrire* in the passage just quoted is an allusion to Sorge's so-called letter of resignation. The way in which this incriminating letter arrives at the desk of his superior provides another example of the dubious status of origins. It is not completely accurate to speak of a pure, original intention which motivates Sorge to keep a diary and which is subsequently corrupted by writing. No such pure motivation for the diary exists. Sorge's transgressive writing does not originate in a willfull, well-thought-out act. If the moment that he writes the sentence in which he makes known his desire to be released of all obligations toward the State marks the origin of his diary, his letter is an *avant propos* which enables him to begin writing. The manner in which it is submitted, however, reveals that this project did not exist as a carefully conceived plan. He never did, in fact, submit the letter; it made its way to Iche's desk "par mégarde" (124).[89] It had accidentally been placed in a dossier by one of Sorge's coworkers; he had never meant to send it to him. Thus, we cannot say that the journal originates in a firm decision made by Sorge; *le hasard* is responsible. His stepfather is not overly concerned by this letter. He downplays its importance when he tells Sorge his initial impression of it, after which he nevertheless gives him a piece of advice. The letter is merely

> un devoir d'écolier. Je l'ai compris dès que la feuille m'est venue sous les yeux, une tâche d'écriture. Vous savez, quand on essaie une nouvelle plume, l'on recourt à des phrases d'un genre spécial, des suites de mots saugrenues, des exemples de grammaire. Tout de même, à l'avenir, faites attention, choisissez dans votre compendium des formules moins voyantes. (123–24)[90]

From the point of view of his stepfather and the State, Sorge's writing constitutes a *tâche* in the service of the State. He writes "compendia": texts that can be reduced (abridged, summarized) to *tasks* of constructive negativity. His stepfather is indeed correct in saying that Sorge is "trying out a new pen," but not in the way he means it. Sorge does not absentmindedly scribble the sentence down to see if his pen works. His pen is new in that it spews forth *taches d'encre* which exceed the appropriating powers of the State. The State, however, sees Sorge's writing only in terms of the regional economy: "devoir," "tâche," and "compendium." Moments later, Sorge refers to his letter of resignation as "ce chiffon de lettre" (125),[91] and we automatically associate the word "chiffon" with the general economy of surplus negativity, expenditure, and worklessness because the *chiffon* is closely related to the *tache humide*, and the paper on which Sorge writes and which absorbs the ink from his pen can be compared to the scrap of red material that soaks up the droplets formed by the humidity in Sorge's room. At the opening of the final chapter, Sorge is engrossed by the contact that takes place between the *tache humide* and the *chiffon*: "Ce chiffon était un morceau d'étoffe rouge très brillant . . . et je le voyais se mêlant dangereusement à des immondices, blotti, brillant et intouchable, dans le seau aux ordures" (225–26).[92] The bucket is situated directly beneath a pipe that runs along one of the walls of his room, and the pipe is sweating. Sorge follows closely the progress of each droplet as it forms on the pipe and grows in size until it falls under its own weight into the bucket, where it is soaked up by the rag. As long as the beads of water are hanging from the pipe, notes Sorge, "l'espoir demeurait encore, et le jour aussi restait intact" (226).[93] The moment of anguish occurs when Sorge hears the splattering sound of the drop landing on the moist cloth:

> je n'avais qu'à entendre le bruit de l'eau pénétrant l'étoffe pour sentir qu'elle rencontrait je ne sais quoi de honteusement humide, de bien plus humide qu'elle, une épaisseur collante, un dépôt saturé d'humidité, inétanchable. Ce bruit me rendait fou. C'était celui d'un liquide qui se corrompait, perdait sa transparence, devenait quelque chose de toujours plus mouillé, sécrété par une existence de rebut, une tache froide, épaisse et noire. (226)[94]

The sound of the water hitting the material is not the only thing that torments Sorge. The other is that the outward appearance of the rag remains unaltered by the moisture which has been sucked inside: "ce qui rendait cette situation si dangereuse . . . [c'était] qu'à chaque nouvelle chute, l'étoffe continuât à offrir le même aspect sec, éclatant, le même rouge luisant et inaltérable. C'était là la ruse maudite de cette histoire" (226).[95] Those who are capable of investing all their energy and attention in the regional economy of productive activity do not have the time or the opportunity to get beyond the outward appearance of the cloth. For them, the regional economy absorbs all, is capable of transforming all negativity into something useful and profitable without being corrupted by it. The cloth (the regional economy) can soak up all the moisture (of the general economy) and still retain its dry permanence. People such as Sorge's stepfather and Bouxx believe that the State or the subversive medical establishment can absorb the malignant infiltration of the epidemic into its fabric of power and mastery. What sets Sorge apart from those who opt unconditionally for the regional economy is that he is not blind to the hidden pocket of water that is contained inside the impeccable, untouched cloth:

> Il ne m'était pas permis d'ignorer comment ce rouge effronté, enfermant dans son enveloppe toujours sèche une réserve d'eau stagnante, me tirait sur le bras, entraînait mon corps, le faisait pencher en avant, donnait à mes doigts une véritable ivresse, à la pensée qu'il leur suffirait de se resserrer soudain sur cette pièce d'étoffe si visible et si nette pour en exprimer l'intimité latente, la faire jaillir au dehors et l'étaler à jamais en une tache ineffaçable, épaisse et noire. (226–27)[96]

Whereas dynamic activity in the regional economy tends to divert our attention from the general economy, the function of the writer is to provide a constant reminder that this second, less palatable version of existence serves as the origin of the regional economy. Sorge is no longer a productive member of society, and he is well aware of the inferior status of his life with respect to the lives of those who are gainfully employed in the building of the State: "je ressentis combien le caractère humiliant de mon existence ici dépassait l'humiliation de toutes les autres, parce que moi je devais lire, écrire, réfléchir" (149).[97] He does not have the luxury of being completely absorbed in the performance of mundane tasks. His new occupation as a patient has endowed him with a different perspective. His withdrawal from society into the essential solitude of his room and the incessant writing of his journal have put him into contact with the undetermined milieu of fascination. He has come to see dissimulation for what it is, as "l'informe lourdeur de l'être présent dans l'absence" (*EL* 351),[98] before it is transformed into constructive negativity. Fascination is "le regard de la solitude, . . . vision qui n'est plus possibilité de voir [this power belongs to the regional economy], mais impossibilité de ne pas voir, l'impossibilité qui se fait voir, qui persévère—toujours et toujours—dans une vision qui n'en finit pas" (*EL* 26).[99] Sorge sees the world through these eyes. It is impossible for him *not* to see the general economy of anonymous being on which the regional economy of differentiation is formed. He is not allowed *not* to know of the dissimulated presence of a reserve of stagnant water (surplus negativity) that dwells within the regional economy which, on the surface, seems to absorb, use up, and eliminate the excess as would a machine that is capable of converting all its fuel into energy that it can use without emitting any wastes in the process. Not only does Sorge's continual state of nocturnal vigilance (he never sleeps) keep his eyes riveted on the general economy; he must go even further by giving himself up to the pressure that the general economy exerts over him by extracting the putrid liquid from its hidden cavity. His task (*tâche*) is to wring out the piece of cloth, to make the usually dormant stagnant water appear to all who are normally too busy in the regional economy to see it by spreading it out in a "tache ineffaçable, épaisse et noire" by writing the indelible ink-stained pages of his journal.

No longer an active representative of the State, Sorge becomes a passive participant in the spreading of the epidemic by writing, which he once again expresses in terms of liquid imagery:

> Réfléchissez à ceci qui est terrible. C'est que moi-même, par bien des côtés, je ne suis qu'une figure. Une figure? Pouvez-vous pénétrer quelle manière de vivre, dangereuse, perfide, sans espoir, un tel mot suppose? Je suis un masque. C'est d'un masque que je tiens lieu et, à ce titre, je joue un rôle de mensonge dans cette affabulation universelle qui, sur l'humanité trop complète de la loi, étale—ainsi qu'un léger vernis, pour en adoucir l'éclat— une humanité plus grossière, plus naïve, rappel des étapes antérieures dans une évolution qui, arrivée à son terme, tente en vain de revenir en arrière. (174)[100]

Sorge sees his task as one of promulgating a lie. He is not writing on behalf of a cause. If he is writing on behalf of anything, it is on behalf of the "fond sans fond anonyme" of causes in general. He views his writing as tantamount to spreading a coat of varnish on the "all-too-complete humanity of the law." The regional economy of power owes its authority to the humanization of death, which is seen exclusively as the source of the power of the negative. Sorge's writing dulls the brilliant finish of the perfection of the law of the regional economy, thereby revealing the crude, unrefined aspect of the underlying layer of the general economy of transgression. The role that Sorge attributes to himself corresponds exactly to the one that Blanchot attributes to the artist on the last page of *L'Espace littéraire*, a passage reminiscent of those in which Heidegger speaks of art as a counterforce to technology:

> plus le monde s'affirme comme l'avenir et le plein jour de la vérité où tout aura valeur, où tout portera sens, où le tout s'accomplira sous la maîtrise de l'homme et pour son usage, plus il semble que l'art doive descendre vers ce point où rien n'a encore de sens, plus il importe qu'il maintienne le mouvement, l'insécurité et le malheur de ce qui échappe à toute saisie et à toute fin. L'artiste et le poète ont comme reçu mission de nous rappeler obstinément à l'erreur, de nous tourner vers cet espace où tout ce que nous proposons, tout ce que nous avons acquis, tout ce que nous sommes, tout ce qui s'ouvre sur la terre et dans le ciel, retourne à l'insignifiant, où ce qui s'approche, c'est le non-sérieux et le non-vrai, comme si peut-être jaillissait là la source de toute authenticité. (*EL* 337)[101]

The more humankind advances in its quest for absolute knowledge, the more incumbent it is on the artist to remind humanity of the nature of the origins whence this progress springs by leading us back to the point where "nothing has meaning yet." Art owes the power that it exerts over us to its ability to provide us with a glimpse of what *is* when the regional economy of power is temporarily suspended. Art offers us "l'ouverture opaque et vide sur ce qui est quand il n'y a plus de monde, quand il n'y a pas encore de monde" (*EL* 28).[102] It exposes us to an intermediary region, a no-man's-land which falls somewhere between the end of history, "when there is no more world," when the power of the negative has gone as far as it can, and the beginning of another history, "when there is no world yet," a moment prior to the reestablishment of a regional economy based on power. During such intervals, the regional economy of power temporarily yields to the general economy of worklessness, the sole ontological exigency of which is the perpetuation of "the formless weight of being present in absence." Sorge's personal history, his alliance with the general economy of the epidemic which culminates in his sacrificial death, inaugurates such an interval, a transhistoric period during which the anonymous, unemployable being of neutrality reigns. On account of the epidemic, usual principles of differentiation that work in the regional economy are temporarily dissolved—rather than enforcing the law, the members of the police force are transformed into the worst felons, for example. It is impossible to say exactly when this interval begins and when it comes to an end. Beginnings and endings apply only to the regional economy, where initiative and decisiveness prevail. The general economy of the neutral is always already there, as a murky undercurrent that flows for the most part imperceptibly beneath the tranquil surface of the waters of the regional economy of the everyday.

What seeps to the surface of the ink-stained pages of his journal is the stagnant water of the plague which he has, in effect, wrung out of the fabric of the regional economy of the State. Instead of revealing in all its glory the "all-too-complete humanity of the law" of the regional economy which he purportedly represents, the true consequence of his writing is to "faire jaillir au dehors" the thick, black oozing of the general economy of the epidemic, "comme si peut-être jaillissait là la source de toute authenticité."

Sorge's "Fable" and Fragments on Narcissus

The encroachment of the general economy on the regional economy makes *Le Très-Haut* a difficult book to read and Henri Sorge a difficult character to fathom. Because of the dual status of death, Sorge's existence moves incessantly back and forth between the two modes. He is simultaneously a representative of the State who knows the ins and outs of the language of power and an infirm member of "la communauté désoeuvrée" who eschews the principles on which such a language is founded. Although it is impossible to single out any particular instance at which time Sorge passes from one role to the other, there is one final anecdote that I would like to consider which underlines his fundamental duplicity and accounts for "the two versions" of Henri Sorge.

The story in question (pp. 83–84) stands out for two reasons in particular. First, it is one of the rare anecdotes told by Sorge to another character, and, second, it is completely removed from any allegorical application regarding the appropriative powers of the State. The gist of the story is this: Sorge tells Bouxx about a strange thing that happened to him at work. There was a colleague with whom he never exchanged a word. They used to see each other quite often and would shake hands, but neither one would say anything to the other. This situation became intolerable for Sorge, so much so that he asked his superior to transfer him to another department where he would no longer be obliged to see his silent partner. Oddly enough, when he did this, Sorge learned that his colleague had already made the same request for the same reason. With that, the story ends as abruptly as it begins. It "comes out of the blue," and Bouxx is at a loss as to what to make of it. "C'est une fable?" he wants to know, to which Sorge responds: "Non . . . pourquoi? Ce n'est pas une fable, c'est un incident de jeunesse. Je vois que vous avez apporté de nouveaux meubles" (83–84).[103] There does not seem to be any point to the story, and their conversation goes off in an entirely different direction immediately after its telling. Sorge is quick to insist that this incident really happened; he is not one to invent fictions whose allusions to the real world need to be deciphered, and he has a deep-seated mistrust for those who do. He does, nevertheless, take a stab at understanding the significance of this rather unusual episode when he says, in the sentence that precedes Bouxx's question, "c'était faux, mais n'était-ce pas arrivé parce que j'étais le même que lui et comment faire comprendre que mon silence n'était peut-être que l'écho du sien?" (83).[104] It is interesting to note that he begins his interpretation with a disclaimer: "c'était faux, mais." We saw Blanchot employ the same tactic in his essay on *The Castle*, in which he simultaneously affirms and denies that the castle represents the neuter. Sorge, too, is reluctant to put forth an interpretation which might be taken as definitive because the *noli me legere* is in force: although he is the author of this episode, he cannot make any claims to be its authoritative reader. One other detail that betrays Sorge's lack of confidence in his ability to interpret this story is the conspicuous absence of any reference to the law. Unlike the other stories in which he demonstrates his mastery of reading, he is not standing on the firm legal ground of the State in this case.

In his fleeting and inconclusive interpretation, he makes the conjecture that his taciturn colleague is somehow related to him, that he is the same as he, some kind of double. This story does not mark the first occasion that Sorge mentions a double who works with him at the ministry. He introduces us to another one in the second chapter. He describes him as a tall, sickly young man whose left arm is paralyzed. Sorge's interest in him is aroused, he says, "car il portait mon prénom et, de plus, à le voir, certains jours, immobile à sa table, le front baissé sur ses registres où il n'écrivait rien, je l'imaginais en proie à des troubles dont j'avais l'expérience et luttant pour surmonter les difficultés du travail" (38).[105] Sorge's overtures of friendship are continually rejected, however, and his feelings vacillate between paranoia and empathy:

Je compris aussitôt à quel complot contre moi participait ce garçon. Je me levai lentement, je le dévisageai: sur cette figure maladive, fermée et cérémonieuse, le mensonge avait sa place, un mensonge qui transformait la comédie

en une scène équivoque, répugnante, avec une vague odeur de délation.
J'eus alors une autre idée. Peut-être n'était-il au courant de rien. Débordé
de travail, il avait vraiment besoin de moi. (38–39)[106]

Sorge is troubled by his namesake's request for help because in the
past, he tells us, "chaque fois que je lui avais offert mes services, il les avait
repoussés de la manière la plus sèche" (38).[107] Why this sudden interest
in getting Sorge to help him? Is his request made in good faith, or is there
some ulterior, less honorable motive behind it? Unable to answer these
questions, Sorge decides to keep his distance and declines to help him.
Sorge's suspicions are confirmed much later on when his stepfather informs him that his double was responsible for delivering his letter of resignation to his superior. Whereas his stepfather believes that it happened
accidentally, Sorge feels like the victim of a set-up, when he exclaims: "Ce
paralytique, je m'en doutais. Il a fouillé sur ma table, il l'a fait exprès"
(124).[108] Sorge's double turned him in, which means that the "odeur de
délation" he had sensed was well founded. This twin is his personal delegate to the State, the supervisor who not only provides moral and technical support to the employee but also keeps a watchful eye on every action
the employee commits. He is there to work with Sorge and to act as an
informant aginst him, should the occasion present itself. By submitting
the letter of resignation that Sorge may never have intended anyone to
see, his double is the instigator of a minor transgression, one which the
State would normally be able to convert to its advantage. His denunciation of Sorge as traitor would normally entail an investigation into the
infraction and an appropriative conversion of it, either by pardon or repri-
mand. The machinery of the State breaks down in this case, however, as
it proves itself incapable of getting to the bottom of the affair.

The double who plays the role of incriminator in the episode of Sorge's
resignation is manifestly not the taciturn coworker in his "fable." With
the former, Sorge is on working, speaking terms, and their relationship of
betrayal which fabricates a normally recuperable transgression which
should contribute to the smooth functioning of the State bears principally on the regional economy of power, although the incident also
points out the State's incapability of converting the transgression into
something it can use. The story of Sorge's silent double, on the contrary,
has repercussions for the general economy. He does exactly what Sorge
does: refuses to speak, finds the situation more and more unbearable, and
finally asks to be moved to a different office. This seemingly insignificant
episode haunts Sorge for some time, and it is only in retrospect that he
can say that perhaps "j'étais le même que lui." The silent *malentendu* that
occurs between Sorge and his colleague is comparable to a Narcissistic
encounter, which allows us to extend an invitation to Blanchot to violate

the *noli me legere* by having him interpret this enigmatic "fable" for us in the context of his remarks on this myth in *L'Ecriture du désastre*.

The essential feature of the myth, according to Blanchot, is that Narcissus does not recognize himself as the person whose reflection captivates him. This state of noncoincidence between Narcissus and his reflected image leads Blanchot to say that in this myth, "il nous est donné d'apprendre l'une des versions de l'imaginaire selon laquelle l'homme— est-ce l'homme?—s'il peut se faire selon l'image, est plus certainement exposé au risque de se défaire selon son image" (*ED* 194).[109] In this relatively recent fragment (1980), Blanchot discusses the myth in terms of "the two versions of the imaginary," and of *ressemblance* which he formulated initially in 1951.

Narcissus's face-to-face encounter with his own image, which he is incapable of recognizing and appropriating for himself, represents in dramatic fashion the surplus of being which exceeds the closure of an integral, fully constituted subject. In an odd sort of way, just as Blanchot gives precedence to the cadaver over the intramundane person with a recognizable identity, we might say (although Blanchot does not explicitly do so himself) that Narcissus's punishment precedes his transgression: the Narcissus who spurns Echo's love (his transgression) is but one manifestation rendered possible by the neutral space created by the "dédoublement initial," Narcissus's fascinated gaze which is unwittingly directed at itself (his punishment). Rather than providing Narcissus with a picture-perfect likeness of himself, his watery reflection plunges him into the undetermined milieu of fascination, where vision is not the ability to see but, on the contrary, the inability *not* to see "l'informe lourdeur de l'être présent dans l'absence" (*EL* 351).[110]

> L'eau où Narcisse voit ce qu'il ne doit pas voir, n'est pas le miroir capable d'une image distincte et définie. Ce qu'il voit, c'est dans le visible l'invisible, dans la figure l'infigurable, l'inconnu instable d'une représentation sans présence, la représentation qui ne renvoie pas à un modèle. (*ED* 204)[111]

The element in which Sorge contemplates himself, the written words of his journal, is every bit as treacherous as the rippling waters of Narcissus's fountain. Instead of faithfully reflecting an image with which he can identify himself, the "miroir d'encre" of his text, to borrow Beaujour's phrase, refracts the image of himself that he expected to see appear, that of a fully constituted, self-present subject. Sorge thought that by writing a day-to-day account of his life during the epidemic, he would come upon "l'épanouissement d'une vérité suprême," that he would arrive at a complete knowledge of himself and of his place in the world (the State). It is just the opposite that occurs, however, as the "secret law of the genre" subverts the "apparent law": his writing takes him back to a moment prior to the subject's integration in the regional economy. He is "unmade" according to his image as he writes. The names that I, as a reader working within the regional economy, have attributed to Sorge to describe this Narcissistic split are Sorge the functionary (in his reductive readings on behalf of the State) and Sorge the subversive (in his sick writings on behalf of the epidemic which make up a major transgression that the State cannot put to use). Sorge's "fable," which tells of his splitting into someone he does not recognize, prefigures this doubling which only seems to be a consequence of his writing. The supposedly integral, original, authoritative subject was already fissured, and it is thanks to this "dédoublement initial," an indeterminate neutrality to which I have tacked on the names "functionary" and "subversive" *a posteriori*, that Sorge can write his self-portrait. If it had not been there to begin with, he would not have felt the need to keep a journal at all.

Had he recognized himself in the reflection, Narcissus would not have remained captivated by it for the rest of his days. He is forbidden to see himself as he is, and Blanchot seizes on his inability to make the connection between himself and the reflection in order to interpret the myth according to his "version of the imaginary" whereby instead of encountering an idealized portrait of himself infused with an added dimension of spirituality, he comes into contact with the illusion "d'une mort évasive qui est toute dans la répétition d'une méconnaissance muette" (*ED* 194).[112] The "evasive death" which Narcissus's gaze ultimately meets is none other than *le mourir*, "la perpétuité de ce qui ne supporte ni commencement ni fin" (*EL* 355).[113] Sorge's "fable" tells the story of a repeated misunderstanding that takes place in silence between him and his colleague. This misunderstanding, moreover, is doubled as it is repeated and maintained in the journal taken in its entirety. No reconciliation between the two Sorges is possible. Neither entity recognizes and appropriates the other; the tension remains unresolved. Sorge is unable to utilize language in order to articulate a form of dialectical communication between the two that would join them together. The language of Sorge the anarchist transgresses the limits that the State would assign to it, but at the same time, it fails to destroy these limits once and for all, as it necessarily remains caught in the "piège du signifiant." Like it or not, no matter how infected with the epidemic of the general economy his language becomes, it will still say something meaningful in the regional economy.

Narcissus and Sorge share the fate of dying elusive deaths; both lack the element of finality. Of the former, Blanchot writes that "il meurt (s'il meurt) d'être immortel, immortalité d'apparence qu'atteste la métamorphose en fleur, fleur funèbre ou fleur de rhétorique" (*ED* 196).[114] Of the latter, we have stressed the incomplete death which leads to a retelling of the story. Like that of Narcissus, Sorge's death or, more properly, the writing that his death provides for, also spawns a rhetorical flower. As is the case with the imaginary, Blanchot speaks of "two versions" of rhetoric. One usually thinks of rhetoric as a set of rules and techniques that writers have at their disposal designed to enable them to have mastery over language and to create certain desired effects in their readers' minds. Blanchot never denies that rhetoric serves the desire to regulate the functioning of language or that it is "l'un de ces moyens de défense, efficacement conçu ... pour conjurer le péril" (*LV* 323)[115] of the intransitive *parole* of the neutral. Rhetoric does not merely constitute an obstacle which protects the integrity of language by nearly reducing the anonymous murmur at its center to silence. It serves also as an invitation, one which exists "pour ... attirer, en la détournant, l'immensité parlante; pour être une avancée au milieu de l'agitation des sables, et non pas un petit rempart de fantaisie que viennent visiter les promeneurs du dimanche" (*LV* 323).[116]

These two versions of rhetoric are present in Sorge's journal. The rhetorical devices at work in journals assure their authors of two things: temporal continuity and identification between themselves and the subject of their entries. Sorge apparently undertook to write a book that would be an eloquent testimonial to the accomplishments of humanity and its harmonious partnership with the world. In the process of writing this book, however, he stumbles upon a rhetoric founded on a different set of principles. A book that started out as being written in accordance with the exigencies of continuity and totalization turns out to respond to a new exigency of writing based on discontinuity and fragmentation. Like Narcissus, Sorge is incapable of recognizing the image of himself that he has created in his writing. Nor does he ever come to terms in any definitive way with the opposing types of rhetoric. The rhetoric of repetition always returns to undo the accomplishments of the rhetoric of continuity, without the latter's being able to harness the transgressive language of the former. Commenting on the idea that all writers are involved with Narcissistic encounters, Blanchot makes the following observation:

> dans le poème où il s'écrit il ne se reconnaît pas, ... il n'y prend pas conscience de lui-même, rejeté de cet espoir facile d'un certain humanisme selon lequel, écrivant ou "créant", il transformerait en plus grande conscience la part d'expérience obscure qu'il subirait: au contraire, rejeté, exclu de ce qui s'écrit et, sans y être même présent par la non-présence de *sa* mort même, il lui faut renoncer à tout rapport de soi (vivant et mourant) avec ce qui appartient désormais à l'autre ou restera sans appartenance. Le poète est Narcisse, dans la mesure où Narcisse est anti-Narcisse: celui qui, détourné de soi, portant et supportant le détour, mourant de ne pas se reconnaître, laisse la trace de ce qui n'a pas eu lieu. (*ED* 205)[117]

Both the myth of Narcissus and Sorge's experience as a writer leave us with the trace of something that never took place—that is, never took place a first time as would an event that begins and ends with respect to other particular points in time. What does not "happen" as far as the myth is concerned? The actual splitting of Narcissus's *moi*. We cannot properly imagine him at a stage prior to his fissured *moi* when he would possess the attributes of a self-sufficient, self-present subject. Narcissus is always already self-centered and deaf to the amorous overtures of Echo, even before he becomes infatuated with his own reflection, as Nemesis's punishment dictated.

Sorge's writings also leave traces of the untraceable. The events of which his journal is the narration are, in fact, nonevents. Moreover, his act of recording them fails to endow them with the characteristics of an event by firmly placing them in some sort of chronological framework. His story is noneventful; his dying words send us back to its beginning. Sorge's book does not begin or end, it just is. Nor does he die once and for all, but he is constantly attentive to the approach of death. Jeanne Galgat[118] is also well aware of the noneventful aspect of Sorge's death which never really comes to pass: "J'ai peine à croire, dit-elle, qu'une chose pareille [Sorge's death] puisse arriver un jour. Est-ce possible? Pourra-t-on jamais dire: c'est à partir de cette date que . . . ?" (234).[119] No, one cannot, just as it is impossible to single out a particular moment when the utopian end of history takes place. The surplus negativity of the epidemic calls into question the closure of totalization purportedly achieved by the State. Another untraceable nonevent is the subversion of one rhetoric by another that goes on within Sorge's book. Like Narcissus, Sorge is always already divided, even prior to his contaminated decision to write, the consequence of which is to reproduce this fissure. Finally, the outbreak of the epidemic, the most fundamental and pervasive element in Sorge's narrative, is untraceable. It never begins or ends; it is ever present as it fluctuates indefinitely between outward virulence and inward remission.

Sorge's Revolt

Sorge is caught in the double bind of the circular exigency: thanks to his writing, it seems possible to him to acquire the aptitude to die content. And yet at the same time, he can write only if he has previously established a rapport with death. We can apply the first half of the circular exigency to his situation ("pour mourir il faut écrire") by recalling his desire to keep a diary. He begins his project enthusiastically. He has a purpose, and in the early going we suppose that it is to compose a homage to the State which has succeeded in achieving mastery over the world and defining humanity's harmonious niche in it. Moreover, he believes he can trust the language he will use in the writing of this book, and he proceeds with the conviction that his book will provide him with more complete knowledge of himself and of his place in the world. If he could accomplish all this by composing the work of his life, he would have nothing left to live for and could, therefore, die content.

We might also approach the statement "pour mourir il faut écrire" from a different angle, that of the sequence of events recounted by the book. In this context, the circular exigency seems to be saying "write first and die later," which in a sense Sorge does. He spends several days writing a thorough account of his activities and thoughts on the events taking place around him, and at the "end," he "dies." We can only imagine what the aftermath of his death might be. Most probably both sides in the conflict (that is, if we pretend for a moment that Bouxx *is* outside the law of the State) would attempt to appropriate Sorge's death, to turn it into something they could use to further their causes. The State-run press agency would no doubt concoct a story of the savage slaying of a government employee at the hands of a group of subversives posing as members of the medical establishment. For his part, Bouxx would circulate a much different story, one that would turn Sorge into a hero and martyr for his cause by making him out to be a disillusioned government official who quit his job and chose to remain with the members of the revolutionary party of his own free will on ideological grounds. In both cases, his death is recuperable.

Thus, as we noted earlier in our discussion of Blanchot's version of the myth of Orpheus, the first half of the circular exigency places us squarely in the regional economy of power: in order for Sorge to die as if it were an act of power (for Orpheus to emerge triumphantly from the underworld with Eurydice by his side), it is necessary for him to write as if language were an instrument of power (for Orpheus to sing as if his music were an instrument of power that would guarantee his success). From this point of view, Sorge's death is not the only thing that is recuperable; his book is as well, a point which his stepfather makes quite clear to him: "Peut-être allez-vous nous donner du tintouin avec les rêves de votre encrier, mais il n'importe, nous ne les laisserons pas se perdre, nous les poursuivrons aussi longtemps qu'il le faudra pour en exprimer la valeur et en tirer parti" (125).[120] The State has people in its employ who will have no trouble reading Sorge's journal in the way that Sorge himself read many of the stories that others told him.

Sorge's exegeses will make pleasant reading for the State's censors, but will they be able to live up to his stepfather's promise by assimilating *all* "the dreams of his inkwell?" Hardly, for they will be bound by the circular exigency every bit as much as Sorge. The second half of the circular exigency states that the ability to write is preconditioned by a rapport with death. In this case, however, "death" does not refer to the power of the negative but instead to the unemployable negativity of the general economy. "Pour écrire il faut mourir," or "die first and write later." In Orpheus's case, in order for him to be able to mobilize his music as a weapon that will protect him as he passes through Hades, he must already have been initiated to *le mourir* by losing Eurydice. The fatal moment of his gaze when he loses Eurydice a second time is nothing more than a repetition of her earlier disappearance. His failure is preordained from the start. He has always been facing her, even before he casts the fatal glance. He is bound to transgress the interdiction not to see her as soon as he makes the transgressive steps of crossing over into the realm of the dead where he does not belong. The myth tells of two failures—Eurydice twice lost—in the midst of which is the interlude of Orpheus's courageous approach when he has a chance to succeed before his music betrays him, which induces him to forget the precondition he would have had to respect in order to complete his mission.

Sorge's interlude consists of his optimistic attitude with which he undertakes the writing of his diary, confident that it will serve some useful purpose for him and the State. Initially, Sorge has as much confidence in his pen as Orpheus does in his lyre. This confidence wanes, however, as he realizes that the conception of language on which his literary project is based is rotten to the core, devoured by the same cancer that is eating away at the system of representation on which the foundations of the State rest. The language of power of his journal, like that of the State's archives and of Bouxx's pamphlets, has already been stricken by this cancer prior to its remission in the regional economy, where language is reduced to only one of its components, ideas. The tissue that connects signified ideas to signifying words is the object of the malignancy, and the only "supreme truth" that is visited upon Sorge as he writes is that this link, far from being the stable, unshakeable connection that the smooth functioning of the regional economy depends on, is at best tangential. Although he does not know it, his journal is doomed to fail even before he begins writing it. Certain passages of his book do fall within the jurisdiction of readings which could be performed from the point of view of the regional economy. His loyalistic interpretations of certain incidents provide the State with textbook illustrations of how the law is supposed to work. His discussions with his stepfather in which he is critical of the State, on the other hand, furnish Bouxx's followers with ample ammunition which they can use to attack the State. Read in its entirety, however, his text can only be seen as exceeding whatever limits he or Bouxx or his stepfather would assign to it. It is irreducible to the work of the negative.

It takes on a secret life of its own; his ink oozes from his pen onto the blank pages of his diary in the same surreptitious way that the spreading epidemic seeps through the walls which separate one house from the next. In short, although portions of the book may be assimilated as instruments of constructive negativity, taken as a whole it does not lend itself to such reductive reading. The major impropriety of Sorge's journal is that it goes beyond his original intentions, and he is as powerless with respect to his contaminated writing as are Bouxx and the State with respect to the epidemic.

On account of the reversibility of the propositions laid forth in Blanchot's circular exigency, it is impossible for us to determine once and for all whether a particular experience of death determines a particular type of writing or vice versa. The torment of the circle cannot be pacified by an either/or. Sorge's book is circular, his death incomplete, and we are unable to say which one of these conditions is responsible for the other. Does the type of death he suffers depend on his experience as a writer, or does the type of book he writes depend on his experience of death? Ideally, he hoped to lay the groundwork for his own *mort contente* by writing his journal, a hymn to the totality, the reconciliation of the individual, the collectivity, and the world. What he produces instead is a fragmentary, unfinished book. Defenders of the faith in totalization would claim that Sorge's death was premature (isn't it always?), an untimely interruption of his quest for absolute knowledge that condemned his book to be fragmentary. From the point of view of the regional economy, Sorge died before his time, and this unfortunate accident prevented him from carrying his plan through to its conclusion. It is only this point of view, however, that authorizes us to make the claim that "the book stops here." At what point does it really end? When Sorge dies? But when does he do that? His last words form such a perfect loop with his first words that we cannot say that his death comprises the final scene; it also serves as an overture to chapter 1. His incomplete death both precedes and proceeds from the writing of the fragmentary journal.

The surplus negativity of *le mourir* predetermines the course that Sorge will follow as he writes his book. It is responsible for the unexpected shape (fragmentary, repetitious, circular) that the book takes as the secret law subverts the apparent law of his original intentions. And his death on the last page is the inevitable consequence of his failure to have complete mastery over the language of his book, the medium in which he, a man of letters, must work. Like Narcissus, Sorge dies of being immortal, of being unable to die completely. His book suffers the same fate: it never gets finished, either. Sorge the user of language fails to gain possession of himself through his literary creation. If his book gets away from him, which means in turn that he gets away from himself, it is because their common denominator of language is also a victim of an incomplete death. "La cruauté du langage vient de ce que sans cesse il évoque sa mort sans pouvoir mourir jamais" (*PF* 30).[121] Sorge and his language are subject to the same prohibition: "Il est interdit de mourir" (*PAD* 133),[122] as if to die were to engage in one final act of negation. Language is not at one with itself. It is made up of elements that are in a state of perpetual contestation with each other. It aspires to accede to the ideal world of pure signification as a purveyor of unequivocal meanings but is unable to do so completely on account of its materiality.

Sorge's diary communicates ideas that have great bearing on the functioning of the regional economy, but at the same time it is irreducible to this dimension. The part of his language that lives on, oblivious to the contribution it ought to make to the regional economy, has the effect of opening up an old wound, one that has existed since time immemorial. His language festers and grows out of control, and Sorge is transformed into a spokesman for the neutrality of the epidemic, a phenomenon of unbridled contestation. The unhealthy condition of his language foretells the failure of his experience as a writer to accomplish what he set out to do. Thus language is the true executioner of Henri Sorge, and his experience with language is responsible for the type of death (the uneventful, unending *mourir*) that he suffers, but this happens only because language has always already been stricken by the *mourir*. It is not so much a question, therefore, of Sorge's death's putting a premature end to his book as it is one of his book's putting him to an unfinished, repetitious death.

Pierre Bouxx, Sorge's personable ideological sparring partner, chooses a very different route from that taken by Sorge. Whereas Sorge quietly retreats into the solitude of his room in order to write and reflect on the events taking place around him, Bouxx enters the fray. He opts for concrete action over abstract meditation. Although he performs a certain amount of reading and writing as an administrator, it is clear that he does so more out of necessity than by choice. "Je n'ai pas le temps de lire" (19),[123] he confides to Sorge in his first conversation with him, and much later on, he confesses: "Mais moi, je hais les idées" (193).[124] He was not always like this, however: "A l'étranger, j'ai beaucoup étudié, j'ai écrit aussi" (19).[125] Perhaps we can explain this change of heart, his choice of action over meditation, by a mistrust of language that he may have developed through his writing. In any case, his philosophy of praxis is predicated on the belief that the direct participation of individuals can alter the course of history.

In the final stage of the novel, when the epidemic is on the wane, Bouxx issues his last order: "Les événements se préparent, chacun doit maintenant prendre part au conflit" (210).[126] Ironically, thanks to Bouxx's efficient management of the medical establishment, the danger of the plague and, therefore, the source of his power have declined. This order constitutes a last-ditch effort to topple the bureaucracy of the State before he and his followers are definitively absorbed by it. It is now or never as far as Bouxx is concerned, time to stand up and be counted.

Sorge is haunted by these words. He cannot seem to escape them. They are repeated incessantly over the loudspeakers in the streets, but it is above all the word "maintenant" that echoes back and forth between the walls of his room. He heeds, however, a different call. Whereas Bouxx goes down swinging, urging his fellow citizens to take part in the conflict, Sorge goes down writing. For him, too, it is now or never. "C'est maintenant que je parle." It is now or never (a first time). It is all the same to him.

SIX

FLAGRANTS DÉLITS

CAUGHT IN THE ACT OF SELF-READING

Discreet Violations of the Noli

D ANS LES ÉLÉGIES, l'affirmation de la vie et celle de la mort
se révèlent comme n'en formant qu'une" (*EL* 170).[1] Rilke is
speaking here as the author of a letter to Hulewicz in which he
embarks on an explanation of the concept of death in the *Duino Elegies*.
To offer interpretations of one's own works is a cardinal sin, an outright
violation of one of the primary commandments in Blanchot's corpus of
critical edicts. *Noli me legere*, "Thou shalt not read me," is the fundamental demand made by the work on its creator that Rilke chose to ignore on
this occasion. Blanchot does not mention this instance to criticize *what*
Rilke had to say about death. He cites him instead for having said anything about its poetic representation at all, evidence of how much "nous
aimons substituer au pur mouvement poétique des idées intéressantes"
(*EL* 170).[2] Blanchot remarks that this letter came to be better known
than the poems themselves on which it was a commentary and that by
writing it, Rilke was laboring under false pretenses, "comme si, dans l'angoisse des mots qu'il n'est appelé qu'à dire et jamais à lire, il voulait se
persuader que, malgré tout, il s'entend, il a droit de lecture et de
compréhension" (*EL* 170).[3] When an author decides to publish a work,
it belongs henceforth to the public domain. He is consequently dismissed
from it, cast out, obliged to give up any claim of authority over it. Rilke
should have written his poetry and left it at that: "c'est en cela que sa
pensée s'élève à une plus haute mesure" (*EL* 179)[4] than that reached in
discursive forms of writing such as his correspondence.

Lest it seem that we are accusing Blanchot of "casting the first stone,"
it would serve us well to remember that his Bataillian-inspired *interdits*
are invitations as well as obstacles. That literary works simultaneously invite and resist interpretations signifies that the *noli* constitutes a weak yet
resilient defense. It is addressed to authors and readers alike, and both
inevitably succumb to the temptation to reduce reading to an act of the
powers of understanding. This impatient impulse leads to failure, however; the work remains unread—unreduced completely to an act of com-

prehension—and the *noli* thus remains intact as it survives the transgression. No, Blanchot is "not without sin." He, too, is guilty of violating the prohibition of self-reading which he characterizes as "une défense qui s'est toujours déjà laissé transgresser" (*AC* 89).[5] He is no more able to abide by this *interdit* than Rilke or, for that matter, any writer is.

Nearly all of Blanchot's critical works are comprised of articles originally written for publication in periodicals and subsequently assembled to form individual volumes. His propensity to write prefaces and *postfaces* springs from the very nature of these books. He no doubt feels compelled to say a few words (these appendices are always brief) about when the essays were written and how they came to be grouped together. Even if he does not attempt to bestow a retrospective unity on his disparate collections of essays in his *pièces liminaires*, he does verge on the activity of self-reading. In his preface to *L'Espace littéraire*, for example, he states that "quand il s'agit d'un livre d'éclaircissements, il y a une sorte de loyauté méthodique à dire vers quel point il semble que le livre se dirige: ici vers les pages intitulées 'Le regard d'Orphée'" (*EL* 5).[6] In this case, the *noli* is barely audible because the book in question is merely "un livre d'éclaircissements," a book of illuminating explanations. In the same way that Blanchot presents Orpheus's transgressive gaze of betrayal as an act of fidelity to a higher law, the primary exigency of failure, he claims to be acting in accordance with a certain "methodological good faith" by writing his preface in which he casts Orphic glances over his own shoulder at texts from which he has long been estranged and by reading them for us, as he directs our gazes to the section of the book that he considers to be the most important.

A rarer but similar kind of self-reading occurs from one book to another, and the fragment on page 97 of *L'Ecriture du désastre* provides us with such an example. It begins with the words "Lisant ces phrases anciennes,"[7] which are followed by two quotations on insomnia and nocturnal vigilance. The author of these "phrases anciennes" is none other than Blanchot himself. The first sentence is taken from an article he wrote in 1953 and that he placed in *L'Espace littéraire* in the section entitled "L'Inspiration, le manque d'inspiration." The second quotation comes from an article on Michel Leiris, "Rêver, écrire," which appeared in the *NRF* in 1961 and resurfaced nine years later as a chapter of *L'Amitié*. That three books, which cover a span of nearly thirty years, are at issue in this fragment helps to explain the somewhat unexpected turn that the fragment takes once Blanchot has quoted himself. In a gesture similar to his commentary on Rilke's self-commentary, in which he was much less concerned with what Rilke had to say about the theme of death in his poems than with the fact that Rilke said anything about it at all, he is not interested in pursuing a meditation on the relationship between dreaming, insomnia, and writing. He ponders instead the ramifications involved in the act of self-quotation that he has just performed. He is less preoccupied with what he means in these sentences than he is with the fact that these sentences continue to haunt him to the point of demanding to be rewritten: "Pourquoi ce rappel? Pourquoi . . . ces paroles semblent-elles avoir besoin d'être reprises, répétées, pour échapper au sens qui les anime et afin d'être détournées d'elles-mêmes, du discours qui les utilise?" (*ED* 97).[8] One of the consequences of rewriting these sentences is to allow them to retain their air of mystery and unknowability. Their repetition makes them unreadable again, for their words exceed the meanings they seem to communicate and the system of discourse that renders these meanings possible. Every *parole* is, nevertheless, "a two-faced monster"; a word is neither entirely neutral nor in the absolute service of the regional economy of power. The essence of language resides in the impossibility of reducing it to either one or the other of these designations. The repetitious copying of these sentences participates in the perpetuation of the anonymous *il y a*, the state of restless contestation that exists at the heart of language and makes of it a "both . . . and" proposition, not an "either . . . or." Words are *both* self-effacing, transparent purveyors of meaning *and* obstinate tactile, acoustic, or visual objects which obscure our attempts to arrive at pure signification. These sentences on *l'autre nuit*, nevertheless, do mean something; they are not total nonsense, and their ability to convey meaning leads to a second consequence of rewriting them which is at odds with the first:

> Mais, reprises, elles [ces phrases] réintroduisent une assurance à laquelle on croyait avoir cessé d'appartenir, elles ont un air de vérité, elles disent quelque chose, elles prétendent à une cohérence, elles disent: tu as pensé cela il y a longtemps, tu es donc autorisé à le penser à nouveau, restaurant cette continuité raisonnable qui fait les systèmes. (*ED* 97)[9]

This is the insurmountable contradiction of Blanchot's entire literary enterprise: the more he writes about the neutral, "la pensée de l'impossible," "la pensée qui ne se laisse pas penser," etc. the more thinkable it becomes. The *pensée* that precedes all systems still lends itself to systematization, to partial degrees of it anyway, whenever the oscillating movement of *mots glissants* such as *le dehors* is arrested and made to correspond to a definable philosophical concept. In this fragment, it almost seems that Blanchot is dismayed by the idea that the regional economy of coherent systems has gotten the upper hand over the general economy of neutrality, ironically thanks to his relentless, single-minded, and consistent efforts of promoting the latter over the years. He need not worry for long, however, because the logic of transgression holds sway here, too: "il n'y a pas loi, interdit, puis transgression, mais transgression sans interdit qui finit par se figer en Loi, en Principe du Sens" (*ED* 121).[10] His transgressive writing on behalf of the general economy lends itself for a time to comprehension, when it temporarily "congeals" long enough to have the consistency of a concept, a "principle of meaning." This law of the regional economy, however, is constantly undermined by the law of the general economy, thanks to the fundamentally ambiguous nature of language. The neutral resists all attempts that would reduce it completely to the level of conceptual knowledge while at the same time surrendering itself partially to such attempts.

A more severe and less frequent violation of the *noli* occurs in connection with his narrative works. Blanchot is less prone to comment on his novels and *récits*, but one notable instance in which he does so is *Après Coup*, a reedition of two stories that had been previously published under the title of *Le Ressassement éternel*, with an afterward by the author in which he reflects on what these stories mean. We witness the same reluctant attitude toward saying anything definitive about "Le Dernier mot" and "L'Idylle" that we noticed in his essay on *The Castle*. Whether reading his own works or those of someone else, it is typical for him to venture forth with an interpretation, immediately after which he beats a hasty retreat by disclaiming the validity of what he has just proposed. This tug of war is a function of the dual nature of the *interdit*. The *noli* is a law begging to be violated, and he obliges it by advancing the hypothesis that the castle represents the locus of the neutral. As soon as he says this, however, he regrets it, just as Orpheus must have regretted having looked at Eurydice. He discreetly withdraws his supposition, labels it a gross simplification, and thereby respectfully allows the *noli* to reassert itself with all the force of an interdiction untouched by his foolhardy transgression. In *Après Coup*, this hesitant movement of advance and retreat is evident in his comments on "L'Idylle": although quick to point out that a reading of this story based on historical events that came to pass after he wrote it would be insufficient, he nevertheless goes on to call it a prophetic tale, a "récit d'avant Auschwitz" (*AC* 99).[11] He admits that it is "impossible de ne pas évoquer ces travaux dérisoires des camps concentrationnaires" (*AC* 95)[12] when reading this story, but he does not think that " 'L'Idylle' puisse s'interpréter comme la lecture d'un avenir déjà menaçant" (*AC* 96).[13] After putting forth a perspective from which this story might be approached, a revelation that we are tempted to adopt as *the* secret key to understanding the story, given its source, he rejects it as inadequate. Moreover, he is conscious of violating the *noli*, so much so that he feels the need to justify his self-commentary by saying that the stories were written so long ago—forty-five years—that it was impossible for him to know who had written them.

Catching Blanchot in the act of violating the prohibition against self-reading in the preface to *L'Espace littéraire* or in the *postface* of *Après Coup* should come as no great surprise. In fact, texts such as these, that were composed as afterthoughts to preexisting works, constitute the most obvious places in which one would expect to find him engaged in this dubious activity. His denunciation of it in the case of another writer, Rilke, and his own transgressive practice of it from one book to the next, are two other examples which are relatively easy to trace. I would like to consider one further type of self-reading which is more subtle and difficult to expose than the ones just mentioned: the kind that takes place within the confines of the same book.

A notable instance of this type of self-reading that occurs in the work as it unfolds can be found in *Le Pas au-delà*. If the *noli* of *L'Espace littéraire* is barely audible because it is a book that is addressed to our discursive intelligence, it would seem to be deafening in a book such as *Le Pas au-delà*, which defies classification. The distinction between theoretical and narrative writing is blurred. This book of fragments is composed of dialogues, vignettes that could be excerpts from his fiction, and mystifying aphorisms. A small constellation of his favorite writers is present (Hegel, Nietzsche, Hölderlin), as well as the themes of the neutral, the dual status of death, the eternal return, and the impersonality of writing, all constant preoccupations over the years. The particular moment in which the *noli* is violated occurs in connection with this enigmatic sentence: "Je ne sais pas, mais je sais que je vais avoir su."[14] It appears on three different occasions during the course of the book (146, 153, 170).[15] On the second of these occasions (here it is slightly modified to "mais je pressens que"), rather than letting us figure it out for ourselves, Blanchot takes the time to give us a veritable *explication de texte* which turns out to be one of the longest fragments in the book (over two pages) and in which he meticulously parses the sentence and explains the negation, the conjunction, the verbs and their tenses. What he demonstrates in so doing is "le défaut d'un sujet . . . capable de porter ce savoir au présent" (*PAD* 156),[16] the "savoir" in question being complete consciousness of death.

Such an immediate juxtaposition of the obscurity of his creative voice and the clarity of his critical style indicates that even a fragmentary work, which is particularly resistant to reductive interpretation, is not immune to analytic explanation and comprehension. For one brief instant he succumbs to Orphic impatience. Having written this fragment and then having been expelled from it (for the fragment, in its isolation, has the same dense plasticity and autonomy that a work does), he could not resist trying to learn its secret by dissecting its syntax. And yet his interpretation fails to reduce it to silence. The sentence resurfaces fifteen pages later, all alone, in a different context (that is, if one can even speak of context where fragments are concerned), and the previous explanation has not succeeded in eliminating its strangeness.

This occurrence of self-reading is noteworthy for two reasons. First, it affords us the rare opportunity to view Blanchot engaged in detailed grammatical analysis, a practice that is virtually nonexistent elsewhere in his critical writings. Second, and more important, the critical distance which served in our previous examples as a motivating factor in his decision to indulge in the transgressive activity of self-commentary has been suppressed. This distance can be measured spatially and chronologically: spatially in that these self-commentaries are most often found in a preface or an afterword or take place from one book to the next, and chronologically with respect to the number of years that have passed between the writing of the work (or sentence, fragment, *récit*, etc.) in question and his commentary of it. The greater these distances, it seems, the easier it is to violate the *noli*. From them Blanchot derives the authority, which he had presumably abdicated, to read his own writings for us in the form of retrospective musings appended to these earlier texts.

Getting Started, Finishing Up
The Pro/Epilogue of *L'Attente L'Oubli*

Notwithstanding the exceptional character of this instance of self-reading, it pales in comparison to the one offered in *L'Attente l'oubli*. Whereas the former is an isolated occurrence, the latter book as a whole presents us with a sustained interaction between the voices of writing and self-reading. In fact, it owes its momentum, even its very existence, to the *entretien* which it creates between these two exigencies. Paul de Man suggests that *L'Attente l'oubli* "could only be the result of a relationship between the completed work and its author. The impossibility of self-reading has itself become the main theme, demanding in its turn to be read and interpreted" (*Blindness and Insight*, 67). As in our example taken from *Le Pas au-delà*, the spatial and temporal interval within which the *noli* usually has jurisdiction has practically been erased. The activities of writing and reading are in a rapport of such immediacy that there is no time for Blanchot to reflect on the consequences of this relationship, something he no doubt would have done in a purely critical context. In his prefaces, *postfaces*, and comments that range from one book to another, he commits violations of the *noli* that are both discrete (isolated) and discreet (done with a sense of culpability, a self-conscious awareness that a law is being broken). In *L'Attente l'oubli*, on the other hand, the transgressions become so indiscrete (continuous) as to be indiscreet (committed with no pangs of remorse).

If I have chosen to conclude my discussion of Blanchot's fiction with an analysis of *L'Attente l'oubli*, it is because it occupies a special place with respect to his other works. Published in 1962, it constitutes not only his final narrative work but also his most experimental attempt to combine narration with fragmentary writing. I use the word "narrative" loosely, for it is not at all certain how this book can be classified generically. Yet it is undoubtedly more of a narrative work than his later fragmentary books. Roger Laporte does not hesitate to call it "le dernier récit de Blanchot" (*Deux Lectures de Maurice Blanchot*, 144).[17] For his part, Michel Deguy says that it occupies some sort of middle ground between philosophy and fiction. He admits that "le commencement du livre paraît le situer dans la tradition du récit" (710),[18] but at the close of this review article he notes the aphoristic character of this book, excerpts of which appeared in a festschrift in honor of Heidegger's seventieth birthday. Michel Foucault, on the contrary, eschews the use of an opposition such as fiction and philosophy when talking about the language of *L'Attente l'oubli*:

> The distinction between "novels," "narratives," and "criticism" is progressively weakened in Blanchot until, in *L'Attente l'oubli*, language alone is allowed to speak—what is no one's, is neither fiction nor reflection, neither already said nor never yet said, but is instead "between them, this place with its fixed open expanse, the retention of things in their latent state." (*Foucault/Blanchot*, 26)

Foucault is correct in alluding to the trajectory that Blanchot's literary history has followed and which took him from the novels of the 1940s, to the *récits* of the 1950s, to the fragmentary works of the 1960s and 1970s. The setting of *L'Attente l'oubli* has been almost completely stripped of any references to concrete reality in favor of a minimalist universe: a hotel room sparsely furnished with a bed, a couch, and a table is where everything takes place. What takes place has also been reduced to the bare essentials. The basic story line concerns the relationship between a man and woman who spend time together talking as they are alternately waiting for something to happen to them that never does and vainly trying to remember something that may have already happened to them. The abstract setting, language, and plot of *L'Attente l'oubli* show how far Blanchot has come from his portrayal of the panic-stricken city in *Le Très-Haut*, which abounds in characters, dramatic situations, and allegorical story-telling. I believe that Foucault goes a little too far, however, when he states that the language of *L'Attente l'oubli* "n'est ni de la fiction ni de la réflexion." I would like to qualify this statement by suggesting that the language of this book is not completely indifferent to designations such as "fiction" and "reflection." Following de Man's lead,[19] I maintain that an examination of the various structures of the fragments that make up this book will reveal traces of the complementary exigencies of creation and analysis, of writing and reading, and that the interdependence of these exigencies is the generating principle responsible for this book's coming into existence.

At first glance, the opening section of *L'Attente l'oubli* apears to be a kind of preface to the fragments proper which begin on page 12. Closer scrutiny, however, reveals Blanchot's skill at confounding the reader's perspective to the point of making it impossible for the latter to determine once and for all what the logical, temporal relationship is between this opening section and the collection of fragments that follows. In the end, all efforts to situate this passage clearly with respect to the rest of the book prove to be futile. Readers must look no farther than the first sentence in order to realize the precarious situation in which they suddenly find themselves implicated: "Ici, et sur cette phrase qui lui était peut-être aussi destinée, il fut contraint de s'arrêter" (7).[20] This sentence comes as a surprise for two reasons. First, it announces the end of something; something is already over just as the book begins. For some reason unknown to us, the protagonist/writer is obliged to stop writing. The other surprising and somewhat bewildering thought expressed in this sentence is that we do not know exactly when he stops writing. What point of his text does "ici" designate? And do the words "cette phrase" refer to the sentence which we have just finished reading and of which they are a part, or does he have another sentence in mind that precedes this one and to which we are not privy?

The second sentence, "C'est presque en l'écoutant parler qu'il avait rédigé ces notes," (7)[21] does more to prolong these questions than to resolve them. If "these notes" are none other than the fragments that we are about to read and which make up the book entitled *L'Attente l'oubli*, the opening section functions more as an epilogue than a prologue; it could have been placed at the end of the book as one last look backward at what had transpired between the writer and his female companion. In spite of what the initial sentence says, there are two factors that prevent us from assuming that this section signals the end of something, above and beyond the most obvious and telling detail: that this passage appears at the beginning of the book. First, the activity of writing has not ceased after all. Contrary to what the first sentence says, in the third one we read: "Il entendait encore sa voix en écrivant" (7).[22] That this section constitutes both an interruption and a continuation of a text already in progress is reaffirmed a few lines further on. He wants to know what she thinks of what he has written, and after he receives her opinion, we are told that "Il résolut de repartir de là" (8); he decides to resume his *récit* from the point she designated as "le plus fidèle" to what had transpired.

The reader's difficulty in determining whether these opening pages constitute a retrospective conclusion or a prospective new beginning has the overall effect of undermining such traditionally useful expressions as prologue and epilogue or primary and secondary texts. From the outset, it is impossible to situate three (separate?) pieces of writing in any kind of stable relationship to each other: what might be called "the preexisting text," referred to as "ces notes"—the pages that the writer asks his friend to read, the opening section of *L'Attente l'oubli*, and the fragments that follow to form the rest of the book. The divisions between these three texts are not clear-cut. The degree to which his notes correspond to the fragments is ultimately unknowable, but the feeling that some overlapping occurs between the preexisting text and the pro/epilogue is particularly striking in what she says in her critical judgment of what he has written. In her verdict, which must cause him some discouragement, she states that "le premier paragraphe lui paraissait le plus fidèle et aussi en peu le second, surtout à la fin" (8).[23] Taking her advice, he resolves to return to this point and to pick it up from there. When he does this, we learn that the passages to which she was referring concern the circumstances in which they first met. Her room was located just down the hall from his, and "il pouvait l'apercevoir, lorsqu'elle était étendue sur le large balcon, et il lui avait fait des signes peu après son arrivée" (8–9).[24] If we, as readers who have finished *L'Attente l'oubli*, repeat the protagonist's gesture of doubling back to reflect on an earlier text, a justifiable act since the opening pages of this book demand to be reread, we realize thanks to the advantage of hindsight that this sentence effectively summarizes the story that is recounted in the rest of the book. After he sees her on the balcony and beckons to her, she responds to his call and comes to his room, where they spend an incalculable amount of time talking. This is what she deems as "the most faithful" of what he has written. Moreover, this sentence appears at the end of the second paragraph of the opening section. The end of the second paragraph of the preexisting text engenders the second paragraph of the text we are presently reading. She directs his attention back to a section that related their initial encounter, which is succinctly reproduced here in the "prologue" at the same point in the text! Because this second paragraph is a reworking of an earlier second paragraph, the question then becomes to what extent the text that we are reading coincides with the previously written text that she has read and commented on. We cannot suppress the uncanny feeling that in some impossible way, the preexisting text could be superimposed on the text that is unfolding before our very eyes.

It seems that what started out as a secondary text, the prologue in which the protagonist pauses to ask his companion for her opinion of what he has written, is suddenly and inexplicably transformed into a double that resembles the primary text so closely that it becomes difficult to distinguish the original from the rewrite. The reading of the primary text that occurs in the secondary text gives rise to a rewriting of the former in the latter. The prologue provides us, therefore, with the first instance of a *flagrant délit*: a violation of the *noli* that is committed indiscreetly on account of the intense proximity of the neighborhoods of reading and writing. The reluctance of the woman to read the primary text—"Elle ne voulait pas lire" (7)—indicates that it is under the protection of the *noli*. To some extent, she is its author: "C'est presque en l'écoutant parler qu'il avait rédigé ces notes." His role was to transcribe as faithfully as possible what she said, and yet she proves herself incapable of reading it. Her first question is "Qui parle?" (7),[25] a sentiment echoed a couple of pages later on in the third fragment: "Mais jamais elle ne reconnaissait en mes paroles les siennes" (13).[26] His writing has had the effect of erecting a barrier which separates her from her own words to the point of rendering them unrecognizable. In spite of *and* because of the fact that her voice was the source of his text, she is unable to perform a definitive reading of it. She makes a vague reference to the two opening paragraphs as being "the most faithful," but her overall reaction is one of disappointment and disillusionment; she cannot bring herself to put her stamp of approval on what he has written: "Elle avait le sentiment d'une erreur qu'elle ne parvenait pas à situer . . . Elle rejeta tous les papiers tristement. Elle avait l'impression que, bien que lui ayant assuré qu'il la croirait en tout, il ne la croyait pas assez, avec la force qui eût rendu la vérité présente" (7).[27]

Having forced her into committing a violation of the *noli* by insisting that she read what he had written, he must suffer the consequences. He does some soul-searching of his own as he tries to analyze her interpretation in an attempt to find out where he went wrong: "D'où venait donc son échec?" (9). Because she faulted him for not believing her enough, his self-analysis revolves around the question of fidelity, and if he can be accused of an act of betrayal, it is in connection with the cardinal (but essential) sin of impatience. He expresses his newly found discovery first in terms of Orphic imagery:

> Etre fidèle, voilà ce qui lui était demandé: tenir cette main un peu froide qui le conduirait par de singuliers méandres jusqu'à un endroit où elle disparaîtrait et le laisserait seul. Mais il lui était difficile de ne pas chercher à qui

appartenait cette main. Il avait toujours été ainsi. C'est à cette main qu'il pensait, à celle qui la lui avait tendue, et non pas à l'itinéraire. Là sans doute était la faute. (10)[28]

He realizes that he was guilty of impatience every time he tried to know the identity of the person whom he should have been content merely to accompany. Their itinerary together—the interminable approach to an elusive point—should have been his main concern, not the destination. He pursues this idea in the paragraph that follows the one just quoted: "C'est cette voix qui lui était confiée. Quelle pensée surprenante! Il reprit les feuillets et écrivit: 'C'est la voix qui t'est confiée, et non pas ce qu'elle dit'" (11).[29] This is the lesson that his analysis of her verdict yields and with which the prologue ends. To record her statements faithfully does not involve getting to the heart of what she means. On the contrary, his responsibility is to concentrate on the fact that any communication between them takes place at all. The conditions of their *entretien* that give rise to the fragmentary text are what must count as the object of his attention, whereas the signifying content of the fragments is of secondary importance.

Two other points must be noted before leaving the prologue. The first is that he writes this revelation on the pages that contain the preexisting text, an action which, once again, has the effect of blurring the distinction between that text and the prologue we are presently reading. The disquieting question concerning the relationship of the primary text to the prologue, the secondary text which is somehow both a commentary and a replica of the former, resurfaces. The second point, which is closely tied to the first, concerns the reemergence of the *noli*: this time, rather than submit his discovery to her for her approval, he refuses to share it with her. "Elle lui demanda ce qu'il venait d'écrire. Mais c'était quelque chose qu'elle ne devait pas entendre" (11–12).[30] One is compelled to ask why she must remain in the dark and why the prologue abruptly concludes on this note. The answers to these questions reside in the power of the *noli* to cover up the faulty or incomplete aspects of the nature of origins. Our inability to situate this prologue with respect to some preexisting text and to the other fragments of which *L'Attente l'oubli* is composed testifies to the lack of any absolute originary point. Moreover, a fragmentary work such as this can be rearranged and reread any number of ways; no particular fragment is necessarily the first or the last of the book. The opening sentence of the prologue, which closes the door on something, shows that the book has a difficult time getting underway, a sentiment that is confirmed ten pages later: "au lieu du commencement, une sorte de vide initial, un refus énergique de laisser l'histoire débuter" (22).[31] De Man suggests that one of the functions of the *noli* is to enable a work to come into being by inducing the author into a state of oblivion which allows him to forget the unpalatable nature of the origin of his work:

> The poet can only start his work because he is willing to forget that this presumed beginning is, in fact, the repetition of a previous failure, resulting precisely from an inability to begin anew. When we think that we are perceiving the assertion of a new origin, we are in fact witnessing the reassertion of a failure to originate. Acceding to the work in its positivity, the reader can very well ignore what the author was forced to forget: that the work asserted in fact the impossibility of its own existence. However, if the writer were really reading himself, in the full interpretative sense of the term, he would necessarily remember the duplicity of his self-induced forgetfulness, and this discovery would paralyze all further attempts at creation. In that sense, Blanchot's *noli me legere*, the rejection of self-interpretation, is an expression of caution, advocating a prudence without which literature might be threatened with extinction. (66)

The protagonist's refusal to let his collaborator in on his discovery indicates that the *noli* will not be violated a second time in the prologue. Furthermore, one has the impression that the reaffirmation of the *noli* with which this section ends makes it possible for the rest of the book to be written. The *mise en abyme* of self-commentary—first, the text of the prologue itself, then her reading of it, and finally his interpretation of her reading—has led him to a paralyzing impasse, "un refus énergique de laisser l'histoire débuter." The only way that the book can begin (as if for a first time) is for him to put an end to the potentially endless activity of self-reflexivity by invoking the *noli*.

Putting Their Story into Words

Sometimes it is best not to look back: consider what happened to Eurydice and Orpheus and Lot's wife. Similarly, the writer realizes at the end of the prologue that if he lingers too long over questions concerning how successful he was in remaining faithful to her words, he runs the risk of never letting the book get under way. He can move forward only by keeping his gaze firmly fixed on what lies ahead, and second thoughts about what he has already written will impede his progress. The *noli* not only ensures the inviolable integrity of a work; it also enables the writer to choose to ignore or forget temporarily certain questions pertaining to the work's origin, namely, the duplicitous nature of the language with which he must necessarily work. Thus the *noli* serves a dual purpose: it protects the work from intrusive glances of its author (and other readers as well) and it protects the author from harmful overexposure to his work. The benefit that the writer derives from the *noli* is that it allows him to close his eyes to the impropriety at the heart of language and to proceed as if the use of language in his book were the same as that in everyday speech. Like Orpheus, who uses his music as an instrument of power while abiding by the *noli* before committing the transgressive gaze, the writer must begin as if the language he has at his disposal were an instrument of power.

On several occasions throughout *L'Attente l'oubli*, the writer's companion instructs him as to what he must do: "Faites en sorte que je puisse vous parler."[32] A description of the hotel room, the setting in which their conversations take place, is what she demands of him and what enables them to enter into a relationship: "C'est comme si elle avait attendu qu'il lui fît une description minutieuse de cette chambre où elle se tenait pourtant avec lui" (16).[33] Elsewhere, we are told that "elle ne cessait de lui demander, avec une insistance silencieuse, de la [la chambre] lui décrire et toujours à nouveau" (33).[34] On the surface, nothing could appear simpler or more straightforward than to write an account of what he sees, which explains why he embarks on this project with no lack of self-confidence whatsoever:

> Avec ses jeunes forces, il n'avait pas hésité alors à répondre. C'était une époque brillante où tout semblait encore possible et où il ne prenait aucune précaution, notant au hasard avec une rectitude souveraine toujours le détail essentiel et se fiant pour le reste à sa mémoire qui n'était jamais en défaut. (15)[35]

This passage portrays someone who has complete mastery over the task at hand and places him squarely in the regional economy of power where "pour dire vrai, il faut penser selon la mesure de l'oeil" (*EI* 38).[36] We have noted more than once, however, that for Blanchot writing is never as inconsequential as everyday speech, even if it is merely an account of the disposition of the pieces of furniture in an ordinary hotel room. A reversal occurs whereby language, instead of being in the service of the optical exigency, contributes to the creation of a state of fascination in which seeing ceases to be a faculty thanks to which revelations can be recorded and processed. Orpheus, who was mesmerized by his own music to the point of forgetting the divine commandment, was a victim of this reversal, as is the writer of a journal, apparently the most carefree of literary endeavors, who unexpectedly finds himself engaged in the process of writing an *autoportrait*. The language of the protagonist's descriptions is susceptible to the same kind of transformation—which his companion desires, for if she insists that he describe the room, she does so "parce qu'elle pressentait que cette description ferait surgir cette même chambre, habitée par quelqu'un d'autre" (16).[37] His descriptive passages do more than set the scene where their story can unfold; they also involve him in a rapport with alterity, the anonymous, unknowable visage of "someone."

Descriptions form an integral part in the telling of a story which, like them, would seem to make use of language in an unproblematical way. Although the description of the room serves as a point of departure in their relationship, what she really expects of him is that he write their story "qu'elle lui ferait une obligation de mener à bien et qui doit avoir pour conséquence sa marche progressive vers un but" (20–21).[38] Both the readers and the characters of the book assume that the story recounted therein will lead them to some sort of goal, a new awareness that they reach after passing through preliminary evolutionary stages. No such evolution takes place, however, and we wait in vain for something to happen to them. Daniel Wilhem explains where we must look in order to find where the "action" takes place: "L'événement de l'attente, ou l'événement de l'oubli, . . . le discours ne le rend pas présent, ne l'actualise pas dans un épisode nommé ou nommable. Cet événement n'est sans doute que ce qui arrive au discours lui-même" (181–82).[39] Whatever transpires in this story does so with respect to the language the characters speak, not to their lives; and if anything can be said to take place (albeit recurrently, not as a unique event), it is the subversion of one *parole* by another, the emergence of the language of worklessness which the language of power cannot contain indefinitely. The language of a diary carries within it the seeds of its own destruction, a condition Blanchot calls the "secret law" of the genre. *L'Attente l'oubli* is governed by the same secret law which is responsible for turning one story, the chance encounter of two strangers in a hotel, into another, language's incapacity to content itself with the telling of the first story, its inability to limit itself to a recitation of the facts. Just as the journal mistakenly appears as a "guardrail against the dangers of writing," the telling of their story is not as simple a proposition as it might at first seem. Like the language in which it is composed, it is double-edged: "Est-ce qu'elle n'essayait pas, et lui avec elle, de se former au sein de cette histoire un abri pour se protéger de quelque chose que l'histoire aussi contribuait à attirer?" (19).[40] The notion of *histoire* as it is presented here recalls the ambivalent structure of the Bataillian *interdit*. The story acts as a shelter within which one may find refuge from the *parole du dehors*, the murmur or state of contestation to which language owes its very existence. It also has the opposite effect of attracting this *parole* because of the dual nature of the language in which it is written. The story puts up an obstacle which pretends to exclude the indeterminacy of language and extends an invitation to it by failing to reduce the irrepressible murmur to absolute, final silence.

The characters' story never gets told. What happens to them is instead supplanted by the very different story of what happens to their language: the disarming from within of the language of power by the *parole du dehors* which emerges principally but not exclusively in the passages written in direct discourse. As Libertson points out, the language of Blanchot's dialogues, the genre which replaced the *récit* as his major preoccupation from the 1960s on, is not maieutic: "When strategically envisaged as a presence of two interlocutors . . . the *parole* is an instance which is essentially irreducible to the notion of dialogue as duality and correlation, comprehension and mutual transitivity" (276). The protagonist's language of power, which is at work in his descriptions of the circumstances that surround their meeting, gives way to the language of passivity in the fragments in which he transcribes the contents of their conversations. She employs language in a manner that is far removed from that of everyday speech: "Elle donnait l'impression, quand elle parlait, de ne pas savoir relier les mots à la richesse d'un langage antérieur. Ils étaient sans histoire, sans lien avec le passé de tous, sans rapport même avec sa vie à elle, ni avec la vie de personne" (24).[41] It is apparent to the narrator that her unusual way of speaking involves a radical break not only from conventional linguistic patterns and codes but also from life itself; for the most part, her utterances have little if anything to do with the world of the everyday. The single most salient feature of her speech which underlines its rupture from the world is her predilection for abstraction. "Bien qu'elle fût apparemment peu savante, elle semblait toujours préférer les mots abstraits, qui n'évoquaient rien" (19).[42] Their exchanges are monopolized by abstract words; in fact, the only sections of the book in which reference is made to concrete objects are the narrator's descriptions of his room. Their conversations, on the other hand, contain almost no words that refer to things or situations that can be easily conceptualized. Thus one-half of the equation which accounts for the smooth functioning of everyday language has been erased. Because reference to the real has been eliminated, the language of their *entretiens* short-circuits the normal sequence whereby naming the thing destroys *and* resuscitates it in the form of an idea which can be mobilized as the object of an act of comprehension which can, in turn, bring about a particular result. Conventional language's usefulness depends on a tacit pact between words and things: for it to work, they have to be on good terms. The language of the dialogues, Blanchot's version of the *parole essentielle*, is so abstract that words are not associated with things at all. Consequently, the operation of the thing's being replaced by its idea is disrupted. Things do not dissolve into notions which are immediately translatable into acts accomplished through comprehension. The recurring terms around which their discussions revolve—*attente, attention, attrait, attraction, détour, oubli,* and *proximité,* just to name a few—do not correspond to concepts that belong to the regional economy of the day. These words are not molds into which we can pour well-understood notions that will enable us to arrive at further accomplishment. Whatever meanings with which we may infuse these signifying vessels will leave them either partially full or overflowing. Conventional language, on the contrary, works as well as it does because the receptacles approximate the perfect size for their signified contents.

One other aspect of conventional language which differentiates it from the speech of the dialogues is that the words fade into the result that they bring about. The words of the interlocutors, however, are not spoken in view of the accomplishment of something. In her statement "Eh bien, c'est là le secret: que je vous avais déjà tout dit" (70),[43] she sets forth the condition that allows for their speech of worklessness to emerge: it can do so only when "everything has been said," that is, when the language of negativity has gone as far as it can go, when all has been said and done. The language of their fragmentary conversations is the useless remainder of the language of power which comes up short in its attempt to attain the impossible limit of "reducing everything to silence, even silence itself." We might say that their language is in a state of suspended animation. It is not completely dead (silent), for it continues to be spoken in spite of the fact that it serves no constructive purpose. But it is not completely alive, either, for its heart and soul have been extracted, its application in the regional economy of power.

This condition undoubtedly explains why nothing really happens in the course of the book. As was the case with *Le Très-Haut,* it is already over before it starts. Everything has been given in advance. We read on, patiently waiting for an event that is bound to happen sooner or later, and yet such a moment never comes because the event we expect to take place is one that has, in fact, always already occurred: the incessant, circular movement of transgression as one *parole* subverts another. Exactly what does happen in *L'Attente l'oubli?* Nowhere else is the "event" presented as succinctly as it is in the third fragment following the prologue:

> Ce n'est pas une fiction, bien qu'il ne soit pas capable de prononcer à propos de tout cela le mot de vérité. Quelque chose lui est arrivé, et il ne peut dire que ce soit vrai, ni le contraire. Plus tard, il pensa que l'événement consistait dans cette manière de n'être ni vrai ni faux. (13)[44]

That the *parole* of neutrality, one that is neither entirely true nor entirely false, rises to the surface from deep within the language of negativity is the event recounted in *L'Attente l'oubli.* What they say cannot be reduced to either of these qualifications; their conversations express neither absolute truth nor utter nonsense. "A travers les mots passait encore un peu de jour" (40).[45] They never speak just the language of truth and comprehension nor that of dissimulation and *non-savoir*. Meaning always manages to creep into the language of passivity just as the murmur can always be heard beneath the surface of the language of discursive knowledge by whoever chooses to listen. Neither excludes the other once and for all. Georges Préli explains the only secret that will be revealed to us: "Il n'y a rien à attendre de l'entretien sinon, tout ayant été dit, le préalable de tout dire, et son horizon, la dissolution de toute parole d'ensemble" (234).[46]

Perspectives of Authority

The major issues raised in the opening pages which I called the prologue will serve as guideposts in our attempt to locate some of the moments when one language encroaches on the terrain occupied by the other. Because the prologue is a reflective pause that signals both the end of something (which is being read) and the beginning of something else (which will be [re]written), our main concern will be to examine the rapport between reading and writing. Other closely related issues that will receive attention are the changing status of the *noli* and the problematic differentiation of primary and secondary texts. The most fundamental question that confronts every reader of this book, however, is none other than the one immediately posed by *elle* upon reading his text: "Qui parle?" What is the nature of the voices engaged in the conversations, and what is their relationship to the authorial narrative voice that is responsible for the very existence of the text known as *L'Attente l'oubli* in its entirety? Detailed analyses of certain representative fragments will yield answers to these questions. I hope to show that the answer to the question "Qui parle?" can be found by means of an examination of the use of personal pronouns and of the functions of direct and indirect discourse. Furthermore, we shall see that the various types of formal composition of the fragments determine to a certain extent who is speaking and that the entities behind the different voices are none other than the exigencies of writing and reading which exist in a rapport of unarrestable circularity.

The fragments of *L'Attente l'oubli* fall into three basic categories. There are, first, those which are written entirely in the mode of direct discourse. Approximately one-eighth of the total number of fragments belong to this group, making it the smallest of the three. Composite fragments, so-called because they are made up of a combination of direct discourse and indirect asides, comprise roughly one-third of the fragments. Finally, the largest group, which numbers slightly more than one-half of the fragments, is completely narrative and contains no direct speech. Moreover, within these major divisions, variations do occur. There are, for example, two types of direct discourse fragments, those in which the interlocutors speak for themselves, respectively, and another subset in which their specificity has been absorbed by a common *nous*. In these fragments, it is virtually impossible to know "who says what." In addition, a small but significant number of narrative fragments contain the pronoun *Je*, which signals an abrupt authorial intervention.

The notion of authority provides us with a foothold from which we may set out on our analysis of the interaction of the different types of fragments. The relationship between a primary and a secondary text or between creative writing and critical reading can be viewed as a matter of perspective, and such perspective carries along with it varying degrees of authority. For the most part but not always, the words of one of the interlocutors are uttered from a standpoint of ignorance. In their repetitious exchanges of questions and answers in the direct fragments, they attempt to arrive at a clear understanding of what is happening to them. The narrative passages that interrupt their bizarre and often incomprehensible conversations, on the other hand, are emitted from a different point of view, one that is, in a sense, superior to that of the two speakers. A shift from direct discourse to objective narration implies a change of perspective. In most cases, the ignorance of the interlocutors in the direct discourse fragments is replaced by the more self-assured voice of someone who seems to be privy to secrets that the partners in the dialogues can only dream of knowing. The direct fragments, therefore, serve as primary texts in which the pulsating *parole* of passivity is clearly audible, whereas the intervening narrative fragments are secondary texts which tend to impose a limit on or put a temporary end to this *parole* in an act of interpretation. Put another way, the writer's rapport is reenacted over and over again in the dialogues that take place between himself and the mysterious visitor to his room. It is in their exchanges that the Orphic protagonist reaches the point of closest proximity to the murmur that is at the origin of the language of his book. The narrative fragments, on the other hand, supply commentaries of this experience which are made from a vantage point one step removed from the experience.

This distinction is, nevertheless, unstable. At times the "primary texts" assume a voice of authority and superiority which is most often associated with the "secondary texts," and the limits that are set up by the seemingly self-assured voice of the readings are not invulnerable barriers. The language of the secondary text is often contaminated by that of the primary text of which it is a commentary. Thus, the authority of the commentaries is undermined by its own language which participates in and helps perpetuate the aimless speech of passivity in spite of its pretentions to contain it. To violate the *noli me legere* is to engage in the activity of reading as if it were an exercise of power, only to discover too late that it leads to a loss of power and failure. Like suicide victims who set out with great determination to seize and appropriate death and yet are forced to realize that in the end it is death which comes to them as they passively await its approach, readers begin as if a concerted effort by their powers of understanding will enable them to have mastery over the work in question, only to find themselves dispossessed of this power as they fall under the spell of the fascination of the image and of the absence of time. We have already witnessed this subversion in Blanchot's criticism—in his account of the Orphic myth, particularly in his discussion of the roles that he assigns to patience and impatience, and in his essay on *The Castle*—and in his fiction—in Sorge's prostate readings that give rise to texts more radical than any of the revolutionary tracts penned by Bouxx. We shall now turn our attention to a few selected fragments of *L'Attente l'oubli* in order to illustrate how this subversion occurs in this work.

There are, first, fragments written in direct discourse in which the statements of either one or both of the interlocutors are spoken from a perspective of ignorance. Their earliest exchange (after the one in the prologue, of course) sets the tone for many that are to follow: " 'Faites en sorte que je puisse vous parler.' —'Oui, mais avez-vous une idée de ce que je devrais faire pour cela?' —'Persuadez-moi que vous m'entendez.' —'Eh bien, commence, parle-moi' " (14).[47] At this early stage in the book, it is virtually impossible to know who says what, and this is the first fragment that shows why the woman's question "Qui parle?" is so pertinent for anyone who reads *L'Attente l'oubli*. The further one reads, however, the clearer the identity of each interlocutor becomes, so that one can determine retrospectively that the woman speaks first. The subject of this initial exchange is what the nature of their rapport is to be. Their conversation functions as a kind of preliminary negotiation which begins to establish the respective responsibilities of each: hers is to speak and his is to listen and to make her voice heard in his writing. *Entendre* describes an important aspect of the writer's attitude toward language which we noted in connection with the myth of Orpheus (who should have contented himself to *hear* the sound of Eurydice's footsteps) and in our discussion of the murmur at the heart of language to which the hearing of Blanchot's writer is particularly attuned.

In this fragment she seems to know more about their rapport than he does; she gives him an order and he then asks her how he can go about executing it. On many occasions, she speaks from a position superior to his, and he is relegated to the role of asking questions as he tries to understand just what is happening between them, as in this exchange in which he wonders why she is so interested in descriptions of the hotel room: "il y a dans vos paroles quelque chose qui parle constamment de ce lieu où nous sommes. Pourquoi? Qu'est-ce donc qui s'y passe? Il faut le dire" (72).[48] His questions fail, however, to elicit a direct response from her: "C'est à vous de le savoir, puisque cela est déjà dit dans mes paroles que vous êtes seul à entendre" (72).[49]

The protagonist and his friend are not always on equal footing as far as what each one knows about their rapport is concerned, but she does not always occupy a position superior to his. Sometimes these perspectives are reversed. In a gross schematization, we might say that her utterances give voice to the neutral *parole* of the general economy, and yet this *parole* can only emerge by rising up through the language of the writer's transcriptions. She has no existence independent of her rapport with him, and she needs his participation so that the special quality of her voice may be heard. Since she can speak only through him, any claim to authority that she might make is ill-founded (not that she wants to make such a claim). At times, therefore, he speaks from a position of superiority, as in this fragment in which he has all the answers: "'Qui es-tu, en réalité? Tu ne peux pas être toi, mais tu es quelqu'un. Qui?' . . . —'Ne doute pas, dit-il doucement. Je choisis d'être ce qui me trouve. Je suis bien ce que tu viens de dire.' —'Qui?' Elle crie presque. 'Oui, ce que tu viens de dire'" (58).[50] Thanks to his contact with her, the protagonist has shed the personal identity which others recognize as his in the world of the everyday, and what is left in its place is the mask of anonymous being, the guise of *quelqu'un*, that is, of no one in particular. She unwittingly answers her own question ("mais tu es quelqu'un"), one that she should not even have to ask in the first place, and it is he who helps uncover for her the truth contained in this seemingly insignificant statement.

There is a third instance in which the conversations are spoken from a perspective of ignorance. What distinguishes it from the two previous instances is that neither speaker has an advantage over the other. In these passages, their ignorance is mutual. They are both reduced to groping around in the dark in their search to deepen their understanding of what has drawn them together. What he must do is to listen to her voice and to try to capture its ineffable quality in his notes. The demand that she makes on him is that "he act in such a way that she might speak to him," which he does by taking the initiative of telling their story or describing the place in which their story unfolds, and to do this involves using language as if it were an instrument of power. She did ask this of him, or did she? This very question is the subject of a fragment which displays their mutual ignorance; neither can recall whether she did, in fact, make such a demand: "'Vous me l'avez demandé parce que c'est impossible.' —'Impossible, mais possible, si j'ai pu vous le demander.' —'Tout dépend donc de cela, si vous me l'avez réellement demandé?' —'Tout dépend de cela'" (82).[51]

The varying degrees of ignorance which hinder the characters' efforts to arrive at a clear understanding of their relationship are offset in many of the narrative segments. The passage from direct discourse to impersonal narration involves a change of voice and perspective, and the questioning voices of the direct fragments which speak from a point of view of uncertainty are replaced by the more authoritative, self-assured voice of an observer who possesses knowledge of the experience which is far superior to theirs. The certainty with which this voice speaks borders on omniscience, especially as far as the experience of the protagonist/writer is concerned. This privileged observer has the capacity to look directly into the writer's mind, to see how it functions, and to discuss the psychological modifications which he undergoes because of his rapport with her. The narrator's propensity for making statements that begin typically with such expressions as "Il se rendait compte que . . . ," "Il s'aperçut que . . . ," "Il sait depuis toujours que . . . ," "Il se demande si . . . ," "Il avait souvent l'impression que . . . ," etc.,[52] shows that he has intimate, firsthand knowledge of the protagonist's mind. Furthermore, this knowledge covers not only the past and present but extends into the future as well. His vantage point is so superior to the protagonist's partial view of the situation that he knows what the protagonist will think even before he thinks it, as in this indirect fragment which tells us of his initial reaction of fear upon hearing the woman speak and which reveals very early on how their story will conclude, before he could possibly be aware of it:

> Quand il comprit qu'elle n'essayait pas de lui dire comment les choses s'étaient passées . . . il éprouva pour la première fois de la peur. D'abord, il ne saurait rien (et il vit combien il avait désiré savoir), et puis il n'apercevrait jamais à quel moment il serait sur le point d'en finir. Quelle existence il en résulterait, sérieuse, frivole, sans dénouement, sans perspective; quant à ses rapports avec elle, un perpétuel mensonge. (16–17)[53]

The function of the narrative voice, however, is not limited to affording us occasional glimpses into the writer's subjective states and to describing to us his doubts, fears, and aspirations. No, it is much more versatile, for it can speak from a variety of perspectives. Not only can this observer occupy a vantage point that lies within the writer's mind, he can also witness what is taking place and being said from without. It goes without saying that there is a dimension of theatricality to this book which is made up in large part of conversations that take place between a man and a woman in a hotel room. If we admit that their relationship lasts one night (and there are indications in the text that suggest that it does), then the classical exigencies of the three unities, time, place, and action, are satisfied. Such a comparison between *L'Attente l'oubli* and a play yields the following distinction between the direct discourse and indirect narrative fragments: the former correspond to the script of the play, the lines that the actors say to each other, and the voice that we hear in the latter is a cross between that of a spectator, who merely watches what transpires, and a director, who is responsible for the blocking and helps the actors with their mannerisms and gestures. When this voice intervenes, the disembodied voices of abstraction are endowed for an instant with the physical attributes of living beings. The presence of the spectator/director emerges in two contexts. First, it may appear in a composite fragment in which scenic indications or stage directions are made in the midst of individual utterances, as in this example:

> —"Je demande très peu cependant, convenez-en." —"Trop peu pour que ma vie y suffise." Elle était debout presque à côté de lui, regardant en avant: "Naturellement, si je mourais, vous ne manqueriez pas de me rappeler à la vie pour me faire encore répondre." —"A moins, dit-il en souriant, que je ne meure le premier." —"J'espère que non, ce serait pis." (36)[54]

This is a composite fragment by virtue of the fact that there is a third party present who can furnish asides that describe her location when she speaks (what she says neatly summarizes the first part of another of Blanchot's books, *L'Arrêt de mort*) and his demeanor in his facetious response. Evidence of this voice is more widespread, however, in narrative fragments such as the lengthy one that begins on page 117 and concludes on page 120. This fragment provides us with the most complete account of their story. We are told of their initial encounter and of his reaction at seeing her enter his room: "il éprouve la froide jubilation du chasseur, lorsque le piège a fonctionné et livre, dans une proximité maintenant sûre, la prise attendue" (118).[55] There follows a brief description of the room, and the last part of the fragment is devoted to the question why she responded to his "invitation autoritaire" (121) by coming to his room. Perhaps in so doing, we read, "elle ne fait que se soumettre à la pratique du lieu, s'il est vrai, comme il croit le savoir, qu'une partie de l'hôtel est réservée à de tels va-et-vient. Cette idée ne lui déplaît pas" (120).[56] This passage is the logical beginning of the book and could have been placed on the first page. Other passages like this one, which retell the story of her arrival in different ways, are interspersed throughout the book, and each time we come upon one, the book in effect starts over again. It is as if the narrator periodically has to regain possession of himself by tearing himself away from the language of the conversations which exerts a hold of fascination over him, and he attempts to do so by returning to the supposedly safer kind of writing involved in straight narration and description.

To the roles of mind reader and theatrical director, both of which I have assigned to the impersonal voice, might be added that of commentator. The narrator often engages in the act of commentary after a conversation has taken place by pursuing the topic further and perhaps by explaining the sense of their conversation in a theoretical claim. An example of such a composite fragment, in which a narrative passage is placed after a direct discourse passage like a clarifying coda, can be found on page 74. The fragment begins with her question "Vous me voyez?" and the rest of their conversation treats the problem of the disruption of the power of seeing in proximity. She questions him about his ability to see her, and at one point she says: "Mais je ne voudrais pas que vous me voyiez pour cette simple raison que je suis visible" (74).[57] The protagonist has difficulty following her and perhaps justifiably so, judging from the almost nonsensical character of this statement: after all, how else can she be seen if it is not because she is visible? Although his confusion is not cleared up in the direct discourse portion of the fragment, ours is to some extent thanks to a narrative intervention at the end: "Si nous sommes visibles par un pouvoir qui nous précède nous-mêmes, alors il la voyait en dehors de ce pouvoir, par un droit sans lumière, et qui évoquait l'idée d'une faute, d'une faute merveilleuse" (75).[58] This commentary of the preceding conversation makes her enigmatic statements more accessible. She is visible to him, but not in the same way as an object toward which we may direct an appropriating gaze. She is visible to him just as Eurydice is to Orpheus; both see only what there is to see when there is nothing left, the dissimulating presence of an absence. Seeing for them is no longer an act of power; rather it is the inability to close their eyes and not to go on seeing something—whatever there is to see when seeing has ceased to be the exercise of power. To see is to be fascinated, to be seen, to be the center of attention under the anonymous gaze of *quelqu'un*. The themes of fascination, *ressemblance*, and the idea that "speaking is not seeing" are well-known concepts in Blanchot's theoretical writings, and the narrative segment helps us make the connection between these writings and what has just been said in a more obscure way in the dialogue.

Although the examples of composite fragments in which the narrative voice provides direct commentary of something that the interlocutors have just said are numerous, it is more common to come across this critical activity in completely narrative fragments which, as I stated earlier, make up the largest group. The voice that we hear in these instances is extremely close to the one we hear when reading Blanchot's criticism, and their superiority resides in the unflinching manner in which they speak and in the authoritative claims they make. Categorical statements made in *L'Espace littéraire*, for example, such as "l'oeuvre d'art, l'oeuvre littéraire n'est ni achevée ni inachevée: elle est. Ce qu'elle dit, c'est exclusivement cela: qu'elle est—et rien de plus" (10–11)[59] or "l'écrivain ne lit jamais son oeuvre" (13)[60] are emitted from a perspective that seems beyond reproach. The same self-assured voice also frequently emerges in *L'Attente l'oubli*, as in this passage which describes the task that the writer must perform in his written versions of the conversations that take place between himself and the woman:

> Mais, avec la patience qui lui est propre, il pense que, s'il pouvait, en lui répondant, attirer hors d'elle et maîtriser l'égalité sans mesure de la rumeur, il s'établirait entre leurs paroles comme une mesure d'égalité, capable de rendre plus parlante et plus silencieuse, jusqu'à l'apaiser, l'affirmation incessante. (151–52)[61]

The narrative voice reiterates an important concept in Blanchot's theoretical writings which I discussed in the first chapter: the writer's relationship with the incessant murmur at the origin of language which can be reproduced in a text thanks to the "triple métamorphose" that words undergo as they are written. If we were to play a game of literary detection with this passage in which we had to guess whence it came, we would be hard pressed to get the right answer. Were it not for the presence of two interlocutors, we might be tempted to say that it comes from the section of *L'Espace littéraire* entitled "L'Oeuvre et la parole errante," say, or from "La Mort du dernier écrivain" in *Le Livre à venir*. Passages such as this, in any case, make it difficult for us to accept Foucault's claim that the language of this book is neither fictional nor critical. On the contrary, it is both one and the other, at different times, and in this narrative fragment on the murmur, the voice of the self-assured critic makes its presence clearly felt.

Another type of intervention in which the narrative voice speaks the language of Blanchot's criticism takes shape in the form of axiomatic statements—definitions of terms or the exposition of ideas whose truths are self-evident. The distinctive quality of this voice is its "matter of fact" tone. The following example, in which death is compared to waiting, could be mistaken for an excerpt of "La Mort possible" in *L'Espace littéraire*:

> La mort, considérée comme un événement attendu, n'est pas capable de mettre fin à l'attente. L'attente transforme le fait de mourir en quelque chose qu'il ne suffit pas d'attendre pour cesser d'attendre. L'attente est ce qui nous permet de savoir que la mort ne peut être attendue. (55)[62]

This passage repeats the lesson on death that we covered in the third chapter: to die is to wait patiently for a moment that never comes. The suicide victim attempts to hasten the arrival of this moment so as to be able to occupy, if only for a fleeting instant, a precarious perch that straddles life and death. This vantage point is an illusion, however, for to die is also to lose the power to accede to such a universal vantage point, and in the end death remains an unsoundable mystery, an event from whose *dénouement* we are ultimately excluded.

Another self-evident truth is enunciated in this excerpt from a narrative fragment in which the capacity to ask questions (in itself, the factor most responsible for generating any conversation at all between the two interlocutors) is compared to writing: "La question de l'attente: l'attente porte une question qui ne se pose pas. Entre l'une et l'autre, il y a en commun l'infini qui est dans la moindre question comme dans la plus faible attente. Dès qu'on questionne, pas une réponse qui épuiserait la question" (96).[63]

The idea that the power to ask questions exceeds the ability to answer them, that no response is perfectly adequate to the question that it seeks to reduce to silence, is the topic of the essay entitled "La Question la plus profonde" from *L'Entretien infini*. Even the simplest question has a way of perpetuating itself, just as the best-conceived answer does not always succeed in making the question go away. Every question contains a reserve that the most cunning mind cannot penetrate. Oedipus learned this lesson in old age; he was blinded by the light of his recognition of the most profound question that the Sphinx's riddle contained and that his brilliant solution failed to conquer. Once again, one could easily mistake this text for part of his essay in *L'Entretien infini*. The voice of the theoretician is loud and clear.

A final case related to the knowledgeability of the narrative voice deserves our attention. It differs fundamentally from all the previous examples. Whereas they involved an exchange between the text of the interlocutors' conversations and the voice of the impersonal author of the narrative fragments, another kind of *entretien* takes place here—between this impersonal author and himself. Such instances are few and far between, and their infrequency causes them to stand out. The precedent for such narrative asides is set early, in the prologue when the protagonist, after having asked the woman to read and comment on his text, reflects on what she says and reaches the following conclusion which he jots down for his own benefit: "C'est sa voix qui t'est confiée, et non pas ce qu'elle dit" (11).[64] If the entity behind the narrative voice possesses a higher degree of knowledge about the characters' experience than they do themselves, it is in the indirect fragments in which the narrator writes notes to, for, and about himself that we see him acquire this level of superiority. To borrow a phrase from Valéry's Monsieur Teste: "Je suis étant, et me voyant; me voyant me voir, et ainsi de suite" (*Oeuvres complètes* II: 25),[65] we might say that the narrator "is being by seeing *them*" (the two speakers) in his narrative commentaries and "by seeing *himself* see them" in his self-conscious messages to himself. Who is speaking now? The narrator himself who instead of merely providing a commentary of the characters' experience from a perspective outside it, implicates himself in the experience by talking about the effect his observing it has had on him: "Ce que tu as écrit détient le secret. Elle, elle ne l'a plus, elle te l'a donné, et toi, c'est parce qu'il t'a échappé que tu as pu le transcrire" (73).[66] This enables us to confirm what we have suspected all along: the protagonist/ writer and the owner of the narrative voice are doubles. His almost omniscient observations are made only in connection with the intimate workings of the writer's mind. This perspective of authority does not extend, however, to the woman's experience: we know what she thinks only through what she says.

This statement also shows that the narrator is in full possession of the secret essence of their relationship. This is the moment when the narrator reaches the highest degree of superiority. He understands something that his shadowy double will never be able to grasp. He knows that the secret resides in what he has written. He also knows that what he has written is possible only because the secret escapes and remains outside his text. This writer, like all of Blanchot's writers, is caught in the Orphic double bind: he loses what he seizes. Just as Orpheus's transgression is caused by the duplicity of his music, the *transgression* of the protagonist of *L'Attente l'oubli* lies in his *transcriptions* of his conversations with the woman. The text that he produces is animated by language that hovers back and forth between two extremes, the authoritative language of power and the passive language of worklessness, without ever stopping once and for all at either one. His decision to record their conversations in writing fails to reproduce the tantalizing, mysterious, whispering qualities of her voice; repetitive music would be an art form that could achieve a closer approximation of this. Thus he loses something, but he does not come up empty-handed. What he does do is to invent a new kind of *parole* previously unheard of, one that proves itself capable of speaking on behalf of the unknowable, unthinkable, ineffable neuter only if one listens closely enough by shutting out the clamor and din that characterizes the bustling activity of everyday language, just as a child must close his ears to the sounds around him if he wishes to hear the sound of the waves in the seashell he is holding (the comparison is Levinas's).

This is the secret that the writing of the book has given its author. At this point, in this brief reminder that he addresses to himself, he seems to know all there is to know about the experience of literature. After putting the two characters on stage, observing them, and considering the significance from a critical distance of what he has them say, this is the lesson that he comes away with. It is important to note, however, that these conversations with himself in which he attains an exceptional degree of immediacy with his *moi* are rare. Moreover, all but one occur in the first half of the book, and the one that does not occurs on page 90, only four pages into the second part. It is almost as if this prophecy comes true: "Avec quelle mélancolie, mais quelle calme certitude, il sentait qu'il ne pourrait plus jamais dire: 'Je'" (34).[67] Perhaps his prolonged advance into the phase of the book dominated by the theme of forgetting causes him to lose the rapport of immediacy with himself. The absence of more notes to himself on the subject of his book confirms that the fissure of his *moi* occasioned by his writing has become more severe.

The Reversal

The infrequency of these interventions, which is eventually followed by their disappearance, is symptomatic of the fragile foundation on which some basic distinctions rest, such as those between primary and secondary text, direct discourse and indirect commentary, or the passive language of writing and the active language of reading. *L'Attente l'oubli* is actually composed of two books, two different experiences of writing and reading, for there are groups of fragments that exist side by side those we have just examined in accordance with these distinctions which have the opposite effect of undermining them and proving them to be unstable. Direct discourse passages previously associated with varying degrees of ignorance on the part of one or both of the interlocutors can also be spoken from a perspective of authority, and, conversely, the language of authority that the narrative voice speaks in the indirect passages can be subverted by the passive language of the dialogues of which it is supposedly a commentary. There is a continual process at work in this book whereby perspectives are constantly reversed: what was once thought to be a perspective of ignorance, the points of view of the characters, for example, at times assumes a position of authority, and by the same token, the narrator loses his privileged vantage point whenever the language of his observations becomes infected with the language of the experience he wishes to analyze.

There are, first, fragments in the mode of direct discourse that resemble the indirect asides in which the narrator speaks to himself. In these situations, the two interlocutors talk about themselves *not* from a perspective of uncertainty but rather with the newly acquired advantage of hindsight. They use the past tense and reflect on what transpired between them as if they can remember everything that happened. The protagonist is obviously speaking retrospectively when he says: "Dès le premier instant, vous m'avez parlé intimement, merveilleusement. Je n'oublierai jamais ces premiers instants où tout était déjà dit entre nous. Mais il m'a manqué de ne pas savoir. Je n'ai jamais pu apprendre que ce que je savais" (69–70).[68] He can summon up their first moments together as though their encounter were an event that could be accurately situated in time with respect to other events at other times. A second example illustrates that on occasions the interlocutors have a fairly good understanding of what they must do and that they are not always groping about in the dark. Here, the protagonist has as clear a notion of what he must do as does the narrator at his most lucid moments of self-presence: " 'Je voulais vous aider.' —'En voulant me conduire jusqu'à moi?' —'Je ne voulais rien que vous aider.' —'Oui, un peu d'aide fait du bien.' —'Je n'avais qu'un rôle modeste, vous le savez. J'étais le mur de cette chambre destiné à vous renvoyer ce que vous auriez aimé dire.' —'Un rôle modeste. Pourtant vous attendiez, vous attendiez tout le temps' " (105).[69] The writer can look back over his experience and explain his role of sounding board. His transcriptions of their conversations enable her words to be deflected back to her, without her being able nonetheless to recognize them as her own. Her original utterances do not coincide with those that are produced by his scriptural mediation. Too much daylight traverses his language, which is what earns him the unfavorable assessment expressed by her on the first page of the book, her feeling that somehow he was not faithful enough to her voice. In light of the myth of Orpheus, however, we know that the highest form of fidelity to the literary experience consists in this inevitable betrayal. What is remarkable about this fragment is that the protagonist can make such an observation in his capacity of protagonist—in her presence—and that it is not something that comes to him thanks to a distancing which endows him with the more objective perspective of an outsider.

The interlocutors are subject to the same phenomenon of division that we witnessed in the narrator. Writing has created a split within him by drawing him into a rapport with alterity in the dialogues from which he tries to extricate himself *après coup* in his indirect commentaries when he tries to paper over the cracks and regain a semblance of wholeness. He is both an unsure participant in the experience of proximity and a knowledgeable observer of this experience from without. This doubling is reproduced in the relationship between the two characters. They cease to be the actors in the leading roles in order to become spectators of the experience of another couple, and the comments and observations that had previously been reserved for narrative passages are now made in direct discourse. There are three variations on the way in which this type of superiority in the direct mode manifests itself, and once again it is a question of which member of the couple speaks with more authority.

In another of the lengthiest fragments of the book, the writer's command of the situation is superior to the woman's. One immediately senses that a major shift is taking place when she cuts short his opening remark, "Quand vous vous approchiez . . . ,"[70] with this question which indicates an element of surprise on her part: "Pourquoi parlez-vous au passé?" (123).[71] To speak in the past tense is to possess the advantage of hindsight, a point of view from which they do not often speak in their conversations. Their points of view, however, are not identical, and she is full of questions about his rapport with another presence, another woman. His superiority over her resides in the fact that he was involved in something from which she was excluded, and she demands a "blow-by-blow" account of everything that happened between them. She is a spectator, but she can witness the action only through the descriptions that he furnishes. His knowledge of the situation, on the contrary, is firsthand. The urgency of her questioning, combined with her thirst for intimate details, suggests an almost jealous reaction to the threatening presence of a rival. Here is a sampling of the kinds of things she wants to know more about: " '—Elle n'est donc plus tournée vers vous?' . . . 'Mais vous, où êtes-vous?' . . . 'A quel moment avez-vous décidé d'aller là-bas [to the sofa]?' . . . —'Et n'avez-vous pas craint de lui faire peur?' . . . 'Quand vous l'avez saisie par les épaules, elle ne s'est pas raidie?' . . . 'N'étiez-vous pas trop sûr de vous?' " (123–25).[72] She wants him to express himself in as precise a manner as possible, and he obliges her, as in this response to her question "où êtes-vous?": "Je crois que je suis venu m'asseoir auprès d'elle, mais un peu en arrière, puisqu'elle est au bout du divan, et assez près pour pouvoir toucher ses épaules que la nuque courbée laisse découvertes" (123).[73] Not only does he exercise great care in telling her where he was at the time, but he also succeeds in adding to the scene an aura of sensuality. The circumstances of their relationship are obviously charged with an erotic content which does not go unnoticed by the protagonist. The most explicit reference to the erotic quality of their rapport occurs in a late narrative fragment: "Il se rappelle qu'elle demeure là immobile, et pendant qu'il l'aide à retirer quelques vêtements . . . il l'attire, la saisit, lui parcourt le visage, tandis qu'elle se laisse glisser, les yeux tranquillement ouverts, présence immobile détournée de la présence. Seule sa main, une main qu'elle lui a docilement abandonnée, se retient encore . . ." (153–54).[74] It is in this kind of fragment that we would expect to find such a descriptive account of their actions. The fact that this type of story-telling occurs in a direct discourse fragment, on the other hand, indicates that our initial distinction between the two modes of discourse can be overturned.

The protagonist does not always have an edge over his companion. In the aforementioned case he does because his identity does not seem to be fissured; in his narrative account to her, he speaks with the authoritative voice of someone who has gone through the experience he is describing. The subject of the experience and the narrator who tells the story in retrospect are supposedly one and the same. She, on the contrary, was not there when it happened; someone else ("cette présence," literally, which is the antecedent to which all the subsequent subject pronouns *elle* refer) was there in her place. Hers is not a full presence. There is a gap with respect to her self-presence which is a consequence of its being in excess over its own closure. Like Eurydice, she escapes from herself and from the hold that the writer would have over her by receding farther into another image of herself, the one created by his story. She anxiously awaits in the hope that the impossible immediacy with herself, a rapport of complete adequation, will come about thanks to the writer's role of intermediary, which enables her to establish a certain degree of communication with herself.

If we wish to cast the writer in the part of Orpheus opposite her Eurydice, however, we must keep in mind that in this role he is bound to succumb to *oubli* and to forget momentarily who he is. Thus the doubling can affect both members of the couple, which means that the protagonist can lose the perspective of authority that he owes to the purported integrity of his self. The fragment on pages 129–30 is exemplary for two reasons. First, it represents a continuation of the major shift that I mentioned earlier: the interlocutors employ the past tense to analyze a scene retrospectively in direct discourse. Second, both members of the couple, not she alone, have undergone a phenomenon of distancing from themselves. The narrator no longer speaks of his experience in the first person, and his sense of authority is gone. Their roles have been switched, and instead of supplying her with all the details of what happened, he is the one who asks all the questions: "Comment en sont-ils venus à se parler?"[75] he wants to know, a line of questioning that he pursues throughout the rest of the fragment: "pourquoi aurait-il été surpris tout à coup de l'entendre?" and "pourquoi eut-il la certitude qu'elle exigeait de lui . . . une confiance à laquelle, malgré son attention, il ne réussissait que difficilement à répondre?" (129–30).[76] If he were endowed with the point of view he possessed in the fragment on page 123, he would not have to ask these questions. The divisiveness of *l'oubli* has taken its toll, causing him to lose sight of something he once knew. And although she hedges, as she usually does, on giving him straight answers to his questions, she nevertheless seems to be the one in the superior position, as her attitude of bemusement toward his questions suggests: his first question "made her laugh," a narrative intervention informs us.

The infiltration of the powers of observation and analysis, traits most often displayed in indirect narrative fragments, in the directly reported conversations of the couple produces a group of fragments which imitate the varying degrees of ignorance that govern the speech of the interlocutors in the fragments not spoken from a retrospective point of view. Whether they are searching for the meaning of their own experience or commenting on the experience of another couple from a point one step removed, there is a constant modulation of perspectives as far as each member of the couple is concerned: she may question him, which gives him the upper hand, he may question her, or they may be on equal footing, in which case a consensus is reached. These are occasions when they achieve a perspective of mutual knowledge which lays to rest, at least for a while, the anxious movement of the interrogative mode of their discussions:

"Oui, je sais, c'était déjà sa manière de lutter contre sa présence." —"Oh, elle ne lutte pas." —"C'est vrai, elle a compris cela merveilleusement, qu'il ne faut ni résister ni consentir, mais glisser en suspens entre les deux, immobile dans la hâte et la lenteur." —"Elle ne fait rien que vous répondre." —"Mais à moi pas plus qu'à tout autre." —"A vous comme à personne: c'est ce qui est extrêmement attirant." —"Ainsi attirée comme hors de sa présence." —"Attirée, mais toutefois pas encore, par l'attirance de ce qui toujours attire mais pas encore." —"Par l'attrait qui force, rejette et occupe toute distance." —"Attirée en elle, en ce lieu de l'attrait qu'elle se sent devenir." —"Partout présente." —"Présente sans présence." (128)[77]

No questions, no answers, rather a common accord between the two. They share in the same knowledge. Their vantage point is the same, which is reflected in the rhythm of the fragment, in the rapidity and the repetitious nature of their exchange. They achieve a degree of superiority which is matched only by the group of fragments in direct discourse spoken by *nous*, such as this one: "'Il y a encore un long chemin.' —'Mais non pas pour nous mener loin.' —'Pour nous conduire au plus proche.' —'Quand tout ce qui est proche est plus loin que tout lointain'" (115).[78] The specificity of each speaker cannot be determined, and the question of who says what is no longer important. Their exchanges are completely indifferent and possess a uniformity in tone that suggests a litany. They speak as if reciting part of a ritual, and their words exert a hypnotic effect over the readers of this book, luring them into a state of fascination. This is the undifferentiated voice of pure passivity speaking, and distinctions such as actor and spectator, primary and secondary text, or the experience itself and a critical observation of it have no place. There is no looking back, no desire to regain possession after the fact of something lost. Ignorance is bliss, and *non-savoir* is superiority.

If the first half of the reversal of the distinction between direct and indirect fragments that I posited initially involves an accession to higher levels of authority on the part of the interlocutors, the second half concerns a diminishing of the authority once enjoyed by the narrative voice. The language of authority spoken in the narrative fragments is undermined by the language of the dialogues of which it is purportedly a commentary, and it abdicates its position of superiority by participating in the experience that at first it pretended merely to observe. We noted earlier that one of the principal characteristics of the narrative voice was its propensity to make authoritative claims in the form of definitions and axiomatic truths. The opening words of the following fragment on forgetting seem to be spoken by the same self-assured voice, but it quickly becomes apparent that the language of this definition has been infected by the very phenomenon that it describes, passivity:

> L'événement qu'ils oublient: l'événement de l'oubli. Et ainsi, d'autant plus présent qu'oublié. Donnant l'oubli et se donnant oublié, mais n'étant pas oublié. Présence d'oubli et en l'oubli. Pouvoir d'oublier sans fin en l'événement qui s'oublie. Oubli sans possibilité d'oublier. Oubliant—oublié sans oubli. (147)[79]

The narrator's language has fallen from its lofty perch and has become a caricature of its former self. The fragment is composed of fragments—incomplete sentences, subjects that wait in vain for a verb and a complement so that some exchange of information might be transacted. The transitive language of the critical observer has been transformed into the intransitive language of the ignorant participants of the direct dialogues. These statements on *oubli* are turned inward toward themselves, unable to break out of their own orbit. The babbling of the entranced narrator (and *bavarder* is *not* a pejorative term for Blanchot) is a far cry from the lucid comparison between waiting and death which bore an uncanny resemblance to arguments presented in his works of criticism and theory. Put another way, the authoritative narrative voice of normative reading has been transformed unwittingly into a passive proponent of the *parole* of transgressive writing.

According to our initial operative distinction, the conversations between the interlocutors, whose principal subject is the nature of the protagonist/writer's rapport with her voice, are allied closely to the experience of writing, whereas the interventions of the narrative voice from a perspective outside this experience constitute a critical activity. This distinction is reversible, however, for we have encountered situations in which the apparently omniscient narrator writes the language of *non-savoir* and when the interlocutors engage in acts of interpretation. Another basic distinction that is put into question for the same reasons is that between primary and secondary texts, according to which the former would correspond to the dialogues and the latter to the impersonal narrative commentaries. This opposition wears dangerously thin when, say, narrative asides participate in the conversations and collaborate with them by helping them along. This type of interaction between the two discourses occurs in the following excerpt from a composite fragment: "Ce qu'elle

disait—il ne manquait pas de l'en avertir—ne cessait de lutter vaillam-
ment, obscurément. 'Contre quoi?' —'Que nous puissions le découvrir,
c'est sans doute aussi le prix de cette lutte.' —'Mais contre quoi?' —'Il
faut que vous luttiez encore pour le savoir'" (90–91).[80] The indirect aside
of the narrator introduces the idea of a struggle (*lutte*). Previous to this,
it had not been mentioned in the fragment. What is most unusual is that
the woman's next utterance picks up on this notion and pursues it: she
asks what he is struggling against, and this becomes the topic of conversation in direct discourse although it emanated from the consciousness of
the narrator, not from something her fellow interlocutor said directly to
her. Does she read the narrator's mind, or does she simply read a portion
of the notes that her friend has written? Either way, it demonstrates the
intense proximity of the neighborhoods of reading and writing, which in
itself explains why neither the characters nor the narrator can be associated in any definitive way with the exigencies of either writing or reading.
To the entities behind the different voices and to the types of fragments
in which they speak cannot be assigned exclusively one of these exigencies. The setting up and tearing down of limits through reading and writing occurs in both contexts.

Flagrants délits

"Il n'est d'explosion qu'un livre,"[81] according to Mallarmé. Applying this
statement to *L'Attente l'oubli* we might also says that "There is no explosion except a fragment," specifically the one that begins at the bottom of
page 136. It runs slightly over four pages, making it the longest in the
book. The volatility of this particular fragment consists in the speed with
which the different perspectives of authority can reverse themselves. If the
other fragments of *L'Attente l'oubli* act as individual fireworks which contribute to the overall pyrotechnic display of the entire book—a bunch of
little explosions that, when brought together, create the "big bang" of
the work as a whole, then this fragment is certainly the *bouquet*. A veritable conflagration erupts on account of the amazing rapidity with which
the exigencies of writing and reading take turns and change camps. The
pattern that we have noticed in isolated situations, whereby the patient
attentiveness to the approaching murmur at the origin of language is interrupted by an impatient urge which forgets that the only positivity in
the existence of the *parole* is that as it approaches it escapes, appears here
in all its different guises. There are *flagrants délits* at every turn. The *noli*
is repeatedly violated, as the reading of the narrator gives way to the
transgressive writing of the protagonists which they in turn seek to read,
while the narrator finds himself engaged in transgressive writing. The

strength of the *noli* is so ephemeral—at one moment it is in force, at the next it is not—and the incessant movement between the transgression and the restoration of limits reaches such a feverish pitch that there is no time to have second thoughts about it, which is why I call them "flagrant" violations of the *interdit*.

The fragment is composed of eleven paragraphs, and each transition from one paragraph to the next involves a change of perspective. The critical voice of the narrator speaks first, on the subject of the relationship between waiting and the story that recounts it. The notion presented here is familiar to readers of Blanchot, and its antecedents in his criticism can be traced back to the well-known opening section of *Le Livre à venir* entitled "La Rencontre de l'imaginaire," in which he explains his theory of the *récit* in an adaptation of the story of Ulysses' encounter with the Sirens. What he calls the "loi secrète du récit" (*LV* 14)[82] repeats what we have studied elsewhere as the circular exigency of writing. In essence, it states that the event itself and the process of its telling are in a rapport of circularity. The conviction that the destination can be reached gives Ulysses' navigational trek its reason for being; he would not have set out on his voyage if he did not believe that he could get where he wanted to go. Yet at the same time, the destination has no existence outside the journey. It is only thanks to the crossing that the destination seems real. Similarly, the story of the couple's journey both makes the patient waiting for an ending bearable and renders the *dénouement* illusory, for the latter has no existence outside the waiting that would put an end to it.

In paragraph two, the authoritative voice of the narrator/theoretician is replaced by the writing of the *parole* of passivity in a direct discourse section spoken by the common "us." The narrative voice of reading returns, however, in the third paragraph. The subject matter is the same—the circular exigency of writing—but it is approached from a different mythic angle. From the recognizable context of Ulysses and *Le Livre à venir*, we have moved to *L'Espace littéraire* and the "mythe inépuisable" of Orpheus. The woman becomes a figure of Eurydice who "attend mystérieusement que la fin lui vienne comme le don de sa mort à lui" (137).[83] Here, circularity is expressed in terms of giving and receiving a gift. In *L'Espace littéraire* we read: "Le regard d'Orphée est le don ultime d'Orphée à l'oeuvre, don où il la refuse, où il la sacrifie en se portant, par le mouvement démesuré du désir, vers l'origine, et où il se porte, à son insu, vers l'oeuvre encore, vers l'origine de l'oeuvre" (232).[84] In this passage, Orpheus is presented as the giver, whereas Eurydice (the work) is on the receiving end. Applying this schema to the fragment yields the following interpretation of the ambiguous phrase, "le don de sa mort à lui." It can be read as "the gift of his death," in which case "à lui" functions as a tag that eliminates the ambiguity of gender contained in the possessive "sa." Orpheus's gaze (the writer's transcription which fixes and arrests her murmuring voice) is the gift to the work that allows it to affirm itself as an impossibility. He puts the work to death (gives it death on his terms) and silences her footsteps (the *ressassement*), but not completely. They rise up again in the language of his work; their echoes can be heard in his transfigured reification. The other half of the circular rapport is condensed in the same words, "le don de sa mort à lui," which can also be read as "the gift of her death to him." This interpretation would make Eurydice the giver, which she is as the victim of a sacrifice who surrenders herself to Orpheus's gaze, like the female character of *L'Attente l'oubli* who waits for the protagonist to put (write) an end to their story.

The *dénouement* that they patiently await—the happy ending of their story—is to arrive at the definitive, final state of plenitude in which they would be fully present to themselves and each other. This theme is established in the opening paragraphs of the fragment and is pursued in the remaining paragraphs from different perspectives. The fourth paragraph gives voice to the exigency of reading through the words of the interlocutors who discuss the experience of another couple. The fifth paragraph also involves the activity of reading, not through the eyes of the interlocutors, however, but rather in the words of the theoretician who reemerges to offer an explanation of the relationship between writing, forgetting, the story, and the general economy. The sixth paragraph is a curious mixture of transgressive writing and legislative reading in direct discourse. A series of hypnotic, ritualistic statements made by *nous* suddenly and inexplicably gives way to an analysis by "us" of "them," another couple: "C'est notre supériorité sur eux: comme si nous étions leur secret" (139).[85] This marks the only occasion when the interlocutors engage in commentary after having lost their specificity in the common *nous*. The exigency of writing returns in the seventh paragraph in an unexpected situation: the language of passivity in a narrative section. Paragraph eight continues the exigency of passive writing in the mode of direct discourse. The two characters assume the roles assigned to them with regard to the basic distinction between the two modes, as actors whose part is to stumble about in the dark as they search for the meaning of their experience. The last three paragraphs of the fragment, on the contrary, present the activities of reading and writing with respect to the reversal of the fundamental distinction. Paragraph nine casts the protagonists in the role of readers as they comment on the experience of another couple. The tenth paragraph consists of a brief narrative intervention, but once again it is not the voice of the authoritative reader that we hear, which spoke the opening words of the fragment, but rather the one that speaks a transgressive *parole* that undoes the limits it usually attempts to assign to this *parole*. The *bouquet*'s final burst allows the exigency of reading to blossom forth one more time, in the reversal of its usual context. Again the characters analyze the experience of another couple from the perspective of mutual superiority. The impossibility of determining who says what, however, and the rapidity and echolike character of their exchanges reveal that the language of passivity has creeped into their commentary. In this case, Foucault's opinion that the language of this book "n'est ni de la fiction ni de la réflexion," seems to hold true; it is a little bit of both.

Thus not only do the exigencies of reading and writing and the perspectives from which they are enunciated reverse themselves and trade places from one paragraph to the next; this transgressive movement also occurs within individual paragraphs themselves. The language of this fragment in particular and of *L'Attente l'oubli* in general cannot content itself by being either exclusively transgressive or normative. It has to do both, and the state of perpetual contestation that animates the very being of the language that the protagonist/narrator has at his disposal obliges him to commit violations of the *noli* and us to catch him at it while he does it, *in flagrante delicto*.

Qui parle?

To answer the fundamental question of the book, "Qui parle?", is first and foremost to identify the various perspectives from which the different voices speak and to characterize the statements that they make. This approach has led us to establish a kind of hierarchy of voices and perspectives. At the top resides the so-called "omniscient" narrator, the creative force behind the work, the entity responsible for the book's existence. Located one rung below is the impersonal voice of the narrator, and the sheer dominance of fragments and asides in which this voice speaks points to the disappearance of a personal author who converses with himself. Elsewhere in the schema, the perspective of the protagonists is located below that of the impersonal narrator, but they are nonetheless superior to another couple that they observe from a distance.

The presence of the omniscient narrator is always felt, but he rarely makes it known to us in a pointedly obvious way. He does so in a few fragments remarkable for their scarcity when he speaks directly to himself about his experience of writing. In these messages to himself, he gives himself advice, notes things down that he does not want to forget, and generally comes to a clearer understanding of certain aspects of his experience than he had previously. Presumably these precious revelations will make a better writer of him if he can succeed in putting this newly acquired knowledge into practice. Instead of reaching an ever-increasing awareness of himself and his art, however, his writing has the opposite effect of estrangement. In an unexpected development, the more he writes, the more alienated he becomes from his work and himself, to such an extent that the narrative interventions in which he confirms something to himself are virtually nonexistent in the second section of the book. This voice makes one final, fleeting apparition in the last fragment of the book, however (not counting the direct discourse passage printed in italics at the very end in the form of an epilogue): "Comme vous parlez peu, vous qui faites signe en dernier" (160).[86] He "signs off" by admitting to himself that he, who is responsible for leaving the traces (signs) of the conversations of the man and woman, has had very little to say about the experience from his own point of view.

Although the answer to the question "Qui parle?" may not be an easy one, it is not difficult to single out someone who does not speak: *Je* is rarely the speaking subject of enunciations that he makes to himself. Such moments of illuminating self-presence are few and far between at best. The question now becomes why *Je* does not speak. What happens to the writer whom we see at rare intervals as he tries to gain greater consciousness of his creative activity?

In his story of an anonymous encounter of a man and a woman in an ordinary hotel room, Blanchot succeeds in dramatizing his version of literary creation. To approach the literary space is to turn one's back on the world of the everyday which, in turn, involves abandoning many of the powers that are in force and that regulate the regional economy. The writer is dispossessed of language viewed exclusively as an instrument of power, of the linear mode of the temporality of becoming, and of the power of sight in which whatever is seen is appropriated by the viewer. The language he uses turns out to have a mind of its own capable of leading him—it should be the other way around—into a state of fascination in which time has a different way of accomplishing itself (repetition and return) and the power of seeing has been transformed into the passive disposition to be seen by the impersonal gaze of Someone. The "essential solitude" of the writer who has penetrated into the undetermined milieu of the space of literature engages him in a rapport with alterity: "Quand je suis seul, je ne suis pas seul, mais, dans ce présent, je reviens déjà à moi sous la forme de Quelqu'un. Quelqu'un est là, où je suis seul . . . Quelqu'un est ce qui est encore présent, quand il n'y a personne. Là où je suis seul, je ne suis pas là, il n'y a personne, mais l'impersonnel est là" (*EL* 24).[87] The locus in which this problematic resurfaces in *L'Attente l'oubli* is the hotel room. Although the narrator is absolutely alone, his writing has the effect of filling his room with voices that belong to many different beings and implicates him in a rapport with alterity that is played out in the texts of the direct dialogues between his alter ego, the male lead, also a writer, and a woman, the mysterious, unknowable, unseizeable figure of the *dehors*. On three exceptional occasions in which the narrator enjoys a rapport of self-presence, he is able to articulate the relationship that exists between himself (the narrative voice who is "in charge" of the proceedings) and the interlocutors:

> Quelqu'un en moi converse avec lui-même.
>
> Quelqu'un en moi converse avec quelqu'un. Je ne les entends pas. Pourtant, sans moi qui les sépare et sans cette séparation que je maintiens entre eux, ils ne s'entendraient pas. (46)
>
> Elle lui parle, il ne l'entend pas. Pourtant, c'est en lui qu'elle se fait entendre de moi.
>
> Je ne sais rien de lui, je ne lui fais aucune place en moi ni hors de moi. Mais si elle lui parle, je l'entends en lui qui ne l'entend pas. (75)
>
> Elle lui parle, il ne l'entend pas, je l'entend en lui. (76)[88]

These three entities exist in a rapport of mutual dependency; the *entretiens* which take place between the members of the couple are possible only because the narrator occupies a space between (*se tient entre*) them. Alterity, therefore, never coincides with any particular entity; it is neither the protagonist's relationship with the woman nor that of the narrator with the protagonist. The Other is neither the one nor the other; it concerns not a term in the relation but the relation as a whole. Moreover, subjectivity (the self-present identity of the narrator) not only has no existence outside its involvement with alterity; it is also both a point of departure *and* a product of this rapport.

> le Même du moi-même ne lui apporte pas l'identité, est seulement canonique, afin de permettre le rapport infini du Même à l'Autre; d'où la tentation (la seule tentation) de redevenir sujet, au lieu de s'exposer à la subjectivité sans sujet, la nudité de l'espace mourant. (*ED* 89)[89]

The self-identical, self-present subject is "canonical," an article of faith on which the possibility of carrying out transactions in the world of the everyday rests. Selfhood is a given, a working hypothesis which allows the rapport of the Same and Other to be thought. This notion of subjectivity as "le privilège du point central" (*PAD* 12)[90] holds sway in the regional economy. In the general economy, however, it loses this privileged perspective and becomes an impersonal attentiveness to "la subjectivité sans sujet" from which it nevertheless periodically attempts to extricate itself and to succumb to the "sole temptation" of reestablishing itself as an authoritative subject. This ebb and flow movement from personal subjectivity to impersonal spontaneity and back characterizes Orpheus's descent. According to Blanchot's account of the myth (which gives us a clue as to how we might understand the title of this book), Orpheus goes through three successive phases. He undertakes his mission as a self-assured poet and saviour who is prepared to *wait* as long as is necessary for Eurydice's ascent from the underworld. He then becomes a dispossessed wanderer mesmerized by his own music. Finally, he *forgets* the divine edict not to look at Eurydice and thereby succumbs to the temptation to extricate himself from his unintentionally self-induced trance and to make a last desperate attempt to hold on to the retreating form of Eurydice.

The same drama, in which a well-conceived act of power is inexplicably transformed into an impulsive act of transgression doomed to fail, is reenacted in *L'Attente l'oubli*. The narrator initially possesses the self-confidence displayed by Orpheus: all he has to do is describe the room and tell the story of the meeting of the man and the woman, that is, to use language as if it were an instrument of power. The telling of the story is eventually waylaid by the interminable, repetitive, circular conversations of the characters. The narrator, the go-between who renders their rapport possible, is involved with them to such an extent that he feels the need to extricate himself from the relationship from time to time, which he does in his Orphic glances when he rereads and comments on the texts of the interlocutors' conversations. Furthermore, the narrator's transgressions fail to extricate him completely from his rapport with alterity and to bestow upon him the vantage point of superiority he seeks. He is toppled from that position whenever his purported discourse of power reveals itself to be contaminated by the spellbinding language of passivity over which it pretended to exercise control. The impersonal narrator, therefore, cannot silence the voices of his protagonists by means of a definitive, authoritative reading in his narrative passages. Nor can the personal self-present narrator reduce the impersonal voice of the narrative to silence in his reminders to himself. On the contrary, this entity falls into oblivion and almost completely disappears from the scene. He is merely one of the by-products of the rapport with alterity which appears in the prologue when everything is all over (or about to begin again) in a vain effort to take stock of what has just taken place. The lesson that he takes away from his experience—that her voice is what has been confided to him—does nothing more than pave the way for another failure in the future of the same sort, which he will try unsuccessfully to reassess from a vantage point of supposed superiority, and so on. This is the vicious circle that, according to Blanchot, the experience of literary creation holds in store for every writer. The narrator of *L'Attente l'oubli* gets entangled in this web, and the interaction of the direct and indirect fragments chronicles his progress as he is lured into a state of fascination by the young woman's sirenlike voice from which he tries to tear himself away, too late, in the language of his commentaries that flails wildly about in a state of self-contestation, vacillating indefinitely between a discourse predicated on power and one that saps the very strength of that power.

This excerpt of a fragment describes the ebb and flow movement which gives *L'Attente l'oubli* its peculiar start again–stop again rhythm:

> (il) ainsi se dédouble en se redoublant indéfiniment: le il sujet et qui en tient la fonction en lançant la phrase, est comme l'alibi d'un autre il, lequel ne jouerait aucun rôle, ne remplirait aucune fonction, sauf celle de se désoeuvrer en se répétant invisiblement en une série infinie que l'analyse essaie de rattraper et ressaisit, après coup, chaque fois. Mais pour cela il semble que, à un bout de la chaîne, il fallait qu'il y eût, pour se charger de figurer la règle d'identité, un moi-même capable de n'être là que pour dire "je." (*PAD* 32)[91]

The transition from the personal to the impersonal inherent in the writer's approach to the space of literature dictates that he become estranged from the identity he possesses in the regional economy of the everyday, a *moi* that, for Blanchot, is "par avance fracturé" (*PAD* 15),[92] and that he become involved with an elusive impersonal spontaneity. The approach to/of alterity in proximity thus opens up a wound in the self that has been there since time immemorial, "dès le jour où le ciel s'ouvrit sur son vide" (*PAD* 9),[93] which the regional economy must overlook. This "initial doubling," a rift within closure that signals a rapport of noncoincidence with itself, renders possible the notion of an integral subject while at the same time undermining its pretensions to primacy. The ubiquitous impersonal narrative voice, which overshadows the voice of the personal self-present narrator to the point of excluding it and making us forget it, contains within it the same capacity of doubling itself: one *il*, the male speaker in the dialogues, performs the function of repeating the *parole* of worklessness "en une série infinie que l'analyse [the voice of another *il*, the narrator] essaie de rattraper et ressaisit, après coup, chaque fois." The ability to carry out retrospective analysis depends on the positing of a subjectivity capable "of acting out the rule of identity," a useful notion but one that lacks any lasting authority: the self-present *Je* is too ephemeral and the perspective of the impersonal *Il* is susceptible to reversals at any moment, given the unreliability of language. The narrative voice that seeks to extricate itself from the rapport with alterity by commenting on the experience of the couple as if from the outside (an illusion) reduces the dimensions of that rapport by talking about "them." Ironically, the transgressive reduction of neutrality is accomplished by putting it into the plural:

> Le rapport au "il": la pluralité que détient le "il" est telle qu'elle ne peut se marquer par quelque signe pluriel; pourquoi? "ils" désignerait encore un ensemble analysable, par conséquent maniable. "Ils" est la manière dont (il) se libère du neutre en empruntant à la pluralité une possibilité de se détermi-

ner, par là retournant commodément à l'indétermination, comme si (il) pouvait y trouver l'indice suffisant qui lui fixerait une place, celle, très déterminée, où s'inscrit tout indéterminé. (*PAD* 10–11)[94]

The narrative voice is not alone in the pluralizing reduction of an irreducible inextrication of terms—the narrator, the protagonist/writer, and his female companion—when he talks about the interlocutors' experience in his indirect commentaries. The interlocutors themselves succumb to the same temptation in their discussions of the experience of another couple. They, too, resort to the "ils" form as a manner of "liberating themselves" from the rapport with alterity of which they are a part. Finally, they also fail in their transgressive readings of the other couple's experience; in the end, they prove themselves incapable of articulating the two experiences together. Their analysis sheds little if any light on their own predicament, and once again, the so-called position of authority achieved by a transgression that has all the trappings of a decisive act of power and initiative is a restricted instance in the general economy, in actuality predicated on failure and the loss of such power. Transgressive gazes of reading, therefore, occur on three levels: (*i*) the authorial *je* tries unsuccessfully to assimilate the experience of his metamorphosis into the impersonal narrator *il*; (*ii*) *il*, like *je* always already divided, is split into two entities, the members of the couple, which he fails to reconcile in his narrative fragments of observation; and (*iii*) the fissure within *il* is reproduced within the couple, previously the object of the narrator's transgressive analyses, when it becomes the observing subject of the experience of another couple.

The narrative subject has thus been split into six different entities. His writing, rather than enabling him to achieve a higher degree of self-presence, has had a disintegrating effect, and he is further removed from a rapport of immediacy with his *moi* than ever. It is as if his foray into the space of literature has led him into a hall of mirrors whose concave and convex surfaces reflect a multiplicity of images back to him (*je* is just one of many) that he is unable to recognize and assimilate as his own. Moreover, one has the impression that the phenomenon of refraction and doubling could go on forever. Blanchot certainly does his best to create this impression, but in the end he has to settle for three levels of *dédoublement*. Given the limits within which he must work, however, this is not an insignificant technical accomplishment. He makes utmost use of the linguistic and syntactic tools that he has at his disposal—all eight subject pronouns, all the tenses, the two modes of discourse—by combining them in every possible way in order to portray the perpetual displacement of subjectivity with respect to itself.

De Man's Blind Spot

I would now like to return to de Man's statements about *L'Attente l'oubli*, the status of the *noli*, and the circular relationship that he sees between Blanchot's criticism and fiction in order to find out how well they fare in the wake of my discussion of the book. I agree with de Man's contention that "the impossibility of self-reading has itself become the theme" of the work. My extensive analysis of the different voices that speak, their relation to each other, and the interaction of the two modes of discourse verifies this claim and at the same time disproves the other one he makes regarding the book, "that it could only be the result of a relationship between the completed work and its author." Why a violation of the *noli* through self-reading should occur only between the completed work and its author is a hypothesis that de Man neglects to work out in his article, and my reading, on the contrary, has shown that the story told in *L'Attente l'oubli* is what takes place between a writer and a work in progress and that what characterizes this relation is an incessant transgressive exchange between the exigencies of writing and reading in which the *noli* is repeatedly violated in the course of the work's being written. According to de Man, the *noli* is in force at the origin of the work and has the positive function of enabling the work to come into being. Writers willfully close their eyes and choose to forget certain aspects of the approach to the space of literature, with which they are undoubtedly familiar thanks to the experiences they have undergone in other books they have written. Complete remembrance of the approach—of the dispossession and failure that it holds in store—would give the writer second thoughts about undertaking a new project. (Rimbaud is Blanchot's example of a writer who could not help having these second thoughts, who was incapable of forgetting.) De Man also believes that the *noli* remains in force until the completion of the project and that violations occur only once the book has been finished.

He seems to speak on good authority, for Blanchot almost invariably describes the *noli* in terms of the rapport between writers and their finished work. In his essay on Louis-René des Forêt's *Le Bavard*, however, his most complete statement on the forces at work in the literary economy of author, text, and reader, a new facet of the *noli* comes to life, one that clarifies de Man's problem of situating the *noli* with respect to its violations. Blanchot repeats the familiar version of the interdiction against self-reading which bars the author from reading his finished work. But he also speaks of another moment of self-reading that he never mentions elsewhere, that which goes on in the course of the work's composition:

A la limite, une fois l'oeuvre terminée, celui qui l'a achevée se trouve expulsé d'elle, renvoyé au dehors et désormais incapable d'y trouver accès, n'ayant du reste plus envie d'y accéder. C'est seulement au cours de la tâche de réalisation, alors que le pouvoir de lire est encore tout intérieur à l'ouvrage qui se fait, que l'auteur, lui-même toujours inexistant, peut se dédoubler en un lecteur encore à venir et chercher, par le biais de ce témoin caché, à vérifier ce que serait le mouvement des mots ressaisi par un autre qui ne serait encore que lui-même, c'est-à-dire ni l'un ni l'autre, mais la seule vérité du dédoublement. (*L'Amitié*, 144)[95]

The new twist that Blanchot adds to his theory regarding the prohibition of self-reading is the distinction between the inside and the outside of the work and the writer's situation with respect to these two terms. Blanchot seems to say that the *noli* is not in force during the period of the work's composition and that to reread and reconsider what has been written is a logical, legitimate, and necessary activity. No transgression is involved when "le pouvoir de lire est encore intérieur à l'ouvrage qui se fait" because there is no taboo in place to be violated. Or is there? For following this initial declaration, which affirms the precedence of the relationship between writers and their works in progress over the jurisdiction of the *noli*, Blanchot describes a state of affairs which belies a hidden presence of the *noli*. In the same breath he claims that writers are perfectly justified in reading their own unfinished texts, *and* he presents this activity of self-reading as an encounter with the *noli*. In spite of what he seems to say at first, he describes a situation in which the *noli* is in force. The only product of this reading, the only secret that this reading yields is "la seule vérité du dédoublement." Reading maintains rather than erases the fissured subjectivity that writing has (re)produced; it repeats on a different level the doubling that subjectivity has undergone in its approach to alterity. Whether authors are rereading the first chapter of a work in progress or the definitive final version, the result is the same: they are already estranged from themselves and dismissed from their work, even if it is a "livre à venir." De Man is thus half right in his assessment of the *noli*: it is in force from the earliest moments of a work's genesis. It does not, on the other hand, maintain a posture of absolute sovereignty that remains untouched by transgressive assaults on it until after the work is completed. The *noli* is always already in force, and because it is an interdiction in the Bataillian sense—both a limit and an invitation to cross over that limit—transgressions occur long before the work reaches its final form. This is only one instance when a violation of the *noli* can occur, and this is the lesson of *L'Attente l'oubli*: that a work owes its very existence *not* to the writer's attitude of respectful obedience to the *noli*, as de Man would have it, but rather to the transgressive rapport of circularity between the exigencies of writing and reading. The *flagrants délits* (repeated violations of the *noli*) within creation prefigure the failure of discrete, respectful, self-conscious violations of the *noli* on the part of not just the author but of all future readers to achieve a rapport of total presence with the work they are reading.

One further contention made by de Man needs to be reevaluated in light of our reading of *L'Attente l'oubli*: his portrayal of the relationship between Blanchot's criticism and his fiction. He states that the former is a "preparatory version" of the latter and that "Blanchot's criticism prefigures the self-reading toward which he is ultimately oriented" in his fiction. De Man compounds his problem in this self-defeating statement which flies in the face of his earlier claim about the *noli*: apparently self-reading *does* occur in his fiction. A problem resides not so much in this blind spot which animates what is nonetheless an insightful discussion of Blanchot as in his model of circularity by which he relates Blanchot's criticism to his fiction. The model is not wrong, but it can be improved upon. Our analysis of *L'Attente l'oubli* bears out his theory that reading and writing are in a rapport of circularity. The comparison of the direct discourse to the indirect narrative fragments reveals a circular relationship between the involvement with alterity that writing produces (in direct discourse) and the unsuccessful attempt of the writer to extricate himself from this rapport by withdrawing into the alluring yet treacherous confines of narrative fragments, a vantage point from which he believes he can read and appropriate the encounter with alterity. The rapport of circularity between the different types of fragments thus confirms de Man's hypothesis. We can go one step further, however, and refine this theory if we recall the reversal that occurs within each type of fragment. The language of each type of fragment carries with it the latent potential to reverse itself, and the so-called "secondary text," the narrative commentaries, sometimes starts to look like the "primary text," and the language that is supposed to circumscribe the language of passivity transgresses the very limits it seeks to restore. Conversely, the primary texts, the aimless speech of the interlocutors, take on the attributes of a critical commentary when the protagonist and his friend analyze the experience of another couple. This reversibility is present not only in the fragments of *L'Attente l'oubli* but is a constitutive element in each of the disciplines which make up Blanchot's *oeuvre* as a whole. We could say with de Man, therefore, that Blanchot's fiction and criticism are related in a circular way, although to do so would be an oversimplification. It is more correct to say that the circular exigency describes not only the relationship *between* criticism and fiction but also that which takes place *within* each of these moments. Thus within de Man's global orbit are two smaller circular exigencies responsible for the activities of creative writing and critical reading, respectively.[96]

The Law of the Genre

L'Attente l'oubli occupies a special place in Blanchot's bibliography. He has tried his hand at many different styles and forms of composition: review articles, philosophical essays, novels, *récits*, and fragmentary books. If *L'Attente l'oubli* stands apart, it is because it represents the extreme limit toward which his theoretical concerns and the working out of these concerns in artistic literary form had tended since his earliest texts of the 1930s. In it, he achieves a blend of the language of criticism and fiction unparalleled elsewhere by managing to set all three circular exigencies into motion at once, quite a juggling act. Since the book cannot be classified as either a *récit* or a collection of philosophical aphorisms (on the order of *Le Pas au-delà* or *L'Ecriture du désastre*), what is it? What is the "law of the genre" to which this book belongs? At the risk of transgressing the "exigence du fragmentaire" by forcing it into a generic paradigm, I would like to suggest that *L'Attente l'oubli* is a rhapsody in the sense that Blanchot himself attributes to the word:

> Lorsque les commentateurs n'ont pas encore imposé leur règne, par exemple au temps de l'épopée, c'est à l'intérieur de l'oeuvre que le redoublement s'accomplit, et nous avons le mode de composition rhapsodique—cette perpétuelle répétition d'épisode en épisode, développement sur place, amplification interminable du même—qui fait de chaque rhapsode non pas un reproducteur fidèle, un répétiteur immobile, mais celui qui porte en avant la répétition, et, par elle, remplit les vides ou les élargit par le moyen de nouvelles péripéties, ouvre, bouche les fissures et, finalement, à force de combler le poème, le distend jusqu'à la volitalisation. (*EI* 571–72)[97]

In this account of the rhapsodic style of composition that Blanchot sees at the heart of epic poetry, he accomplishes in one swift gesture a reversal of a commonly held notion, which by now we are accustomed to. The opposition that he calls into question is that between creative and critical activity. Common sense tells us that the artifact precedes the critical appreciation of it. Blanchot disrupts this distinction, however, by placing the origin of criticism within the work of art itself. Thus prior to a clearcut distinction between creation and commentary, artists and critics, is the work of literature seen as a hybrid text. In the beginning is an incessant exchange between two irreducible, inseparable exigencies, a "dédoublement initial," a "disparité de fond" which renders possible their subsequent division into two separate and often opposed categories. Just as Homer doubles back to amplify or reflect further on the significance of an episode he has just recounted, the narrator of *L'Attente l'oubli* constantly casts Orphic glimpses over his own shoulder at the dialogues upon which he expounds in his indirect asides. Moreover, in spite of the furious pace with which the transgressions are committed, the narrator does not succeed in "filling in all the gaps." Instead his frantic activity distends his book "jusqu'à la volitalisation" in the fragment that I designated as the *bouquet*.

Other meanings contained in the word "rhapsody" lend themselves as well to our task of trying to classify *L'Attente l'oubli* according to genre. Besides being a compositional element of an epic poem, as Blanchot has indicated, it can be defined as "a series of disconnected and often extravagant sentences, extracts, or utterances, gathered or composed under excitement; rapt or rapturous utterance" (Funk and Wagnall's *Standard College Dictionary*). One would be hard pressed to formulate a more concise and accurate characterization of most of the direct discourse fragments. Another definition is "an instrumental composition of irregular form," such as a medley. This meaning is closest to the etymology of the word: "songs that are stitched together." What is *L'Attente l'oubli*, if not a medley of fragments which tries unsuccessfully to weave a textual thread that would serve as a "suture parfaite" for a fragmented subject who seeks to sew up his wounds? "Là où, selon la loi générale, une suture parfaite cache le secret du raccord, le secret ici, à la manière d'une déchirure, se montre en son trait caché. De ce vide, tous deux, selon leurs voies, sont les témoins" (*AO* 142).[98] This book, like the subjects who are both the participants and the witnesses of the adventure that is recounted therein, is bursting at the seams.

CONCLUSION

BLANCHOT'S POSTMODERN LEGACY

I N THE preceding chapters, our overriding concern was to examine
two representative works of fiction by Blanchot, one fairly tradi-
tional-looking novel and one highly experimental fragmentary text,
through the lense of his theoretical writings. The decision to engage in
close readings of each of these modes of writing and to play them off each
other necessitated a certain willingness on our part to remain within the
circular trajectory described by the constant movement back and forth
between his criticism and his fiction. Whereas I hope that this methodological approach was far from inhibitive, it did not lend itself to address-
ing questions pertaining to the place that Blanchot occupies with respect
to other important figures involved in contemporary French critical theory. As a manner of concluding, therefore, I would like to entertain the
problem of how to situate Blanchot in this context by stepping outside
the relatively closed circuit that connects his critical and narrative works.
The task of locating Blanchot's position within the recent history of
philosophical criticism in France is not self-evident, and as Joseph Libertson explains, the difficulty resides in the potential misunderstanding
and misapplication of certain key terms which belong to the vocabulary of
Blanchot's critical discourse:

> The opacity of Blanchot's theoretical text . . . is its mimicry of phenomenol-
> ogical procedures and existential themes, and its description of a reality
> which is as incomprehensible to phenomenology as it is to the formalisms
> which succeeded phenomenology. . . . Where the humanist subject suffered
> the anguish of his freedom, and where the formalist subject disappears (or
> assumes an ontological insignificance which approximates disappearance) in
> the freeplay of signs or structures, the subject in proximity persists as an
> indecision, a fascination, and a passivity which are produced by differentia-
> tion itself, and which are uneliminable. . . . To the former tradition, the ex-
> pression "essential solitude" must seem pertinent and yet insufficient (given
> Blanchot's insistence on passivity); to the latter, the expression "impersonal-
> ity" must have the same attraction and deception (given Blanchot's insis-
> tence on the multiple remainders which contaminate dispersion, including
> subjectivity itself). To the reader who is conscious of their historical circum-
> stances, Blanchot's theoretical publications present an extraordinarily per-
> verse aspect of accessibility and mystery. (76)

Blanchot's texts must surely be relegated to the sidelines when considered from the points of view of existential humanism and structuralism in its various guises, two of the intellectual currents that have dominated the discursive field of play during the past half-century. In a provocative and self-admittedly "extravagant claim," however, Geoffrey Hartman dismisses the idea that Blanchot will continue to be seen as a marginal thinker: "When we come to write the history of criticism for the 1940 to 1980 period, it will be found that Blanchot, together with Sartre, made French 'discourse' possible, both in its relentlessness and its acuity" (*GO*, xi). I would like to suggest that Hartman's claim is not so extravagant as it might at first sound and that certain aspects of the discourse which Blanchot had an indispensable role in forming are developed along various lines by such diverse poststructuralist thinkers as Jean-François Lyotard, Gilles Deleuze, Jean Baudrillard, Michel Foucault, and Jacques Derrida. Each of these figures has contributed substantially to the thematization of the postmodern, and it is with respect to this context that we may perhaps best begin to ascertain how to situate Blanchot in the recent history of French critical theory.

I propose to undertake this project of contextualization by means of an examination of four different but not unrelated problems. First, I will consider some ways in which Blanchot's writing can be qualified as postmodern in the sense that Lyotard gives to this term. I will then take up the question of representation and its subversion by the simulacrum, which occupies an important place in the thought not only of Deleuze and Baudrillard but of Blanchot as well, since we have seen that the neuter functions as a simulacrum. We will discover, however, that there is an important difference of opinion concerning power's relationship to the irreducible alterity of the simulacrum, which gives rise to two opposing points of view regarding the advent of the postmodern condition. One of these perspectives is essentially affirmative and is maintained, as we shall see, in various ways by Blanchot, Deleuze, Lyotard, Foucault, and Derrida, whereas the other, fundamentally negative position is that assumed by Baudrillard. After entertaining the nature of this difference, I will end my discussion by drawing some parallels between the work of Blanchot and Foucault, on the one hand, and that of Blanchot and Derrida, on the other, particularly with respect to the power/alterity question. But before we turn our attention to what is at stake for the respective projects of these thinkers as far as their assimilation of Blanchot is concerned, a brief preambulary detour by way of Nietzsche is in order, for it is he who defined to a large extent many of the key terms of the discussion in which all of them have participated.

In the course of this study, Nietzsche's name was generally evoked in order to designate a stance with respect to history which contested

Hegel's teleologically oriented conception. And, in a more specific instance, we examined in our discussion of *Le Très-Haut* how repetition and return functioned strategically as tropes of a new, radically different form of writing based on fragmentation which prefigured Blanchot's turn away from his more traditional early novels in favor of the *récits* of the 1950s and the fragmentary books that became a central preoccupation from the 1960s onward. The main concern shared by Nietzsche and Blanchot that interests us here has to do with Nietzsche's denial of the privileged status of truth, or the idea that truth is the product of error. Figures who commit errors in the name of truth abound in Blanchot's theoretical texts: the suicide victim mistakes *le mourir* for *la mort heureuse*, Orpheus his music for a weapon, Oedipus *la question profonde* for a *question d'ensemble*, and readers the work for the book. We also know, moreover, that Blanchot insists on the limited, restricted nature of the truths produced by such errors.

Blanchot follows Nietzsche in the latter's rejection of two fundamental doctrines of epistemology, the correspondence theory of truth, which presupposes the conformity of mind with object, and the referential theory of meaning, which ensures this conformity by maintaining that language enjoys a relation of adequation with the world. It is precisely this view of language as a faithful, nondistorting mirror of nature that arouses Nietzsche's suspicion, and in his essay "On Truth and Lies in an Extramoral Sense," he examines this problem by distinguishing between metaphors and concepts. Whereas Heidegger summed up the history of Western philosophy as a progressive forgetting of the question of Being, we might say that for Nietzsche, it is more a case of philosophy's forgetting the metaphorical origins that lie hidden deep within concepts. Concepts are actually congealed metaphors, and the error of philosophy resides in its blindness to the fact that concepts succeed in passing themselves off as something they are not:

> What then is truth? A mobile army of metaphors, metonymies, and anthropomorphisms—in short, a sum of human relations which have been poetically and rhetorically intensified, transferred, and embellished, and which, after long usage, seem to a people to be fixed, canonical, and binding. Truths are illusions which we have forgotten are illusions; they are metaphors that have become worn out and have been drained of sensuous force, coins which have lost their embossing and are now considered as metal and no longer coins. ("On Truth and Lies in an Extramoral Sense" in *Philosophy and Truth*, 84)

To understand what Nietzsche means when he says that "knowledge is nothing but working with the favorite metaphors" ("The Last Philosopher" in *Philosophy and Truth*, 51), recourse to the etymology of the word is necessary. "Metaphor" is derived from a verb whose Greek roots express the action of "carrying over," "carrying across," or "transferring." Rather than confining it to rhetorical applications, Nietzsche broadens this notion to cover the transferences from one sphere to another inherent in all cognitive activity which entails the observation of something and the putting into words of what has been observed. On the way from the initial perception to the concept that has something truthful to say about the initial perception, three metaphorical translations take place: (*i*) a nerve impulse is converted into a mental image, (*ii*) this mental image is transformed into an acoustical image/word, and (*iii*) the word is turned into a concept.

Nietzsche denies the possibility of ever achieving an adequate, proper translation between such different spheres while insisting that this process of metaphor formation in no way corresponds to the model of knowledge according to which the unproblematic use of a transparent language is capable of bridging the gap between subject and object. Concepts' contributions to truth claims are also suspect because they are reductive dissimulations of reality. "Every concept arises from the equation of unequal things" ("On Truth and Lie in an Extramoral Sense," 83). Concepts are generalized abstractions which are designed to be applicable to different cases that possess a certain degree of similarity and, therefore, they deprive objects of their exceptional character, their uniqueness. On account of the metaphoric transferences involved in forming concepts, access to the truth of the thing-in-itself is unavailable to us. Concepts are subjective projections on reality, anthropomorphic illusions that tell us more about ourselves, the investigating subjects, than about the object of study. Truth is thus not a given, latently inherent in things and patiently waiting to be unearthed by reason. On the contrary, truth is a construct, something appended to things from without, the inevitable and desired product of the self-fulfilling epistemological drive.

The precedence that Nietzsche accords to metaphor over concept recalls the priority that Blanchot grants to poetry over everyday language. Blanchot defines poetic language as the intrication of and incessant movement between sound and sense, materiality and ideality. Everyday, practical language, on the other hand, is possible thanks to the suppression of language's materiality, which puts a halt to the oscillating movement between the two components of language characteristic of poetry. Transitive language subordinated to the logic of means and ends arrests the murmur of contestation at the origin of language just as metaphors solidify to become concepts. In both instances, knowledge, which puts a premium on stasis, freezes the dynamic flux of becoming, whether by reducing language to a transparent medium of communication or by glossing over the metaphoric conversions upon which concept-making depends.

In her book entitled *Nietzsche et la métaphore*, Sarah Kofman analyzes the architectural metaphors that Nietzsche self-consciously employs in his descriptions of how epistemological systems are built in order to expose the occulted metaphoricity of concepts. The beehive, the medieval fortress, the Egyptian pyramid, and the spider's web are some of the structures to which Nietzsche compares conceptual edifices erected by culture. It is the metaphor of the Roman columbarium, however, which comes closest to the image Blanchot frequently uses to express culture's way of domesticating death: "Le columbarium romain ne conserve plus que les cendres du défunt comme le concept est seulement 'résidu' de métaphores. Les cendres sont l'effacement complet de toute effigie, la volatilisation de toute singularité: ne plus conserver de la vie que les cendres, c'est réduire jusqu'à l'extrême les différences" (Kofman 98).[1]

As we noted during our discussion of Lazarus, Blanchot's metaphor of the tomb is similar in that it constitutes the resting place from which an intact and perfectly preserved Lazarus (for Nietzsche, concepts, immutable truths that cannot be tainted by decomposition) can be summoned forth. One of Blanchot's versions of the tomb is thus that it possesses the ability to contain death and to render it authentic, human, and usable. He always insists, however, on the persistence of another form of death which is completely indifferent to such human concerns as authenticity and mastery, the other, decomposing Lazarus around whom culture erects funerary monuments so as not to have to acknowledge him. The act of reading implicates the reader in a confrontation with the dual status of death, and the presence of the two negativities accounts for the work's state of noncoincidence with itself. Whereas the book, the index of constructive negativity, lends itself to reading conceived as an act of power, the work possesses a reserve of excess negativity which disrupts the closure of the book and undermines the totalizing pretentions of acts of reading predicated on and directed toward the closure of the book. The work is irreducible to the book, and, at the same time, the destiny of every work is to become a book, just as for Nietzsche, the destiny of any metaphorical translation is to solidify into a concept. The work, always in a state of self-contesting flux, does not constitute a thing-in-itself of which interpretation can provide an adequate translation, and because it is not identical to itself, it possesses no voice in which it speaks for itself that an interpreter can hope to reproduce in his or her own words. We can see how close Nietzsche and Blanchot are on this score by considering Alan Schrift's characterization of Nietzsche's transvalued conception of the text; he could not have been more accurate had he been describing Blanchot's conception of the work:

> the "text" is not an independently existing object but the heuristic aggregate of all possible interpretations which can be imposed on it. This is to say,

a text is distinct from any *particular* interpretation, but it *is* nothing other than a product of interpretive activity. The text and its interpretations exist only in a relationship of *reciprocal* creation: the "text" is fabricated from the totality of possible interpretations which themselves emerge in response to the text. As a consequence, there can be no single totalizing interpretation which completely masters the "essential meaning" or "truth" of the text; no one interpretation will exactly replicate the text, nor will any one interpretation get the text "exactly right," for it is the "nature" of the text as an infinite reservoir of possible signification to exceed all attempts at totalization. (*Nietzsche and the Question of Interpretation*, 196)

There is always some unfinished business when it comes to interpretation because the object of interpretation, the text or work, never completely present unto itself, never surrenders itself in exactly the same way to different interpreters. The text/work does not exist in the mode of a brute fact, which is the point that Foucault makes in the paper entitled "Nietzsche, Freud, Marx" that he presented at the colloquium on Nietzsche held in 1964 at Royaumont: "if interpretation can never be brought to an end, it is simply because there is nothing to interpret. There is nothing absolutely primary to interpret, because at bottom everything is already interpretation. Each sign is in itself not the thing that presents itself to interpretation, but the interpretation of other signs" (*Transforming the Hermeneutic Context*, 64).

In our discussion of *Le Très-Haut*, we encountered a situation that exemplifies the interpreter's inability to have access to brute phenomena which exist in pristine form, untouched by a previous act of interpretation: the two differing versions of how the fire broke out in the Roste family's apartment. At issue may very well be the explanation of how the very first case of the epidemic was contracted. Dorte's retelling with variations of the anecdote recounted earlier to Sorge by Marie has the effect of obscuring the original event that gave rise to the conflicting stories in the first place. Exactly how the epidemic began remains shrouded in mystery; no one can get close to the first case by breaking out of the web of interpretations which compete for legitimacy: whereas the politically nonpartisan Marie speculates as to why the usually efficient police failed to act, Dorte makes Roste's (unclear) actions out to be the stuff of which legends are made, in the eyes of the revolutionaries.

Nietzsche's questioning of the correspondence theory of truth and the referential theory of meaning, his assertion regarding the hidden metaphoric nature of concepts, and his doctrine of the eternal return opened the way to a new mode of reflection on these problems that have come to be associated with the postmodern: a reexamination of the status of representation, a break with the methods of post-Cartesian rationalism, a contesting of the humanist subject viewed as an autonomous being capable of achieving mastery over his or her destiny and the world thanks to rigorous applications of rationalist methods, and a critique of totalizing systems in general and of teleological conceptions of history predicated on closure in particular. This radical rethinking has had as its effect the undermining of the authority of the most fundamental categories that have served to organize and account for the modernist project of the progressive acquisition of knowledge since the Enlightenment. The loss of confidence in the ability of these categories to continue to serve as the grounds which would assure the legitimacy of this project has created a breach within it. Those who are obliged to write and reflect in this newly opened space find themselves implicated in the postmodern condition, which Jean-François Lyotard has characterized as an attitude of "incredulity toward metanarratives" (*The Postmodern Condition*, xxiv). In spite of the various forms these metanarratives can assume, they are motivated by two common concerns: the ideas that history is the progressive movement toward a desired, if unreachable, finality and that this desired end involves the emancipation of humanity from the bonds of some sort of subjugation. Some examples of these grand narratives which, according to Lyotard, tell the tale of mankind's progressive liberation are

> the Christian narrative of the redemption of original sin through love; the *Aufklärer* narrative of emancipation from ignorance and servitude through knowledge and egalitarianism; the speculative narrative of the realization of the universal Idea through the dialectic of the concrete; the Marxist narrative of emancipation and alienation through the socialization of work; and the capitalist narrative of emancipation from poverty through technoindustrial development. (*The Postmodern Explained*, 25)

Blanchot most certainly qualifies as a writer working in the postmodern condition as it is understood here, and the metanarrative toward which he is particularly incredulous is, of course, the third one mentioned above, the "speculative narrative" of Hegelianism. He also qualifies on the basis of his views on the work of art and literary creation. Let us consider the following distinction that Lyotard makes between modern and postmodern art:

> Modern aesthetics is an aesthetic of the sublime, though a nostalgic one. It allows the unpresentable to be put forward only as the missing contents; but the form, because of its recognizable consistency, continues to offer the reader or viewer matter for solace and pleasure. . . . The postmodern would be that which . . . denies itself the solace of good forms, the consensus of a taste which would make it possible to share collectively the nostalgia for the unattainable; that which searches for new presentations, not in order to enjoy them but in order to impart a stronger sense of the unpresentable. ("What is Postmodernism?" in *The Postmodern Condition*, 81)

This last statement on the search for new presentations constitutes an accurate description of Blanchot's literary experimentation, which consists of an exploration of different modes of writing and genres—essays, novels, short narratives, fragmentary books—that would be capable of expressing something ineffable. Blanchot's unpresentable, the neuter, is surely a far cry from the nostalgia for a lost unity that Lyotard sees as the essential theme underlying modern art, and whereas modern art seeks to palliate the suffering that its negative message visits upon its public by means of an aesthetic pleasure derived from "the solace of good forms," Blanchot's work does nothing of the kind. He steadfastly holds on to the belief expressed in his introduction to *Lautréamont et Sade*, "Qu'en est-il de la critique?" that value judgments of works of art made in accordance with a criterion such as taste are foreign to the experience that art affords us. He never concerns himself with appealing to the taste of his readers; if anything, his journey from novels to *récits* to works composed of fragments testifies to his wish to strip away the veneer of the solace that good forms offer "in order to impart a stronger sense of the unpresentable."

Lyotard's refusal to think of the postmodern in periodizing terms also has its equivalent in Blanchot's account of the space of literature. Many critical theorists view the postmodern as a critical moment of modernism, the period that follows chronologically on the heels of a failed or worn-out modernist aesthetic. For Lyotard, however, the postmodern does not consist of a subsequent break with modernism. On the contrary, it "marks a temporal aporia—a gap in the thinking of time which is constitutive of the modernist concept of time as succession or progress" (Readings 53). In a reversal reminiscent of some of those effected by Blanchot, Lyotard grants precedence to the postmodern over the modern: "A work can become modern only if it is first postmodern. Postmodernism thus understood is not modernism at its end but in the nascent state, and this state is constant" (*The Postmodern Condition*, 79). Theorizations of the postmodern as a distinct period that comes after modernism treat the postmodern as a *moment*, but Lyotard insists that it must be seen as an *event*. In his terminology, moments are reductive reifications of events. Events have precedence over moments. They render moments (interpretations) possible and at the same time are irreducible to them. Events are in excess over the closure of well-defined and locatable moments. As Bill Readings explains, "The postmodern is thus an alien temporality that in a sense precedes and constitutes *modernism*, always inscribing the possibility of a radical revision of modernism against itself, specifically in the thinking of the event" (xxxiv). Lyotard draws his distinctions between, for example, the postmodern and the modern, the event and the moment, and figure and discourse in accordance with a logic of reversal that is also at work in Blanchot and which gives rise to similar kinds of distinctions such as those between poetry and utilitarian language, *la ressem-blance* and representation, and the work and the book. The outbreak of the epidemic in *Le Très-Haut*, which I mentioned earlier in connection with Nietzsche's denial of the existence of brute facts, is an event in Lyotard's sense of the term: it lends itself to reductive appropriations as *moments* in the histories of both the State and the subversive movement while exceeding and contesting the intentions of these organizations to achieve mastery over it. Just as the State and the revolutionary party are two ways in which the pure dissimulation of the epidemic can dissimulate itself, thereby seemingly manifesting itself as negation, we might say that for Lyotard, modernism is a regional aesthetic economy, one way in which the general economy of the postmodern can manifest itself.

The temporal aporia that renders problematic the situating of the postmodern with respect to the modern has ramifications as far as the relationship of artists to their work is concerned. A consequence of the eventhood of the postmodern—the idea that it cannot be reduced to an autonomous, well-delineated, self-present moment—is that writers working in this condition do not enjoy a rapport of presence with their work. Lyotard's examination of the etymology of "postmodern" fur-nishes him with a compact demonstration of the inability of presence to render a satisfactory account of these situations and of the verbal tense that is capable of doing so: "*Post modern* would have to be understood according to the paradox of the future (*post*) anterior (*modo*)" (*The Postmodern Condition*, 81). The future perfect best describes the relation-ship that exists between a postmodern artist or writer and his work because

> the text he writes, the work he produces are not in principle governed by preestablished rules, and they cannot be judged according to a determining judgment, by applying familiar categories to the text or to the work. Those rules and categories are what the work of art is itself looking for. The artist and the writer, then, are working without rules in order to formulate the rules of what *will have been done*. Hence the fact that the work and text have the characters of an *event*; hence also, they always come too late for their author, or, what amounts to the same thing, their being put into work, their realization (*mise en oeuvre*) always begins too soon. (*The Postmodern Condition*, 81)

Lyotard is clearly making a broad claim meant to embrace postmodern artists and writers in general, but he could not have been closer to the mark had he been talking about Blanchot's work in particular. When Blanchot speaks of the "essential solitude" of the work and of the writer involved in its creation, he affirms the work's independence from criteria extrinsic to the work that would serve either as a standard against which the relative success or failure of the work could be measured or as prescriptive formula which the writer would have only to follow in order to produce good art. The work is indifferent to such criteria. Instead it turns inward, thus implicating its author in the search for its origin. In this quest, the Orphic writer does not occupy a position of masterful omniscience thanks to which he or she can know in advance and control how everything will turn out. Belatedness, not presence, characterizes the rapport that exists between writers and their works: either Eurydice is too late in arriving at Orpheus's side, or Orpheus turns around too soon. If writers can know anything about what transpires in the course of the composition of their work, they can do so only retrospectively and imperfectly.

Blanchot's writer is caught in the temporal paradox that Lyotard ascribes to postmodern art and literature, and the paradigm that I have used to organize my presentation of Blanchot, the circular movement of the transgression and the restitution of limits, accounts for this paradox. Let us take as an illustration the transgressive relationship that exists between the narrator of *L'Attente l'oubli* and his work. He begins by undertaking a relatively straightforward form of writing, his descriptive passages of the hotel room, as if writing were an exercise of power. As he continues to write, however, he becomes fascinated by his encounter with alterity, succumbing to the spells of the image and the absence of time as he undergoes a transformation from a personalized subjectivity into an impersonal spontaneity. This passive state is interrupted when impulsive impatience intervenes, thereby signaling a return of the lost subject who tries to seize what has taken place after the fact, in an impossible act of self-interpretation. This incessant circular movement is the principle that generates this work: the transgressive writing of passivity (the general economy) lets itself be partially seized by transgressive gazes of impatience (the regional economy) which set up provisional limits of understanding that will subsequently be subverted by more transgressive writing, and so on. To cast this movement, which is economically contained in the two words that make up the title of this work, *L'Attente l'oubli*, in terms of Lyotard's future anterior, we might say that the writer's passive attitude of the patient waiting for a desired moment in the future—the possibility of being complete consciousness at the origin of the work or of seeing Eurydice in her nocturnal element—is cut short by a fit of impatience which forgets that the only positivity of this moment is this moment as an approach and attempts to capture the anterior state of passivity by means of appropriating gazes cast from the presumed vantage point of mastery. The writing of passive patience is directed forward to an awaited future moment, and the reading of active impatience represents the reader's effort to go back to this prior phase of passivity that has already been endured for a time in order to formulate the rules of what occurred, but never the twain shall meet in a moment when they would be subsumed by a common present, or in Blanchot's words, "ce qui fut écrit au passé sera lu à l'avenir, sans qu'aucun rapport de présence puisse s'établir *entre* écriture et lecture" (*PAD* 45–46).[2] Thus, the uncanny temporal mode of the future anterior, which accounts for the rapport of belatedness that exists between artists and their work, is what enables Lyotard to characterize a work as an event, and for Blanchot as well as for Lyotard, art remains the privileged site of resistance to the totalizing effects of metanarratives.

Gilles Deleuze, too, is a proponent of the idea that the authority of metanarratives must be contested. In chapter 2, I associated Blanchot with Deleuze in connection with the problem of representation, and we saw that Blanchot's theorization of *la ressemblance* and "the two versions of the imaginary" places him squarely in the philosophical countertradition that traces its lineage from Nietzsche and whose task, according to Deleuze, is to respond to the former's challenge to overthrow Platonism by affirming the existence of simulacra and reappraising their status. The simulacrum upsets the hierarchical ordering that Platonism sets up in relation to the idea, the model, and the copy. Through an exclusionary gesture, Platonism trivializes simulacra, reducing them to mere bad copies so far removed from the truth contained in the original that they need not be taken seriously. Platonic mimesis thinks of difference as an aftereffect produced by a preexisting, self-identical plenitude. Consequently, good copies can be distinguished from bad on the basis of their similarity to the original plenitude: if they are to be deemed good, difference must be kept to a minimum, and, conversely, copies are considered bad (simulacra) when they stray too far from the original idea and the faithful model, when their differences outweigh the similarities to such a degree that they are no longer of any use as far as the representation of the truth, the preexisting idea, is concerned.

To overthrow Platonism is to demarginalize the simulacrum. Rather than viewing simulacra as regrettable but ultimately negligible aftereffects, works that do not come close to measuring up to the original idea on which they were based, Blanchot, Deleuze, and other philosophers of difference give priority to the simulacrum, which leads to a complete undoing of the Platonic scheme of things since it implies that similitude and even identity itself are the products of an "initial doubling" (Blanchot) or a "deep disparity" (Deleuze). No longer simply a bad copy, the simulacrum is a groundless ground which both enables the restricted economy of representation to appear and subverts the pretentions of this economy to totalization. The regional economy must covertly appeal to this heterogeneous intensity in order to exist. It must also overtly denounce simulacra as inauthentic and unthinkable so as to affirm its desired supremacy over them.

In *Le Très-Haut* and *L'Attente l'oubli*, which comprise two very different modes of narration, Blanchot represents this unpresentable phenomenon. In the former work, the epidemic functions as a simulacrum which not only renders possible the opposed yet all-too-familiar institutions of the State and the revolutionary movement but also perpetually resists the attempts of these institutions to domesticate its energy and to turn it completely into something they can use to further their respective agendas. In the case of *L'Attente l'oubli*, we witnessed how selfhood, the pretention of a self-present, self-identical subject to primacy in the form of a first-person narrator, is a regional instance which is conditioned by an initial rapport with alterity and which makes fleeting appearances whenever the impersonal spontaneity throws off a remainder, the guise of a subject who seeks to extricate himself from this rapport in order to assume a purported position of ascendancy and mastery over it. Blanchot and Deleuze thus pursue the same line of thinking as far as difference's status as being constitutive of identity is concerned. What separates them, however, is the ways in which they apply this fundamental insight. Whereas Blanchot concentrates first and foremost on language and the approach to a work of literature by reading and writing, Deleuze "extends the analysis of difference in philosophical discourse to embrace difference in its physical, biological, mathematical, and psychological manifestations" (Bogue 162).

A similar rapprochement can be made between Blanchot's revision of classical representation in his discussions of *ressemblance* and Jean Baudrillard's analyses of the structure of communication in advanced industrial society which is characterized by the all-pervasive presence of the media. It is not at all common to associate the work of these two figures; on the contrary, one is much more likely to see Baudrillard portrayed as having taken his cue from certain questions (such as that of the gift) raised in the political and socioeconomic writings of Blanchot's friend, Georges Bataille. Admittedly, the comparison may be a bit strained—after all, how can Blanchot's account of the space of literature be likened, for example, to Baudrillard's semiologically informed presentation of consumer goods and capital that circulate in the manner of linguistic codes?—but it is warranted, I think, at least in the context of Baudrillard's remarks on simulation and simulacra, which can be read as an adaptation of the theory of the simulacrum, as it is found in Deleuze and Blanchot, pushed to (and perhaps beyond) the limit as he applies it to the domains of politics, economics, and media and culture studies. It seems to me that Baudrillard takes this theory so far that it leads to a parting of the ways as far as his affinities with Deleuze and Blanchot are concerned. How does this come about? Let us first look at the affinities, after which we will be better able to account for the parting of the ways.

Baudrillard states that "the age of simulation . . . begins with a liquidation of all referentials" (*Selected Writings*, 167). In so doing, like Deleuze and Blanchot, he posits a general economy of communication which renders inoperable distinctions that have currency in the regional economy of power such as those between fact and interpretation, original and copy, object and image, the real and the imaginary. He also notes the contentious relationship that exists between these two rival economies in the failed attempts of the regional economy of representation to achieve mastery over the general economy of simulation by assimilating it completely: "Whereas representation tries to absorb simulation by interpreting it as false representation, simulation envelops the whole edifice of representation as itself a simulacrum" (*Selected Writings*, 170). The general economy of simulation dissimulates itself, thus appearing falsely as negation, the regional economy of representation. The regional economy is itself, therefore, a product of simulation, an imperfect copy of an original "deep disparity." So far, Baudrillard could not be any closer to the critique of classical representation found in Deleuze and Blanchot. The similarities between Baudrillard and Blanchot become even more pronounced, however, in the former's delineation of "the successive phases of the image" (*Selected Writings*, 170). He isolates four stages in the evolution of the image into a simulacrum: (*i*) the image as a faithful copy of a basic reality, (*ii*) the image as an unfaithful copy of a basic reality, (*iii*) the image as a stand-in that masks the absence of a basic reality to be represented, and (*iv*) the image as simulacrum, an empty reflection of itself which no longer has any connection to a preexisting reality. The passage by Baudrillard that I have just paraphrased can itself be read as a paraphrase of Blanchot's "two versions of the imaginary," and the affinity between the two reaches its highest degree of intensity in a sentence in which Baudrillard interprets the significance of the shift that occurs between the first two stages of the image, the regional economy of representation, and the last two, the general economy of simulation—or *ressemblance*, for Blanchot:

> The transition from signs which dissimulate something to signs which dissimulate that there is nothing marks the decisive turning point. The first implies a theology of truth and secrecy (to which the notion of ideology belongs). The second inaugurates an age of simulacra and simulation, in which there is no longer any God to recognize his own, nor any last judgment to separate the true from the false, the real from its artificial resurrection, since everything is already dead and risen in advance. (*Selected Writings*, 170–71)

A reader familiar with Blanchot's work cannot help being struck by the language that Baudrillard uses to describe the region where simulacra reign, imagery that harks directly back to Blanchot's discussions of Lazarus and *la ressemblance cadavérique*.

The similarity of imagery aside, however, the thinking of Deleuze, Blanchot, and other philosophers of difference diverges greatly from that of Baudrillard when it comes to answering the questions of when, where, and how simulacra manifest themselves. We have seen that for Blanchot, literature possesses the dubious distinction of being able to allow repressed simulacra to rise to the surface thanks to the duplicitous nature of words, the writer's medium. Moreover, the exposition of this unavowable excess negativity is the task to which the writer must relentlessly dedicate himself, as we saw in our analysis of the ink-stained pages of Henri Sorge's journal. But this exposition can only be apprehended fleetingly. The pulse of anonymous being, the neuter, can never be experienced as such. Its tendency to manifest itself as negativity is in itself a dissimulation, but the appearance of negativity is all the encouragement the regional economy needs to reassert itself, and when it does, it mistakes this *paraître*, which is nothing less than the indifferent movement of initial doubling and dissimulation in the general economy, for an *être*, which would have a proper place in the regional economy, in a reductive and incomplete gesture of appropriation. The regional economy is allergic to the excess negativity of the neuter, and the epistemological drive to convert this negativity into something it can use to consolidate its standing is provoked by an allergic reaction that is quick to declare itself, which explains why encounters with the neuter are necessarily brief, situated in intervals when the regional economy of power is only temporarily withdrawn.

According to Baudrillard, on the other hand, simulacra and simulation do not make themselves felt in periodic, fleeting ways. On the contrary, the age of simulation is upon us and has been for some time. A new culture has emerged in which simulacra dominate: the hyperreal. Julian Pefanis casts Baudrillard's point of view in terms of the Platonic scheme of representation: "But unlike Plato—who would like to draw a categorical distinction between the second and third orders, because the latter 'does not appeal to reason'—for Baudrillard the entire second order, which is the order of Plato's production, along with the immense edifice of its theoretical, philosophical, and cultural discourses, has collapsed into the third order" (*Heterology and the Postmodern*, 60). Thus, the general economy of simulation is everywhere, and unemployable negativity, far from being repressed and hidden, runs rampant out in the open in the form of the anonymous circulation of signifiers (capital, consumer goods, information transmitted in the codes of the mass media and advertising) which have been severed from referents grounded in reality. The ubiquity of the general economy is what distinguishes Baudrillard from philosophers of difference, who maintain that this radical heterogeneity is a latent phenomenon that must be ferreted out (of philosophical texts, for example) in order to be made manifest.

Perhaps this distinction can be illustrated by comparing their respective interpretations of fascism. Philosophers of difference would tend to portray fascism as the ultimate example of a failed political system predicated on the flawed logic of totalization. Fascism would then be another name to designate the systematic execution of the project of the suppression of difference and the reduction of alterity to identity. For Baudrillard, however, fascism did not result from a society's desire to purge a heterogeneous element from its midst that it stubbornly refused to acknowledge. On the contrary, fascism was a product of a society adrift in an already hyperreal world that could not cope with the loss of its moorings to reality. He defines fascism as an "overdose of a powerful referential in a society which cannot terminate its mourning" (*Selected Writings*, 181), occasioned by the loss of the real which used to and presumably still could function as a guarantor of authenticity. Here we see power's precarious position with respect to simulation. Simulation is the enemy of power, and yet power enlists simulation to combat the destabilizing effects of simulation. Baudrillard cites Watergate as an example of the semblance of a political scandal staged by power to rejuvenate itself. Whether "Deep Throat" was a Republican or a Democrat is of no consequence, for, as Baudrillard says, in the hyperreal "the work of the Right is done very well, and spontaneously, by the Left on its own" (*Selected Writings*, 174). What power needs in order to perpetuate itself is to make it seem that such dialectical oppositions exist. In short, then, the ruse that power must exercise in the general economy of the hyperreal is to conceal the fact that the second order—the regional economy of power anchored firmly in the real—does not exist.

The idea that power stages minor transgressions specifically designed to allow power to reassert itself applies to the State in *Le Très-Haut*, and much of what Baudrillard says about power's relationship to simulation holds true as far as Blanchot's novel is concerned—except for one major difference: what is all-pervasive in *Le Très-Haut*, State power, becomes for Baudrillard a pathetic, ineffectual, reactionary apparatus whose main function is to convince its citizens that debates about what is right or wrong which are conducted in language that deals with brute facts and reality still matter. The culprit in *Le Très-Haut* is the all-encompassing power of the totalitarian state which has infiltrated every aspect of existence. Sorge learns in the course of keeping his diary that the State's power can be undermined. Nevertheless, the State remains supremely confident in its abilities to assimilate the dreams that flow from Sorge's pen. Sorge (and Blanchot) are primarily interested in contesting the legitimacy of claims issued by totalizing systems—be they political or philosophical—and, consequently, they do not underestimate or gloss over the formidable appropriative powers of these systems which are for them very real. Thus, the regional economy almost always has the upper hand, and the general economy can rise up only surreptitiously.

For his part, Baudrillard apparently no longer feels the need to write against totalizing forms of thought which have presumably been sufficiently discredited by other earlier thinkers such as Bataille and Blanchot. In his theorization of the hyperreal, Baudrillard appears to take Blanchot further that Blanchot himself would probably like by imagining a world that Sorge, Blanchot, and Bataille would never even have dreamed of, one in which simulacra and *ressemblance* are the order of the day and where the regional economy of power is *truly* regional, a caricature of its former self. Thus, Nietzsche's plea to overthrow Platonism, which is heeded by Lyotard, Deleuze, and Blanchot in their own ways, falls on deaf ears in Baudrillard's case, for as far as he is concerned, this has already come to pass. We can now see why Baudrillard and these philosophers of difference find themselves on opposite sides of the debate concerning how the advent of the postmodern condition ought to be interpreted in spite of so many similarities: what the philosophers of difference call for has, for him, already happened, and, furthermore, this development has led to a state of affairs that he bemoans. Whereas the philosophers of difference can still engage themselves in the subversion of totalizing systems through a Nietzschean affirmation of heterogeneity, Baudrillard no longer allows himself this attitude, which must appear to him as a luxury, and the bleak and pessimistic resignation that one often senses when reading Baudrillard is no doubt a consequence of the lack of a site to be contested, for how is resistance even possible in a hyperreal world where dialectic polarities which would designate opposing positions have no place?

If the association of Baudrillard and Blanchot appears as somewhat strained, the same cannot be said of Michel Foucault's relationship with Blanchot's writings. As evidence of his indebtedness to Blanchot that he has acknowledged publicly, two statements can be mentioned. Didier Eribon reports that once while reminiscing about the fifties with his friend Paul Veyne, Foucault confided: "A cette époque, je rêvais d'être Blanchot" (79).[3] And in an interview with Raymond Bellour, he stated (extravagantly?): "Il est vrai que c'est Blanchot qui a rendu possible tout discours sur la littérature" (113).[4] Foucault's affinities with Blanchot on the question of power's relationship to language serves as an interesting counterpoint to the position taken up by Baudrillard, and it is to these affinities that we shall now turn.

In *The Order of Things*, Foucault credits Nietzsche with ushering in the episteme of the twentieth century, for it was he who was the "first to connect the philosophical task with a radical reflection upon language" (305). No longer the medium in which things can be classified and known, the position it held under the reign of the classical episteme, language acquires its own density and becomes itself one more object of knowledge among others. Mallarmé, too, conducted his own meditation on language as if, suggests Foucault, in response to Nietzsche's questioning:

> For Nietzsche, it was not a matter of knowing what good and evil were in themselves, but of who was being designated, or rather *who was speaking* when one said *Agathos* to designate oneself and *Deilos* to designate others. For it is there, in the *holder* of discourse and, more profoundly still, in the *possessor* of the word, that language is gathered together in its entirety. To the Nietzschean question: 'Who is speaking?', Mallarmé replies—and constantly reverts to that reply—by saying that what is speaking is, in its solitude, in its fragile vibration, in its nothingness, the word itself—not the meaning of the word, but its enigmatic and precarious being. (305)

The work of both Foucault and Blanchot has been carried out within the parameters described here and represented by the respective attitudes of Nietzsche and Mallarmé toward language. In his analyses of the histories of institutions as functions of power/knowledge networks, the methodological stance suggested by Nietzsche's geneology of the will to power, Foucault approaches the question of "who is speaking" by concentrating on the speaking subject and by trying to expose the relations of force that subtend the claims of a given sector of society to have the right to speak on behalf of certain cultural values at the expense of the silencing of other sectors of society. Foucault's geneology tries to see behind the inaugural prejudice, the preemptive, self-validating gesture whereby the law of the Same not only delimits alterity by simultaneously circumscribing and marginalizing it but also sets itself up as the power capable of reappropriating alterity and bringing it back into the fold of the Same. Mallarmé took a different tack in his response to Nietzsche's question. Rather than emphasizing the enabling conditions of the speaking subject, his radical reflection on language led him to posit the disappearance of this subject, dismissed from the scene of writing by the anonymous being of language capable of speaking on its own. Blanchot's work, as we have seen, clearly takes place in the wake of Mallarmé's solution to the problem initially formulated by Nietzsche. Foucault can be aligned on this side of the problematic as well, albeit in a less obvious way since it is in his relatively less-studied essays on literature that he takes up the themes, inherited from Blanchot, of the unlocatable and unpresentable murmur at the origin of language and of language's impossible movement toward its own disappearance. In order to explore further the affinities between Foucault and Blanchot, we will reconsider briefly *Le Très-Haut*, the fictional work in which Blanchot deals most explicitly with the relationships of power and subversion to language, problems that are Foucault's stock in trade.

In his essay on Blanchot entitled "The Thought from Outside," Foucault describes in a section devoted to *Le Très-Haut* the retreat of the law, the temporary withdrawal of the State's power when the epidemic is at its most contagious, in the following way:

> The order of the law was never so sovereign than at this moment, when it envelops precisely what had tried to overturn it. Anyone who attempts to oppose the law in order to found a new order, to organize a second police force, to institute a new state, will only encounter the silent and infinitely accommodating welcome of the law. The law does not change: it subsided into the grave once and for all, and *each of its forms is only a metamorphosis of that never-ending death.* (*Foucault/Blanchot*, 38–39)

The excess negativity of the general economy of the epidemic, "that never-ending death," gives rise to various limited responses to it: it furnishes the State with a pretext to flex its muscles by "cleaning up" the infested quarters which just so happen to house the subversive movement, and at the same time it energizes the cause of the revolutionaries who seek to infiltrate and undermine the harried State's power by gaining control of the medical establishment. The epidemic itself is the truly subversive element, however, for neither side can lay total claim to it.

David Carroll has noted that Foucault's analyses aim to show that at the heart of order, whether epistemological or political, resides a secret, generally unacknowledged yet fundamental disorder or impropriety:

> The archeologist focuses on the systems of opposition, classification, and analogy that arise to cover over the dissipation of being, the void at the origin of language. He digs beneath the surface in order to discover the rules which make possible and regulate the different orders of words and things, the knowledge that is produced in spite of (or is it not, rather, because of?) the abyss at the heart of the "being of order." (*Paraesthetics*, 74)

Henri Sorge, the novel's main character and narrator, accomplishes (albeit unwittingly, given his vacillation) the work of Foucault's archeologist as it is presented here. From his perspective of convalescing writer, he is in a better position to see the disorder (the general economy of contagion) lurking beneath the apparently stable forms of order (the State and the subversive movement located in the regional economy). He maintains his residence in a quarantined section of the city and refuses to take sides, ultimately choosing instead to align himself with the epidemic and becoming, as it were, a kind of spokesman for the general economy.

Sorge's ambivalent stance with respect to both the State and the revolution manifests itself throughout the novel in his lively debates with his stepfather and Bouxx in which he criticizes their pretentions of harnessing the epidemic and of mobilizing it as an arm that could serve their respective interests. There is one particular situation, however, which shows us more clearly than all the others Sorge in the role of archeologist bent on exposing the disorder at the heart of order: his interpretation of the anecdote about the photo opportunity that his stepfather recounted to him. During a groundbreaking ceremony performed by government officials to commemorate the State's ability to construct a new building on the ashes of one that had been destroyed by the revolutionaries, the crowd of onlookers became unruly on account of an overzealous expression of their patriotic fervor and had to be dispersed by the police. Normally such ceremonies are held before the appreciative gaze of the people, but this time the State had to "faire le vide," thereby excluding one of two participants in this political spectacle, the public. According to Sorge, this is not so strange as one might think: "C'est bizarre, mais justement c'est là qu'apparaît la profondeur de la loi: il faut que chacun s'efface, il ne faut pas être là, en personne, mais en général, d'une manière invisible" (68–69).[5] Sorge understands the secret truth about power: that it rests on the precarious foundation of *personne*. The people, from which the State derives its power, cannot be identified with any particular political exigency. On the contrary, its essence resides in its "déclaration d'impuissance" (*CI* 54), which renders the State ultimately powerless in its attempts to have complete mastery over it. Instead of viewing the dispersal of the crowd merely as the assertive, self-defensive gesture of the State's erecting a protective cushion around itself, Sorge sees it as a telling indication that power and order are delicately poised, superimposed on the anonymous being of the collectivity, a condition that the State does not wish to acknowledge.

In the context of our discussion of *Le Très-Haut*, it is at the point where we compared the sovereignty of the people to that of the work of literature, the will to power's anguish of governing to the will to knowledge's anguish of reading, that we can see Blanchot coming closest to anticipating some of Foucault's most important insights regarding power. Because it lends itself to reductive strategies of reading predicated on representational thinking—even as it exceeds the boundaries set up by such reading, every work is destined to become a book. Similarly, the sovereignty of the people is bound to be compromised by institutional powers. As Foucault has demonstrated, power and knowledge join forces in the development of disciplines and technologies of control whose object is to transform a faceless mass into discrete, classifiable, manageable entities. In *Discipline and Punish*, Foucault studies how power extends its effects and how it masks itself while doing so. Power's greatest ruse is its ability to cast the increasing subjection of the individual in terms of enlightened humanitarian progress. According to the official version promulgated by the government in *Le Très-Haut*, the State derives its power from a symbiotic relationship with its citizens, who enjoy a personal, one-on-one relationship with representatives of the law. Behind the State's avowed goal of providing each citizen with a personal delegate to the State—political representation carried to the extreme—lurks an ulterior motive: the creation of a panoptical society in which each member of society is under constant surveillance. Sorge's stepfather is surprisingly frank in characterizing the duplicitous nature of the motives that fuel the State's aspirations to achieve a society of pure visibility: "derrière chaque travailleur, il y a un délégué qui incarne en chair et en os la raison de son travail. En principe, le délégué est là pour apporter une aide technique et morale, mais aussi, ma foi, pour contrôler les activités" (127).[6]

On the surface, the will to power of the modern state presents itself as benevolent. Foucault looks beneath this seemingly tranquil surface to examine the exclusions accomplished by power and the hidden agendas that motivate these exclusions. Like Blanchot, he posits two economies of power, one regional—the disciplines (bodies of knowledge) that are produced by essentially negative, subjecting applications of power—the other general—the anonymous, ubiquitous negativity that is not a thing-in-itself and which no one can either possess or resist. The will to knowledge is a restricted instance of the powerless power of the general economy and constitutes an insatiable drive toward totalization. This variety of power abhors a vacuum and irresistibly rushes to fill it in. Although Foucault and Blanchot are in agreement concerning these two economies of power, however, there is a fundamental difference: whereas Foucault spends most of his time chronicling power's successes in the regional economy, its uncanny ability to preserve itself by dissimulating the impropriety of its origin, Blanchot emphasizes "what happens" when the regional economy of power retreats and is eclipsed by the general economy of worklessness, especially as this occurs in the neighborhood of a work of literature.

Like Foucault, Jacques Derrida sets out to expose the ruses that power employs in order to dissimulate its origins. The places where he locates this power and analyzes its effects are quite different, however, from those frequented by Foucault. Rather than looking for hidden effects of power by excavating the layers of assumptions and practices on which the human sciences and the social institutions created by them are founded, Derrida digs through the semantic and structural layers of the major texts of Western philosophy from Plato to Heidegger in an effort to show how philosophy's quest for absolute truth is a self-deluding one on account of its unwillingness to take into account its own textual constitution. In his theorization of a general economy of archi-writing which both renders possible the regional economy of logocentric writing and undermines its pretentions to totalization, Derrida enlists several important insights previously developed by Blanchot in the 1940s and 1950s. To find evidence of Derrida's association with Blanchot, one need look no further than his essays on Blanchot that have been gathered together and published under the title *Parages*. Two of these essays, "LIVING ON. Border Lines" and "La Loi du genre" first appeared in American publications and were instrumental in introducing Blanchot to a new audience. Now, though, I would like to reverse this trend: instead of viewing Derrida as an important mediator of Blanchot's work, we might ask ourselves what questions were taken up by Derridean deconstruction thanks to the mediating influence of Blanchot's texts on his work.

One of the most persistent themes that occurs throughout Derrida's work is the derivative status that the logocentric tradition accords writing with respect to speech. He finds the earliest disparaging remarks about writing in Plato, and it may very well be that we can trace his interest in this problem to an essay on René Char entitled "La Bête de Lascaux" originally published by Blanchot in the *Nouvelle Revue Française* in 1953. Summarizing the mistrust of the written word expressed by Socrates in the *Phaedrus*, Blanchot states: "Socrate propose donc que, de cette parole, l'on s'écarte le plus possible, comme d'une dangereuse maladie, et que l'on s'en tienne au vrai langage, qui est le langage parlé, où la parole est sûre de trouver dans la présence de celui qui l'exprime une garantie vivante" (12).[7] Socrates does, however, make allowances for a certain type of writing, one that is "capable tout au plus de commémorer les oeuvres ou les événements du savoir, sans avoir nulle part au travail de leur découverte" (17–18).[8] Derrida's entire enterprise can be seen as an attempt to think through the reasons that account for philosophy's ambivalent attitude toward writing, its declaration of independence from writing that can be accomplished only through writing, a double gesture which testifies to philosophy's irreducible intrication with and dependence on writing. And to understand the sense of this double gesture, why the formerly debased term in the conceptual speech/writing opposition is called upon by the primary term to authenticate the latter's status as primary, Derrida devises a strategy of reading that involves a double gesture of its own, that of reversal and displacement. He describes the first moment of his "double science" in the following way:

> On the one hand, we must traverse a phase of *overturning*. To do justice to this necessity is to recognize that in a classical philosophical opposition we are not dealing with the peaceful coexistence of a *vis-à-vis*, but rather with a violent hierarchy. One of the two terms governs the other (axiologically, logically, etc.), or has the upper hand. To deconstruct the opposition, first of all, is to overturn the hierarchy at a given moment. To overlook this phase of overturning is to forget the conflictual and subordinating structure of opposition. (*Positions*, 41)

The purpose of this reversal is not to rehabilitate the debased term by endowing it with a new, long-overdue prestige that it somehow deserves, for to do so would leave intact the same structure of hierarchical ordering. A critical rethinking of the very notion of hierarchy is what is at stake in the second part of the operation, which concerns the reinscription or displacement of the formerly derivative term: "By means of this double . . . writing, we must also mark the interval between inversion, which brings low what was high, and the irruptive emergence of a new 'concept,' a concept that can no longer be, and never could be, included in the previous regime" (*Positions*, 42). The new "concepts" produced by the phase of reinscription, which Derrida variously calls "undecidables" and "infrastructures," do not belong, properly speaking, to the vocabulary of logocentric philosophy and are unthinkable for this tradition. They are what makes possible systematization predicated on representational-calculative thinking and at the same time not being self-identical identities, they exceed the attempts of such thinking to assign them a specific place within the hierarchical scheme which they ground. Thus, as Rodolphe Gasché notes, a relationship of exorbitant incommensurability characterizes the shift from the first operation of the double science to the second: "Whereas the first gesture plays entirely within the closure of metaphysics, the second attempts a breakthrough toward a certain outside of philosophy" (173).

So as to be able to draw a clear parallel between Derrida's double science and Blanchot's account of the approach to/of the space of literature, it is not inappropriate to consider rapidly how the deconstruction of a conceptual dyad unfolds. Let us take as an example the following related sets of oppositions: philosophy/literature, *logos/mythos*, proper/figural, and concept/metaphor. The first terms of the couples that form this series are not mere dialectical opposites of the second terms; they are also superior in quality to them. Thus, serious philosophy is favored over frivolous literature as a more reliable discipline to be mobilized in the quest for truth thanks to its ability to marshal thought. Similarly, a certain type of language is befitting to philosophy, carefully formed concepts are the best vehicles for conveying truth, and metaphors and other tropes normally confined to literature are permissable as long as the deliberate act of misnaming that the use of such figures implies is subordinated to truth and provided that the resulting loss of meaning is only temporary, certain to be recuperated later on. The first stage of the deconstruction, the reversal (one reminiscent of Nietzsche's—concepts as worn-out metaphors), grants priority to metaphorical literary language over the purported objective conceptual language of philosophy. The second operation, the radical displacement, causes figural language to return in its reinscribed form as a general economy of metaphoricity that allows for an opposition such as that between metaphor and concept to appear in the regional economy of representational thinking even as it escapes determination at the hands of the system it renders possible. The notions of "concept" and its inferior opposite "metaphor" are aftereffects, ways in which metaphoricity can manifest itself. Gasché explains how this infrastructure both enables and disables concepts' claims to universality:

> Although the concept in its universality is irreducible to metaphor, figure, or trope, its status *as* concept (its intelligibility and universality) hinges on its possibility of lending itself to metaphorization. General metaphoricity . . . is the name for that possibility that inaugurates the concept's universality. At the same time it limits this universality by virtue of its generality, a generality that cannot be subsumed under universality inasmuch as the latter has grown on its soil. (314)

Infrastructures such as general metaphoricity, the supplement, and the pharmakon are produced by the general economy which serves as a kind of ground for the regional economy inasmuch as it renders this latter economy possible. It would be more correct, however, to think of this ground in terms of a "fond sans fond anonyme." This simulacrum of a concept, unthinkable within the bounds of traditional metaphysics of presence, designates a ground in that it allows for the conceptual oppositions that organize the discourse of this metaphysics, and yet it is groundless in the sense that the very notion of "ground" is a product of differentiation and belongs exclusively to the regional economy. By definition, a ground must be different from that which it grounds. Philosophy, however, justifies itself on grounds that it determines itself: it produces truth in the name of truth.

This self-constituting, self-validating gesture of self-reflection is possible only by assuming an attitude of partial blindness, the refusal to acknowledge the trace of an irreducible alterity within the closure that philosphy presupposes at its beginning and foresees as its *telos*. The closure of totalization is not, however, the be-all and end-all of philosophy; there is something even more fundamental. The dream of philosophy, the apotheosis of the coming into being of Truth, depends on the harmonious collaboration of self-present, self-identical beings and language, but such integral entities of the order of the Same can only be posited after the fact of a preliminary detour by way of the Other. To assert its claim to primacy, the Same must appeal to the Other (for example, speech appeals to writing, melody to harmony, concepts to metaphors) in order to constitute itself (happily) as what the Other is not. This uneasy alliance that identity forms with alterity belies a condition of initial doubling within identity, without which identity could not proclaim its primacy in the first place. The undecidable infrastructures of the general economy account both for this originary duplicity and for the dissimulating, reductive metamorphosis of this duplicity into unicity in the regional economy:

> As all the infrastructures demonstrate, such a whole is only an aftereffect, a necessary illusion produced by the play of the undecidables. To explain duplicity and doubling presupposes an originary doubling, which would not be preceded by any unity, and which thus annuls the traditional restriction of doubling to a matter of accidentality and secondariness. . . . Indeed, if the simple could not be doubled, the simple would not be what it is. As a consequence of its identity, the simple must inscribe the possibility of being divided within itself; in order to be simple, the simple must already be double. (Gasché 225–26)

In his discussions of this fissure or lack at the hidden center of a plenitude, Derrida resumes Blanchot's meditations on the "dédoublement initial" and *ressemblance*. Derrida's "double science" of reading involving reversal and reinscription and his discovery of a heterogeneous economy of difference, of which the economy predicated on identity and power is merely a restricted instance, also have their antecedents in Blanchot. We might even go so far as to say that in his work, Derrida has in a sense codified the basic moves of reversal and reinscription already present in Blanchot in a less explicit, less systematic way on account of his responses to the repeated demands that he clarify and justify his "method," something never asked of the more elusive, less public Blanchot. Two conceptual dyads that we saw Blanchot "deconstruct" (*avant la lettre*) are the opposition between object and image and that between everyday language and poetry. In both cases, Blanchot begins by recognizing the inequality of the terms: images are secondary with respect to objects, copies of an original, and poetry is derivative of everyday language, a flowery, diverting deformation of "normal" language. He then reverses the received ordering of these terms and reinscribes them to produce the respective infrastructures of *ressemblance* and the murmur, both of which are produced by the groundless ground of the general economy of the neuter, "l'ouverture opaque et vide sur ce qui est quand il n'y a plus de monde, quand il n'y a pas encore de monde" (*EL* 28).[9]

The same logic of supplementarity is also in effect in Blanchot's deconstruction of the relationship that exists between law and transgression. The proverbial expression "laws are made to be broken" reflects the priority that common sense grants to the law: in order for there to be transgression, there first has to be something to transgress. Just as Derrida makes a distinction between good writing and bad writing, as does Blanchot between good and bad versions of the imaginary (in both cases "bad" referring to infrastructures of the general economy upon which logocentrism depends but which it cannot acknowledge), we may distinguish between two versions of transgression. According to the good version, transgressions are sanctioned by and performed in accordance with the law of the regional economy. They represent a temporary suspension of the law, a calculated risk the law is willing to take, after which power returns in all its mastery, rejuvinated by the minor transgressions enacted on its behalf. The reversal and reinscription of this schema produces the bad version, which is encapsulated in the following statement: "il n'y a pas loi, interdit, puis transgression, mais transgression sans interdit qui finit par se figer en Loi, en Principe du Sens" (*ED* 121).[10] In this case, a general state of transgression precedes and makes possible the regional economy of power (where, as we just noted, minor transgressions occur), which, in turn, fails to arrest the differential play at its origin. To be able to do so would result in the regional economy's totalizing assimilation of the general economy, but the transformation of assimilation into dissimulation, the attempt of the regional economy to cover up or to avoid acknowledging the play of difference, marks the failure of totalization.

The notions of transgression and subversion occupy a prominent place in Blanchot's accounts, both theoretical and narrative, of the approach to the space of literature by writing and reading. The adventures of the figures employed by Blanchot to portray this approach—the journal writer, Orpheus, Jesus, and Oedipus in his critical texts; Sorge and the nameless narrator of *L'Attente l'oubli* in his fiction—all tell of the undoing of previously well-conceived plans. They commence their undertakings by overlooking the fact that negativity has a dual status: it lends itself to partial domestication while at the same time exceeding exorbitantly attempts to gain complete mastery over it. This error enables them to begin in the first place, and it also implicates them in the committing of a transgression during the course of which they discover—too late—that their fundamental rapport with their work is one predicated on the primary exigencies of impossibility and failure. They are forced to confront the marginality of the very notion of accomplishment as their dynamic projects are unexpectedly transformed into the patient waiting for a moment that never comes to pass, a transformation that occurs on account of the double bind in which they are caught but that they cannot recognize as such: that of pitting writing against itself as if the language of the regional economy, the univocal, transparent purveyor of meaning that establishes a relationship of adequation between mind and object, could silence once and for all the murmur of differential play thanks to which it exists at all. The incommensurable difference between these two levels of language explains why Orpheus's initial decision to view his music solely as a weapon or Sorge's original intention to write solely on behalf of the State are so contaminated by alterity as to be doomed from the start.

Whereas Foucault concentrates on the successful ruses devised by power to dissimulate its origins that are unthinkable by it, Derrida delights in exposing the heretofore effective textual ruses employed by philosophy to exclude what is unthinkable for it. Blanchot can be seen as an important precursor whose meditations also take place within the problematization of the unavowed exclusion of the Other by the Same. What distinguishes Blanchot from both Foucault and Derrida is a difference more of degree or emphasis than of essence. As the creator of a hybrid oeuvre, which responds to the exigencies of criticism and creation, and like the figures of writers that he elaborates in specific works, which reproduce individually the hybridity characteristic of his oeuvre taken in its entirety, Blanchot establishes residence (that is, if one can equate wandering and residing) in the neutral space outside philosophy much more readily than can Foucault or Derrida. This is especially true in narrative and fragmentary works but somewhat less so in a "livre d'éclaircissements" such as *L'Espace littéraire*, whose goals are of a more expository nature. Given the critical perspectives within which Foucault and Derrida work, it is inevitable that they remain constrained, more closely tied to the disciplines and the philosophical tradition that they respectively excavate and deconstruct. Blanchot's orientation, on the other hand, leads him more directly to the exploration of what transpires in subjectivity's encounter with alterity than to considerations about how alterity itself is denied and concealed by social practices or intellectual traditions.

A constellation of words just used, "ruse," "tied to," and "exploration" summons up the image of one final mythical figure adapted by Blanchot in a critical text that I would like to evoke here. I am thinking of Ulysses, who appears in the opening section of *Le Livre à venir* entitled "Le Chant des Sirènes." In contrast to his admiring portrayal of Orpheus, his description of Ulysses' clever solution to the problem of how to listen to the Sirens' music without being engulfed by it is less than flattering; he comes across as more underhanded than noble. In the following characterization of Ulysses' victory over the Sirens, Blanchot's disapproval of his attitude borders on contempt:

Il est vrai, Ulysse les a vaincues, mais de quelle manière? Ulysse, l'entêtement et la prudence d'Ulysse, sa perfidie qui l'a conduit à jouir du spectacle
des Sirènes, sans risques et sans en accepter les conséquences, cette lâche,
médiocre et tranquille jouissance, mesurée, comme il convient à un Grec de
la décadence qui ne mérita jamais d'être le héros de *L'Iliade*. (*LV* 11)[11]

Ulysses' treachery consists in his decision to stop up the ears of his crew
members with wax, so that they would hear nothing, and in his ordering
them to lash him to the mainmast, so that he could listen to the Sirens
from a safe distance. His ruse allows him to listen to the music from the
point of view of mastery, thereby chalking up yet one more exploit, while
depriving his men, absorbed in the task of their rowing, of this pleasure.
His strategy procures him a cheap thrill: it gives him a taste of the absolute, an experience that he can appropriate personally, after which he can
proceed on his way.

This version of Ulysses, however, tells only half the story, for he succumbs unwittingly to the "loi secrète du récit" in a manner that parallels
the transgressions suffered by Orpheus and by Sorge and other journal
writers who fall prey to its secret law. The apparent law of the epic poem
(and, by extension, of the novel, its successor) holds that the events to be
recounted, whether produced by the imagination or drawn from reality,
precede their being cast into narrative form. In other words, Ulysses had
to complete his voyage before Homer could commit it to paper. The subversive, secret law of the *récit* emerges as the result of the double gesture
of reversal and reinscription: the transcription of the event has precedence
over events as in-themselves and is reinscribed as *récit*, whose textual
economy exceeds while rendering possible that of the epic/novel. (The
incommensurable relationship that exists between the *récit* and the novel
is a corollary of that which exists between the work and the book.) In
connection with Orpheus, we said that every song tells of an Orphic encounter, even those sung on the way to that encounter. Like Orpheus,
Ulysses loses what he seizes in his encounter with the Sirens (although for
different, less honorable reasons), and we could say that every epic/novel
tells of such an encounter, even the episodes recounted on the way there.
Every novel contains secretly invaginated within it a *récit*, "une poche
interne plus grande que le tout" (*Parages*, 256).[12] Ulysses' meeting with
the Sirens does not, therefore, constitute a self-same, delimitable event;
on the contrary, it has always already been taking place before it can be
represented *as if* it were merely an allegory of his power and mastery, and
the *récit* is an "infragenre" (to coin a new term) that accounts for this
paradoxical mode of existence of a narrative work.[13]

A limited parallel can be drawn between the figure of Ulysses, on the
one hand, and Lyotard, Deleuze, Foucault, and Derrida, on the other,
which we can use to illuminate the difference of orientation that distin-

guishes their work from that of Blanchot. Like Ulysses, they are "tied to the masts," so to speak, of the traditions that they criticize. Their resemblance to Ulysses ends here, however, for unlike him, they are not the instigators of a ruse; such ruses are precisely their point of departure from which they work backward in order to expose the disorder of alterity on which the order of the Same depends. Nor does their legacy consist in the stopping up of the ears of their readers. Speaking critically of the philosophical tradition comprised of philosophers who deal exclusively in the currency of concepts, old, worn-out, petrified metaphors, Nietzsche writes:

> They . . . thought that the senses might lure them away from their own world, from the cold realm of "ideas," to some dangerous southern island where they feared that their philosopher's virtues might melt away like snow in the sun. Having "wax in one's ears" was then almost a condition of philosophizing; a real philosopher no longer listened to life insofar as life is music; he *denied* the music of life—it is an ancient philosopher's superstition that all music is sirens' music. (*The Gay Science*, 332)

Blanchot, Lyotard, Deleuze, Foucault, and Derrida are all dedicated to the proposition that the wax in our ears be removed. Each in his own way exhorts us to listen to the "music of life," the irreducible, unarrestable murmur that secretly resides at the heart of all discourses as both their enabling condition and their ultimate impossibility. Taken collectively, their work constitutes a relentless effort to attune our hearing to the affirmation contained in this strange, unworldly music, to give it its due, "comme si peut-être jaillissait là la source de toute authenticité" (*EL* 337).[14]

NOTES

INTRODUCTION

1. *L'Entretien infini* ought to be distinguished, however, from the two preceding collections of essays on account of its stylistic variety. This book includes not only essays but also subversive parodies of Platonic dialogues and fragmentary pieces which prefigure the books to come that will be composed entirely of fragments. As for *L'Amitié*, like *L'Entretien infini* it does contain some fragmentary pieces, but as a fairly heterogeneous collection of essays written between 1950 and 1970, it resembles *Faux Pas* and *La Part du feu* more closely than it does *L'Espace littéraire* or *Le Livre à venir*.

2. Some noteworthy exceptions to the statement that Blanchot's narrative works are less widely read are the following studies: Evelyne Londyn's *Maurice Blanchot Romancier* (Paris: Nizet, 1976); Jacques Derrida's extended commentaries of *L'Arrêt de mort*, originally published as "LIVING ON. Border Lines" in *Deconstruction and Criticism* (New York: Seabury Press, 1979); and of *La Folie du jour* entitled "La loi du genre," which appeared first in *Glyph* 7 (1980): 202–29—these pieces have since been gathered together with others Derrida has written on Blanchot in *Parages* (Paris: Éditions Galilée, 1986)—and more recently Steven Shaviro's discussions of *L'Arrêt de mort* and *Au moment voulu* in *Passion and Excess: Blanchot, Bataille and Literary Theory* (Tallahassee: Florida State University Press, 1990).

3. "Criticism is no longer a judgment exterior to the work which puts the work's qualities on display and makes retrospective pronouncements as to the work's value. It has become inseparable from the work's intimacy; it belongs to the movement by means of which the work comes to itself, searches for itself, and is the experience of its own possibility."

4. "just as Kant's critical reason is the examination of the conditions that make scientific experimentation possible, criticism is implicated in the search for that which makes the experience of literature possible."

5. "The word 'search' ought not to be understood in its intellectual sense but rather as action taken at the heart of and with an eye toward the space of creation."

6. "strange dialogue . . . between critical and 'creative' speech."

7. *Noli me legere* is the injunction uttered by the work to its potential readers, including its author, and it signifies the work's irreducibility to acts of interpretation predicated on power and mastery. This law will receive extensive treatment in chapter 4.

8. "It would be an amazing thing for a critic to become a poet, and it is impossible for a poet not to contain a critic."

CHAPTER ONE
LITERATURE AND TRANSGRESSION

1. "As early as the end of 1940, he meets Maurice Blanchot, with whom ties of admiration and agreement are quickly established."

2. "Death, Finitude, Determination, Negativity are closely related in a rational philosophy of becoming, where the affirmation and destruction of the particular unceasingly form the ground of a universal which comes to fruition in the movement itself."

3. For an in-depth account of the reception of Hegel in France, see Michael S. Roth's *Knowing and History: Appropriations of Hegel in Twentieth-Century France* (Ithaca: Cornell University Press, 1988).

4. "power to exercise totally, that is, *transform into action* all his negativity" (*IC* 205).

5. "If action ('doing') is—as Hegel says—negativity, the question then becomes one of knowing if the negativity of someone who has 'nothing more to do' disappears or subsists in a state of 'unemployable negativity': personally, I can settle this question in one way only, being myself exactly this 'unemployable negativity' (I could not define myself any more precisely)."

6. "Consciousness is the condition of the perfectly complete death. I die to the extent that I have consciousness of dying: at the same time, death deprives me of this consciousness."

7. "a breaking of the rule permitted by the rule"

8. "The interdiction is there to be violated"

9. "the interdiction is no less an invitation that it is, at the same time, an obstacle."

10. "an aspiration to destruction explodes during the festival, but a conservative wisdom orders and limits it."

11. "Through the sacrifice, the faithful one has become the creditor and waits for the powers that he reveres to settle the debt that they have incurred at his expense by answering his prayers."

12. "the impossibility of death in its most naked possibility (the knife meant to cut the victim's throat and which, with the same movement, would cut off the head of the 'executioner')" (*UC* 14).

13. I am greatly indebted throughout to Joseph Libertson's outstanding study *Proximity: Levinas, Blanchot, Bataille and Communication* (The Hague: Martinus Nijhoff, 1982) and, more precisely here, to his discussion of transgression which appears in the second chapter of his book.

14. "*The interdiction marks the point at which power ceases.* Transgression is not an act of which the force and the mastery of certain men, under certain conditions, would still be capable. Transgression designates what is radically out of reach: assailment of the inaccessible, a surpassing of what cannot be surpassed. It opens to man when power ceases to be man's ultimate dimension" (*IC* 453, note 3).

15. "The 'I' will never arrive at it, nor will the individual, this particle of dust that I am, nor even the self of all of us that is supposed to represent absolute self-consciousness. Only the ignorance that the I-who-dies would incarnate by acceding to the space where in dying it never dies in the first person as an 'I' will reach it" (*IC* 209–10).

16. "There is no clear consciousness of what the festival is *at the time* (at the very instant that its energies are unleashed), and the festival is distinctly situated in consciousness only to the extent that it is integrated in the duration of the community."

17. "The work is never that in anticipation of which one is able to write (in anticipation of which one would relate to writing as to the exercise of some power" (*SL* 26).

18. "The book, the written thing, enters the world and carries out its work of transformation and negation" (*GO* 34).

19. "the stubbornness of what remains when everything vanishes and the dumbfoundedness of what appears when nothing exists" (*GO* 47).

20. ". . . what never happens to me, so that never do I die, but 'they die,' people always die other than themselves, at the level of the neutrality and the impersonality of an eternal They" (*SL* 241).

21. "The task of culture has always been to restore a kind of purity to death, to make it authentic, personal, proper—but also to make it possible" (*IC* 180).

CHAPTER TWO
LANGUAGE, HISTORY, AND THEIR DESTINIES
OF INCOMPLETION

1. "The word has meaning only if it rids us of the object it names: it must spare us its presence or 'concrete reminder.' In authentic language, speech has not only a representative but also a destructive function. It brings about disappearances; it renders the object absent and annihilates it."

2. "as if words, far from leading us away from things, were supposed to be carbon copies of them: in this case, language is carried away by its sensuality, and the word dreams of being wed to the object whose weight, color, and heavy, dormant appearance it possesses."

3. "Not only are the figures abbreviated, oblique, and diffuse, but they follow one another according to a rhythm rapid enough to ensure that none of them provides the reality it circumscribes with the time to exist or to become present to us through its intermediary."

4. "an absence of words and an absence of things, a simultaneous void, nothing supported by nothing."

5. "a two-faced monster, the reality of its material presence and the ideal absence of its meaning" (*GO* 59).

6. "the relentless pursuit by means of which words, thanks to their abstract value, destroy the materiality of things, then, thanks to their power of sensorial evocation, destroy this abstract value, and finally, through their mobility and their ability to keep things unresolved, attempt to vanish into thin air and to extinguish each other behind the reciprocity of their fires."

7. "certain words betray a hypertrophy of matter and language at the expense of ideas."

8. "One is that Terror freely admits that an idea is worth more than a word and that mind is superior to matter: between these first and second terms there is no less a difference of dignity than of nature. Such is its article of faith or, if you prefer, its prejudice. The second maintains that language is essentially dangerous for thought: always ready to oppress it, if one is not careful. The simplest definition that one can give of a Terrorist is that he is a misologist."

9. "the verbal material disappears with respect to ideas or facts and promptly lets itself be forgotten."

10. "words do not allow themselves to be used up but remain inseperable from the state of mind they evoke."

11. "it is a question of isolating momentarily for the sake of analysis elements which do not exist in a state of isolation outside the analysis and which can, therefore, justifiably be viewed as distinct only within the limits of the analysis."

12. "In other words, in poetry, only the tension that unites these terms exists, and these terms are distinct in appearance only and from a posterior point of view, from the point of view of language which is itself an outgrowth of poetry."

13. "by talent or by creative savoir faire is content to change 'crude or immediate' language into essential language" (*SL* 48).

14. "relations which precede any objective and technical accomplishment"

15. "According to the common analysis, the image comes after the object. It is the object's continuation. We see, then we imagine. After the object comes the image. 'After' seems to indicate subordination . . . But perhaps the common analysis is mistaken" (*SL* 34).

16. "the initial division that then permits the thing to be figured" (*IC* 30).

17. "here the distance is at the heart of the thing" (*SL* 255).

18. "By analogy, we might also recall that a tool, when damaged, becomes its *image* . . . In this case the tool, no longer disappearing into its use, *appears*. This appearance of the object is that of resemblance and reflection: the object's double, if you will. The category of art is linked to this possibility for objects to 'appear,' to surrender, that is, to the pure and simple resemblance behind which there is nothing—but being" (*SL* 258–59).

19. "what reveals itself does not give itself up to sight, just as it does not take refuge in simple invisibility" (*IC* 29).

20. "Something that one can sense when one thinks that even if there were nothing, the fact that 'there is' is undeniable. Not that there is this or that in particular, but the very scene of being is opened: there is."

21. "what is given us by a contact at a distance" (*SL* 32).

22. "What is there, with the absolute calm of something that has found its place, does not, however, succeed in being convincingly here. Death suspends the relation to place, even though the deceased rests heavily in his spot as if upon the only basis left him. To be precise, this basis lacks, the place is missing, the corpse is not in its place. Where is it? It is not here, and yet it is not anywhere else. Nowhere? But then nowhere is here. The cadaverous presence establishes a relation between here and nowhere" (*SL* 256).

23. "Yes, it is he, the dear living person, but all the same it is more than he. He is more beautiful, more imposing; he is already monumental and so absolutely himself that it is as if he were *doubled* by himself, joined to his solemn impersonality by resemblance and by the image. This magnified being, imposing and proud, which impresses the living as *the appearance of the original never perceived until now* [my italics] . . . may well bring to mind the great images of classical art" (*SL* 257–58).

24. "the possibility of a world behind the world, of a regression, an indefinite subsistence, undetermined and indifferent, about which we only know that human reality, upon finishing, reconstitutes its presence and its proximity" (*SL* 257).

25. "In the tranquility of ordinary life, dissimulation is hidden. In action, true action—the action which is history's laborious unfolding—concealment tends to become negation" (*SL* 253).

26. "the formless weight of being, present in absence" (*SL* 258)

27. "Reality is not anterior to the 'unreal' and is not richer than its copy; one should say that on the contrary, the unreal is first and that reality is formed upon it."

28. "We have spoken of two versions of the imaginary: the image can certainly help us to grasp the thing ideally, and in this perspective it is the life-giving negation of the thing; but at the level to which its particular weight drags us, it also threatens constantly to relegate us, not to the absent thing, but to its absence as presence, to the neutral double of the object in which all belonging to the world is dissipated. This duplicity, we must stress, is not such as to be mastered by the discernment of an either-or in that it could authorize a choice and lift from the choice the ambiguity that makes choosing possible" (*SL* 262–63).

29. "To write is to coordinate the elements of language in a state of fascination; it is to remain in contact, through language, in language, with the absolute milieu where the thing turns back into an image, where the image, instead of alluding to some particular figure, becomes the allusion to the figureless, and instead of a form drawn upon absence, becomes the formless presence of this absence, the opaque, empty opening onto that which is when there is no longer any world, when there is no world yet" (*SL* 33).

30. "To live an event as an image is not to see an image of this event, nor is it to attribute to the event the gratuitous character of the imaginary . . . The occurrence commands us, as the image would command us. That is, it releases us, from it and from ourselves. It keeps us outside; it makes of this outside a presence where 'I' doesn't recognize 'itself'" (*SL* 262).

31. "the life-giving negation, the ideal operation by which man, capable of negating nature, raises it to a higher meaning, either to know it or to enjoy it admiringly" (*SL* 260).

32. "The central point of the work is the work as origin, the point that cannot be reached, yet the only one which is worth reaching" (*SL* 54).

33. "an intimate relationship with the initial murmur. He must pay this price so as to be able to impose silence on it, to hear it in this silence, and then to express it, after having transformed it."

34. "It is necessary to impose silence on it . . . For an instant, it must forget itself so that by means of a triple metamorphosis, it can come into existence as a true utterance: that of The Book, as Mallarmé would say."

35. "no longer that which speaks, but that which is, language having become the workless depth of being, the milieu where the name becomes being but where it neither signifies nor reveals."

36. "to utter everything and reduce everything to silence, even silence itself"

37. "At all levels of language there is a relationship of contestation and restlessness from which it cannot free itself. As soon as something is said, something else needs to be said. Then, once again, something different still needs to be said so as to make up for the tendency of everything that is said to become definitive,

to slip into the imperturbable world of things. There is no repose, either at the level of a sentence or on the scale of a work."

38. "the language of literature is a search for this moment that precedes literature" (*GO* 46).

39. "the fact remains that what 'is' has, in effect, disappeared: something was there that is there no longer. How can I find it again, how can I, in my speech, recapture this prior presence that I must exclude in order to speak, in order to speak it?" (*IC* 36).

40. "Language strives for self-fulfillment. It lays claim to a veritable absolute in the most complete manner, and not only for itself in its totality but for each of its parts, demanding to be entirely words, entirely signification, entirely words and signification, in a selfsame and constant affirmation that cannot bear the thought that the parts which clash come together in harmonious accord, nor that discord disrupts this accord, nor that this accord is the harmony of a conflict."

41. "Ponge's descriptions begin at that hypothetical moment after the world has been achieved, history completed, nature almost made human, when speech advances to meet the thing and the thing learns to speak" (*GO* 53).

42. "a kind of relation with the earth, a certain sense of fusion, a relationship of the totality with death."

43. "it seems that he chose a rapid means to realize symbolically our common desire to exist at last in the manner of the in-itself. What fascinates him as far as the thing is concerned is its mode of existence, its total adhesion to itself, its repose. No more anxious flight, anger, or anguish: the unfeeling imperturbability of the pebble. I have observed elsewhere that the desire of each of us is to exist *consciously* in the mode of being of the thing. To be entirely consciousness and stone at the same time."

44. "for lack of a real fusion of consciousness and the thing, Ponge makes us oscillate from one to the other at a very great speed, hoping to achieve the fusion at the highest limit of this speed. But that is not possible."

45. "The cruelty of language is a consequence of the fact that it unceasingly evokes its death without ever being able to die."

CHAPTER THREE
BLANCHOT'S SUICIDAL ARTIST:
WRITING AND THE (IM)POSSIBILITY OF DEATH

1. "The best of what I have written is based on this capacity to die content" (*SL* 91).

2. "one must be capable of satisfaction in death" (*SL* 91).

3. "To die well means to die with propriety . . . and this good death shows more consideration for the world than regard for the depth of the abyss" (*SL* 100).

4. "will have been conscious of disappearing and not consciousness disappearing; he will have entirely annexed to his consciousness its own disappearance; he will be, thus, a realized totality, the realization of the whole, the absolute" (*SL* 99).

5. "An act in which one hopes against hope (without hope) to unify the duplicity of death and to bring together in one, single occurrence by a decision of impatience the eternal repetitions of that which, dying, does not die. Then the temptation to name, that is, to personalize, by attributing it to oneself, the anonymous, that which is spoken only in the third person and in the neuter. Or again the power to enlarge, as if in proportion to it, in localizing and dating it, the infinitely small and ever evasive dimension of death" (*SNB* 97–98).

6. The distinction between the book and the work will be explored more fully in the following chapter.

7. "Even when, with an ideal and heroic resolve, I decide to meet death, isn't it death which possesses me, dispossesses me, hands me over to that which cannot be possessed?" (*SL* 98)

8. For more on the circular exigency, see my discussion of the myth of Orpheus in the following chapter.

9. "The shortcut does not allow one to arrive someplace more directly (more quickly), but rather to lose the way that ought to lead there" (*WD* 113).

10. "a guardrail against the danger of writing."

11. "the writer increasingly feels the need to maintain a relation to himself. His feeling is one of extreme repugnance at losing his grasp upon himself in the interests of that neutral force, formless and bereft of any destiny, which is behind everything that gets written" (*SL* 28).

12. "Here, whoever speaks retains his name and speaks in this name, and the dates he notes down belong in a shared time where what happens really happens" (*SL* 29).

13. "Kafka wrote everything that mattered to him: events in his personal life, meditations upon these events, descriptions of persons and places, descriptions of his dreams, narratives begun, interrupted, begun again. His is thus not only a 'Journal' as we understand this genre today, but the very movement of the experience of writing, very close to its beginning and in the essential sense which Kafka was led to give to this term. It is from this perspective that his diaries must be read and explored" (*SL* 57).

14. The same critical posture is expressed in *L'Amitié*: "Je reprends l'idée d'un récit qui va de livre en livre, où celui qui écrit se raconte afin de se chercher, puis de chercher le mouvement de la recherche, c'est-à-dire comment il est possible de raconter, donc d'écrire" (174). ["I come back to the idea of a narrative that continues from book to book, in which the person writing tells his own story first in order to discover himself, then to look for the movement of this discovery, that is, how it is possible to tell a story at all and, therefore, to write."] This is perhaps the first principle of Blanchot's "method."

15. "This diary can be written only by becoming imaginary and by being immersed, like the one who writes it, in the unreality of fiction."

16. "One of the secret laws of these works is that the farther the movement advances, the closer it tends to approach the impersonality of abstraction."

17. "There is no self-portrait which is not that of a writer as writer, and his or her guilt is the guilt of writing in the midst of a culture where rhetoric has broken down, where utilitarian or intransitive writing takes turns conferring power and

powerlessness, where the subject seeks out kindred spirits, affirming his or her absolute difference all the while. This is why the only true readers of self-portraits are writers who are badly in need of them."

18. "indiscriminately change both meaning and sign" (*GO* 60).

19. "one who speaks poetically is exposed to the kind of death that is necessarily at work in essential speech."

20. "Literature is the experience by which consciousness discovers its being in its inability to lose consciousness, in the movement whereby it is transformed, as it disappears and is torn away from the well-delineated confines of a self, into an impersonal spontaneity beyond unconsciousness" (*GO* 50).

21. "The self-portraitist is always already an *Other*, 'dead as so and so,' 'the omission of oneself,' according to Mallarmé's formulations, which could also be written as 'dead as So and So,' absent from the text just as Christ's body was from the tomb."

22. "The most frequent figures in the self-portrait are those of Christ and Socrates at the moment of their deaths. The self-portrait is haunted by the Passion and the story of the *Phaedo*."

23. "The self-portraitist must become the artisan of his own resurrection."

24. "I cannot say, strictly speaking, that *I die*, since—whether dying a violent death or not—I am present for only part of the event. And to a large extent, the terror I feel at the idea of death may be a result of this: the dizzying spectacle of being left hanging in the middle of a crisis from which my disappearance will forever prevent me from knowing the outcome. This kind of unreality, of *absurdity* of death is . . . its radically terrible element."

25. "We want to be certain of death as being finished . . . we wish to be able to see ourselves dead, to assure ourselves of our death by casting upon our nothingness, from a point situated beyond death, a veritable gaze from beyond the grave."

26. "The myth of the resurrected one (Lazarus, Christ) stresses the paradox of the self-portrait which assures an afterlife to *no one*, in such a way that no one is ever represented there, at least in the specificity of a unique, irreplaceable body. And yet in the self-portrait, this very body seeks its revenge against the impersonal logos of philosophy."

27. "Death is the only act possible. Cornered as we are between a true material world whose chance combinations take place in us regardless of us, and a false ideal world whose lie paralyzes and bewitches us, we have only one means of no longer being at the mercy either of nothingness or of chance. This unique means, this unique act, is death. Voluntary death. Through it we abolish ourselves, but through it we also found ourselves . . . It is this act of voluntary death that Mallarmé committed. He committed it in *Igitur*" (*SL* 44).

28. "Nietzsche had already come up against the same contradiction when he said, 'Die at the right time.' That right moment which alone will balance our life by placing opposite it on the scales a sovereignly balanced death can be grasped only as the unknowable secret: only as that which could never be elucidated unless, already dead, we could look at ourselves from a point from which it would be granted us to embrace as a whole both our life and our death—the point which is perhaps the truth of the night from which Igiture would like, precisely, to take

his leave, in order to render his leave-taking possible and correct, but which he reduces to the poverty of a reflection" (*SL* 116–17).

29. "*Igitur* does not seek to surpass itself or to discover, through this voluntary move, a new point of view on the other side of life" (*SL* 111).

30. "To write one's autobiography, in order either to confess or to engage in self-analysis, or in order to expose oneself, like a work of art, to the gaze of all, is perhaps to seek to survive, but through a perpetual suicide—a death which is total inasmuch as fragmentary" (*WD* 64).

31. "the inevitable accomplishment of what is *impossible* to accomplish—and this would be dying itself" (*SNB* 107).

32. "To die has no inflected forms" (*SNB* 107).

33. "The moribund utterance (not a dying utterance but the utterance of dying itself) has perhaps always already passed the limit that life does not pass, obliviously following the path that writing traced out while marking it as untraceable" (*SNB* 93).

CHAPTER FOUR
MYTHICAL PORTRAYALS OF WRITING AND READING

1. "The central point of the work is the work as origin, the point which cannot be reached, yet the only one which is worth reaching" (*SL* 54).

2. "the furthest that art can reach" (*SL* 171).

3. "To look at Eurydice, without regard for the song, in the impatience and imprudence of desire which forgets the law: *that* is *inspiration*" (*SL* 173).

4. "The desire that carries Orpheus forward . . . is not an impetus able to clear the interval . . . Desire is separation itself become that which attracts: an interval become *sensible*" (*IC* 188).

5. "His error is to want to exhaust the infinite, to put a term to the interminable" (*SL* 173).

6. "Everything proceeds as if, by disobeying the law, by looking at Eurydice, Orpheus had only obeyed the deep demand of the work" (*SL* 173).

7. "Orpheus . . . forgets the work he is to achieve and he forgets it necessarily, for the ultimate demand which his movement makes is not that there be a work, but that someone face this 'point'" (*SL* 171).

8. "But not to turn toward Eurydice would be no less untrue. Not to look would be infidelity to the measureless, imprudent force of his movement, which does not want Eurydice in her daytime truth and her everyday appeal, but wants her in her nocturnal obscurity, in her distance, with her closed body and sealed face—wants to see her not when she is visible, but when she is invisible" (*SL* 172).

9. "Writing begins with Orpheus's gaze . . . But in order to descend toward this instant, Orpheus has to possess the power of art already. This is to say: one writes only if one reaches that instant which nevertheless one can only approach in the space opened by writing. To write, one has to write already" (*SL* 176).

10. "It is inevitable that Orpheus transgress the law which forbids him to 'turn back,' for he already violated it with his first steps toward the shades. This remark implies that Orpheus has in fact never ceased to be turned toward Eurydice" (*SL* 172).

11. "Only in the song does Orpheus have power over Eurydice. But in the song too, Eurydice is already lost, and Orpheus himself is the dispersed Orpheus; the song immediately makes him 'infinitely dead'" (*SL* 173).

12. "can indiscriminately change both its meaning and its sign" (*GO* 85).

13. "Patience is the ruse which seeks to master this absence of time by making of it another time, measured otherwise" (*SL* 173).

14. "true patience does not exclude impatience. It is intimacy with impatience—impatience suffered and endured endlessly" (*SL* 173).

15. "impatience must be the heart of profound patience" (*SL* 176).

16. "institute a limit, pronounce the inaugural, break the movement of ceaseless repetition."

17. "the one who writes is . . . one who has 'heard' the interminable and incessant, who has heard it as speech, has entered into this understanding with it, . . . has become lost in it and yet, in order to have sustained it, has necessarily made it stop, . . . has proffered it by firmly reconciling it with this limit. He has mastered it by imposing measure" (*SL* 37).

18. "the work can surpass itself, be united with its origin and consecrated in impossibility" (*SL* 174).

19. "All the glory of his work, all the power of his art, and even the desire for a happy life in the lovely, clear light of day are sacrificed to this sole aim: to look in the night at what night hides, the *other* night, the dissimulation that appears" (*SL* 172).

20. "should he come to sense this surplus of nothingness, . . . then he must respond to another exigency—no longer that of producing but of spending, no longer that of succeeding but of failing, no longer that of turning out works . . . but . . . of reducing himself to worklessness" (*IC* 206).

21. "The movement toward the other—the movement Bataille calls heterology—precedes, in his work, what the words 'gift' or 'expenditure' are meant to designate: the subversion of order, transgression, restitution of a more general economy which would not be dominated by the administration of objects (utility). But impossible loss—linked to the idea of sacrifice and to the experience of sovereign instants—does not allow the tensions which rip thought apart, and which the harshness of a restless language maintains, to congeal into a system" (*WD* 109).

22. "of which . . . the force and mastery of certain men would still be capable . . . It [transgression] opens to man when power ceases to be man's ultimate dimension" (*IC* 453, note 3).

23. "whose substance is all levity, unconcern, innocence" (*SL* 175).

24. "leave by means of a project the domain of the project."

25. He claims that it is "the opposite of action," action being "entirely dependent on the project," and that "discursive thought is itself engaged in the mode of existence of the project."

26. "The inner experience is conducted by discursive reason."

27. "whose strange effect is to attract literature to an unstable point where it can indiscriminately change both its meaning and its sign" (*GO* 60).

28. "May words cease to be arms; means of action, means of salvation. Let us count, rather, on disarray" (*WD* 11).

29. "If the written word, which is always impersonal, changes, dismisses, and abolishes the writer as writer, . . . then how can he turn back (ah, the guilty Orpheus) to what he believes he is leading into the light—to judge it, to consider it, to recognize himself in it and, in the end, to make himself the privileged reader of it, the principal commentator or simply the zealous helper who gives or imposes his version, resolves the enigma, reveals the secret and authoritatively interrupts (we are, after all, talking about the author) the hermeneutic chain, since he claims to be the adequate interpreter, the first or the last?" (*VC* 61)

30. "the volume takes place all alone: finished, being."

31. "dead as so and so"

32. "sacrifice, relative to his personality"

33. "The moment when that which is glorified in the work *is* the work, when the work ceases in some way to have been made, to refer back to someone who made it, . . . this moment which cancels the author is also the moment when . . . reading finds its origin" (*SL* 200).

34. "Not personified, the volume does not cry out for the approach of a reader."

35. "Reading is ignorant . . . It is receiving and hearing, not the power to decipher and analyze . . . it does not comprehend (strictly speaking), it attends. A marvelous innocence" (*IC* 320).

36. "The book is there, then, but the work is still hidden, absent, perhaps radically so; in any case it is concealed, obfuscated by the evident presence of the book, behind which it awaits the liberating decision, the 'Lazare, veni foras'" (*SL* 195).

37. "the Book always indicates an order that submits to *unity*, a system of notions in which are affirmed the primacy of speech over writing, of thought over language, and the promise of a communication that would one day be immediate and transparent" (*IC* xii).

38. "always diverging, always without a relation of presence with itself" (*IC* 427).

39. "what was written in the past will be read in the future, without any relation of presence being able to establish itself *between* writing and reading" (*SNB* 30).

40. "he who, without being engulfed in cadaverous reality and even while looking steadily at it, is able to name it, 'comprehend' it, and, by this understanding, pronounce the *Lazare veni foras* through which death will become a principle, the terrible force in which the life that bears it must maintain itself in order to master it and find there the accomplishment of its mastery" (*IC* 35).

41. "what does he have to do with what is lying there and makes you draw back, the anonymous corruption of the tomb, the lost Lazarus who already smells bad and not the one restored to life?" (*IC* 35–36)

42. "The book, the written thing, enters the world and carries out its work of transformation and negation. It, too, is the future of many other things, and not only books . . . it is an infinite source of new realities, and because of these new realities existence will be something it was not before" (*GO* 34).

43. "a violent rupture, the passage from the world where everything has more or less meaning, where there is obscurity and clarity, into a space where, properly

speaking, nothing has meaning yet, toward which nevertheless everything which does have meaning returns as toward its origin" (*SL* 196).

44. "when there is no more world, when there is no world yet" (*SL* 33)

45. "where being ceaselessly perpetuates itself as nothingness" (*SL* 243)

46. "The work, even if it is without an author and always becoming in relation to itself, delimits a space that attracts names, a possibility of reading that is determined every time, a system of references, a theory that appropriates it, a meaning that clarifies it" (*SNB* 36).

47. "the impersonal affirmation that it is" (*SL* 23)

48. "communication of a given thing" (*SL* 205)

49. "for instruction, for increased self-knowledge, or to cultivate the mind" (*SL* 205).

50. "Reading is anguish, and this is because any text, however important, or amusing, or interesting it may be [and the more engaging it seems to be], is empty—at bottom, it doesn't exist; you have to cross an abyss, and if you do not jump, you do not comprehend" (*WD* 10).

51. "In order to leap there must be a free space, there must be firm ground, and there must be a force that, starting from a secure foothold, changes the movement into a jump" (*IC* 19).

52. "there is nothing sure, nothing firm" (*IC* 19).

53. "the question of the totality in its proper meaning, the preeminent metaphysical question, which is situated in the realm of truth where the symbol is a guarantee of knowledge."

54. "memorable confrontation of the profound question and the question of the whole" (*IC* 18).

55. "Certainly, he *knew* how to answer, but this knowing did no more than affirm his ignorance of himself, his answer being possible only by reason of this profound ignorance" (*IC* 18).

56. "a felicitous activity which requires more innocence and freedom than careful thought."

57. "Symbolic reading is probably the worst way to approach a literary text."

58. "It is strange; one can go looking for the supreme designations that humanity has been perfecting for thousands of years to characterize the Unique. One may well say: 'But the Castle is Grace; the *Graf* (the Count) is *Gott*, as the identity of the capital letters proves; or it is the Transcendence of Being, or the Transcendence of Nothingness, Olympus, or the bureaucratic administration of the universe.' Yes, one may say all this . . . The fact nonetheless remains that all these profound identifications . . . do not fail to disappoint us: as though the Castle were always infinitely more than this—infinitely more and thus also infinitely less" (*IC* 395).

59. "What, then, is above Transcendence, what below Transcendence?"

60. "Well (let us hasten to respond, as haste alone authorizes the response)" (*IC* 395).

61. "that before which all evaluation reveals itself to be inadequate" (*IC* 395)

62. "have we the right to suggest that the Castle, the count's residence, would

be nothing other than the sovereignty of the neutral and the site of this strange sovereignty?" (*IC* 395–96)

63. "Unfortunately, one cannot say this so simply" (*IC* 396).

64. "the neutral cannot be represented, cannot be symbolized or even signified and . . . inasmuch as it is borne by the infinite indifference of the entire narrative, it is everywhere . . . as though it were the infinite vanishing point from which the speech of the narrative, and within it all narratives and all speech about every narrative, would receive and lose their perspective: the infinite distance of their relations, their perpetual overturning and annulment. But let us stop here, for fear of engaging in our turn in an infinite movement" (*IC* 396).

65. "To read would mean to read in the book the absence of the book, and, as a consequence, to produce this absence" (*IC* 427).

66. "it is the pledge of its own death."

67. "The neuter can be named, since it is named (even if this is not a proof). But what is designated by this name? The desire to dominate the neuter, a desire to which the neuter immediately lends itself, all the more so as it is foreign to any domination and as it has always already marked, with its passive insistence, the desire that thus infects its object and every object with it" (*SNB* 83).

68. "The circle of the law is this: there must be a crossing in order for there to be a limit, but only the limit, in as much as it is uncrossable, summons to cross, affirms the desire (the false step) that has always already, through an unforeseeable movement, crossed the line" (*SNB* 24).

69. "Lazarus in the tomb and not Lazarus brought back into the daylight, the one who already smells bad, who is Evil, Lazarus lost and not Lazarus saved and brought back to life" (*GO* 46)

70. "It would seem, then, that to read is not to write the book again, but to allow the book to *be*: written—this time all by itself, without the intermediary of the writer, without anyone's writing it" (*SL* 193).

71. "The virgin envelope of the book, once again, lends itself to a sacrifice which made the red-edged pages of ancient volumes bleed; the introduction of a weapon, or letter opener, to establish the taking of possession of it."

CHAPTER FIVE
WRITING THE DISASTER: HENRI SORGE'S JOURNAL

1. "The disaster defined—hinted at—not as an event of the past, but as the immemorial past (*Le Très-Haut*) which returns, dispersing by its return the present, where, ghostly, it would be experienced as returning" (*WD* 17).

2. For further discussion of the significance of Sorge's name, see Pierre Klossowski's piece on Blanchot in *Un si funeste désir* (Paris: Gallimard, 1963).

3. "I would have liked to write an account of that day, as well as of the rest of my life, for that matter: an account, that is, a simple diary . . . I then felt certain that I would only have to write an hourly commentary of my actions in order to discover therein the glorious revelation of a supreme truth, the very one which circulated actively among us all and which public life incessantly maintained, watched over, reabsorbed, and threw back in an obsessing and reflexive game."

4. "not because he is outside the judicial system but because the State needs his example."

5. "an infinitely more serious crime is committed through the robbery, the most terrible of all, and, moreover, one which is not realized, which fails."

6. "I clearly saw that even if I succeeded, by summoning up all my strengths, in changing only one, single thing, in affecting only a piece of straw, it would not be useless. And perhaps I would also accomplish much more."

7. "You believed it was intelligent to ensconce yourselves in your cells, but what did you accomplish? Nothing, except conform to the desire of the State, for its most cherished wish was to keep you in prison, on account of your illegal activities, and to make you stay there of your own free will, because this conquest of your freedon was the true objective of your detention."

8. "insignificant story, idle gossip."

9. "they are made-up stories . . . I can't stand this manner of self-expression."

10. "stories that are staged from beginning to end"

11. "give the impression that things are not going perfectly well, that the system's net, in spite of its ever-tightening mesh, always lets the particles of a few miserable, distressing cases fall through."

12. "Acquittal could only signify the presence of a woman, but I could only look for acquittal in prisons where there were no women. Therein lay the punishment."

13. "Your dream illustrates the unhealthy, depraved nature of your thoughts . . . I understand your allusions. But this thinly veiled chatter has gone on long enough. If it is my neighbor and my walk with her this evening which are lurking behind your riddles, forget it."

14. "from the bailiff to the highest commissioner, we were all like this: indulgent, understanding and clarifying everything, transforming into normal acts, by means of a reverse decoding process, the worst infractions of the rules."

15. "you don't teach me anything; you do nothing except express what I think, and when you speak, it is not you who are speaking; I am."

16. "a handful of men against a mass of them"

17. "You don't surprise me. You don't shock me, either. You are nothing but an out of print book without a date."

18. "The truth is that all your criticisms are whispered to you by the law itself: it needs them and appreciates what you do for it."

19. "What about outlaws?"

20. "But you are mad! That is a story from another time, a reminiscence. You are a book; you do not exist."

21. "I have read your papers. You haven't asked me for any advice, but for several days I have wanted to give you some, this piece in particular: you write too much. You have superstitious beliefs about the written word. You are excessively preoccupied with commentaries, orders, and reports. In addition, your expressions lack a certain precision. They are ignorant copies, cast in a language you have learned by rote which tends to ressuscitate past situations that have little bearing on what is happening now, in such a way that the past appears to return, but it does so as the caricature of a prophecy which makes everything that one undertakes seem illusory."

22. "a narrative, complete and finished, of all the events of an endless day."

23. "at every step I take, I am able to remember, from beginning to end, the movement full of suffering and triumphs which enables all of us to say the last word while justifying the first."

24. "The regimes of times past could fear new measures because the movement toward the future threatened them. But we have nothing similar to fear: we are this future; the future is progressing toward its own realization, and it is our existence that lights the way for it."

25. "there are no more convictions because there are no more infractions. Interior and exterior coincide; the decisions made in the innermost recesses of the State are immediately integrated in outward forms of public utility from which they are inseparable."

26. "all the events of all of history are here, around us, just like dead people. From the very depths of time, they flow back onto today; they most certainly existed, but not completely: when they occurred, they were only incomprehensible, absurd preliminary sketches, atrocious dreams, a prophecy. People lived through them without understanding them. But now? Now, they are really going to exist; it is time, everything is reappearing and being revealed in the light and the truth."

27. "I sense perfectly that if I were to change or to lose my head, history would collapse."

28. "I was carried away by a feeling of triumph, by the certainty, of which I would henceforth be aware, that the heavens belonged to us as well, that we were responsible for administering them along with all the rest, that at every instant I touched and surveyed them from on high."

29. "the river, too, seemed to have flowed throughout time, affirming with its vast tranquillity that there was neither a beginning nor an end, that history constructed nothing, that man still did not exist, what do I know? From this conviction rose, like a suffocating deception, the reminder of a lie, of an endless fraud, an insinuation made in order to degrade noble sentiments."

30. "why doesn't a question as serious as this one—since it contains the future of humanity, a question such that to answer it would presuppose the existence of a radically new mode of thought—renew the language that carries it? And why does it only give rise to remarks that are either partial (and biased, in any case, when they are political in nature) or moving and compelling, when they are spiritual in nature, yet identical to the ones we have been hearing in vain for two thousand years?"

31. "Classical language, Foucault states in the clearest formula, 'does not exist, but functions.' It represents thought in identical fashion, and in it (which is not), thought represents itself according to identity, equality, and simultaneity . . . The response to Pascal's challenge comes in the project of a universal tongue, the *mathesis universalis*: a discourse in which order is to dispose itself in the simultaneity of space, that is, the hierarchized equality of all that is representable; it comes in the analytical vocation of this functional language that does not speak but classifies, organizes, and makes order" (*IC* 254).

32. "when you speak, it is not you who are speaking; I am."

33. "Did you like this story? Were you touched by it? Did you have a good sense of my narrative intentions?"

34. "It was you who sabotaged the machine because his work was already no longer sufficient and he talked too much."

35. "That is how their minds work. They can't take a story seriously anymore; they transpose it, dissect it, draw a lesson from it. Undoubtedly I was the saboteur, but what difference does that make? The anecdote did not exist any less, something that I presented to her as a gift, without an ulterior motive, because I am a human being like her and upon seeing her, I regained my youth and my years of apprenticeship. I don't blame her; she was right, and if she had merely appreciated the purely historical side of my tale, its aesthetic value, I would have said to myself: foolish little girl, sentimental little goose."

36. "my intention was to make her say something against you. It had to be done; it was my duty to approach all the widespread rumors about you from the perspective of their greatest plausibility."

37. "My insipid words began to cast off foam, as if they were fermenting. She discovered something in this; she was fascinated. I can say that I know how to recognize this dizziness from afar. I follow its phases. It is a complete breakdown whose outcome is no less familiar to me: a thousand avowals of negligence, of complicity, an obliviousness which abruptly appears and denounces itself on the basis of an infinite amount of evidence, too much evidence."

38. "Instead of heaping incriminations on you, from the depths of her distress, the poor girl did just the opposite: she no longer saw in your name anything except a way to ingratiate herself with me, a connection, an opportunity. You were no longer the suspect that she was supposed to turn in; you became the only one who could exonerate her."

39. "After such miscalculations, one learns to be patient, and one realizes how long history is, how slowly it passes, even if it is finished."

40. "I am a trap for you. Even if I tell you everything, it will be of no use. The more loyal I am, the more I will deceive you. My candor will be your undoing."

41. "they are, rather, administrative cases, an idea to get rid of the squalor of the old sections of the city and to modernize an underdeveloped region."

42. "staged, . . . a plan to justify certain administrative measures."

43. "people against whom the State protects itself by means of barriers and police crackdowns, who escape from the State, whom the State no longer recognizes and can no longer treat like everyone else. We are outside the law."

44. "sickness contaminates the law when the law takes care of the sick."

45. "one no longer seizes the law; one contemplates it, and that is bad."

46. "you talk about it too much, you think too much; that isn't natural"

47. "my ideas smell of the disease."

48. "it is not a question of privileging in *Le Très-Haut* subversion with respect to the state or the simulacrum with respect to the good copy of the law, the model of which would reign in the inaccessible world of ideas sheltered from all corruption. What must be privileged—the fourth term in *Le Très-Haut*—is the disease itself, as the radical subversion of the world of representation from one end of the spectrum to the other, from the *eidos*, represented in the world by the copy, to the simulacrum that reproduces it."

49. "You had to disperse the crowd, chase the people away, create a vacuum: no one has the right to attend your ceremonies, and yet they are performed for everyone. It is strange, but this is precisely where the depth of the law appears: each individual must fade away and not be there in person but rather in general, in an invisible way, such as at the movies, for example. And you, you come, but to do what? To make an official gesture which is honorary, a simple allegory. Before you, anyone who had come to take a look at the ruins had already begun a new edifice, had turned those crumbling remains into materials that could be used for reconstruction. And even the arsonists, if only because they watched the building burn, had already put out the fire and restored the house."

50. "in their instinctive refusal to accept any power, in their absolute mistrust in identifying with a power to which they would delegate themselves, thus in their *declaration of powerlessness*" (*UC* 31).

51. "the impersonal, anonymous affirmation that it is—and nothing more" (*SL* 23).

52. "Reading is anguish, and this is because any text . . . is empty—at bottom it doesn't exist" (*WD* 10).

53. "The people are there, then they are no longer there; they ignore the structures that could stabilize them. Presence and absence, if not merged, at least exchange themselves virtually. That is what makes them formidable for the holders of a power that does not acknowledge them: not letting themselves be grasped, being as much the dissolution of the social fact as the restive obstinacy to reinvent the latter in a sovereignty the law cannot circumscribe, as it challenges it while maintaining itself as its foundation" (*UC* 33).

54. "You are on the wrong track; you are fighting against this regime as if it were like all the others . . . It has permeated the world so thoroughly that it can no longer be separated from it. It does not only consist of a political organization or a social system: all people, things, and, as the proverbs say, heaven and earth are the law, obedient to the State because they are the State. You attack the commissioners of the State, the public figures, but it would not be any less useful to attack all the inhabitants, all the houses, then this table and this sheet of paper. You know that you will have to attack yourself. There is not a speck of dust that you should not view as an obstacle. Everything that you want to overthrow conspires against you."

55. "Interior and exterior coincide; the decisions made at the innermost recesses of the State are immediately integrated in outward forms of public utility from which they are inseparable."

56. "It is a matter of shattering the framework once and for all, of eliminating the divisions that separate those who administer from the things they administer. You already know how this works: for every position, there is a representative of the administration; behind every worker is a delegate who embodies in flesh and blood the idea of the worker's job. In principle, the delegates are there to provide technical and moral assistance, but, in fact, they are also there to control the workers' activities and to enable us to maximize them. The results are so-so; the system does have its weaknesses."

57. "Your observations would please one of my colleagues, who would not fail to ask you his favorite question that is always on the tip of his tongue: 'And

what is your fly for today?' The fly is a thought that is too brilliant or too subtle, the spirit of truth and depth at the moment it takes wing and seeks to separate itself from the movement. It buzzes and hears itself vibrate. You see, that is another allegory."

58. "his department is the object of severe criticism"

59. "a simulacrum, a kind of game to make the law circulate."

60. "The law's scheme: that prisoners construct their prison themselves. This is the culmination of the concept, and the concept is the mark of the system" (*WD* 45).

61. "victims of a system of illusion capable of making them work enthusiastically toward their own servitude."

62. "writing belongs to the fragmentary when everything has been said. There would have to have been the exhaustion of the word and by the word and the accomplishment of the totality (of presence as totality) as logos for fragmentary writing to let itself be re-marked. Still, we cannot, writing, free ourselves from a logic of the totality by considering it as ideally completed in order to maintain as 'pure remainder' a possibility of writing, outside everything, useless or endless, the study of which a completely different logic, still difficult to make out (that of repetition, limits, and return), would claim to guarantee us" (*SNB* 42).

63. "There is not, to begin with, law, prohibition, and then transgression, but rather there is transgression in the absence of any prohibition, which eventually freezes into Law, the Principle of Meaning" (*WD* 75).

64. "if to write is to arrange marks of singularity (fragments) . . . , there is always a risk that reading, instead of animating the multiplicity of crossing routes, will reconstitute a new totality from them" (*SNB* 51).

65. "an insignificant story, idle gossip"

66. "You don't hold anything against him? He did, after all, take your father's place."

67. "Yes, my father. You know, I didn't know him very well; I hardly remember him."

68. This comparison was first suggested by Foucault who, in "The Thought from Outside," calls Sorge an "Orestes in submission" (*Foucault/Blanchot*, 39). The resemblance of the families of these two characters supports this comparison, and the paradoxical notion of a submissive Orestes accurately describes the ambivalency of Sorge's political position with regard to the State. He is a figure of Orestes insofar as he articulates a radical brand of subversion, and he is submissive to the extent that it takes place in the confines of his journal, where the logic of transgression reigns. Orestes is probably more often viewed, however, as an unsubmissive man of action who succeeds in creating a new order through an act of constructive negativity, his crime. Blanchot discusses this version of Orestes in his essay on Sartre's *Les Mouches* in *Faux Pas*. Such a character does, in fact, exist in *Le Très-Haut*: Roste, an anagram of Oreste. In addition, the association of this name with the German word for "rust" suggests that the machinery of the regional economy that is driven by the power of the negative is worn-out, obsolete, and in need of an overhaul.

69. "Whenever Louise spoke of her, she referred to her as 'the queen.'"

70. "And my mother cannot even look me in the eye. She broods over me and spies on me, but never face to face, so afraid is she that her gaze might summon forth from behind me a terrible figure, a reminiscence that she must not see."

71. "Where there was once an unjust death will be a just death; blood once spilled in a heinous crime will be spilled again in a vengeful one."

72. "This is what 'family' is: the reminder of a time prior to the law, a cry, ignorant utterances from the past."

73. "All the photographs resembled each other, as is the case for those taken by professional photographers. The pose was the same; the clothes, always of the kind that would be appropriate for some festivity, passed from one person to the next; the different physical traits disappeared beneath the sameness of the expressions. In short, they were highly monotonous. And yet I did not grow tired of looking at them; I kept needing more. They were the same, but the same in infinite quantity. I plunged my hands into the pile and ran my fingers over them; I was intoxicated."

74. "I looked at this long, bony, largely inexpressive face—except for the eyes. They possessed a savage steadiness that was striking in this nondescript countenance. Undoubtedly a man of duty, approximately forty years old. Louise held up the frame from behind, and at the same time I could see her face and the one depicted in the portrait, as well as her equally cold, keen gaze which slid, with jealous haste, from the top of the frame to the image, as if to verify its material identity. I then remembered all those other photographs, behind which there was also something to look for. Today they all seemed to refer me to this face with the savage gaze of which only the piercing eyes were visible."

75. "in the background, there were certainly many details, but wear had gotten the better of the colors, the lines, and the print itself on the cross threads. By stepping back, I could discern nothing more, and when I moved closer, everything became blurred. When standing completely motionless, I felt a light reflection pass behind this tattered chaos and slide across its surface. Obviously, something was moving. The image kept itself in the background. It looked out at me as I looked in at it. What was it? The ruins of a stairway? Columns? Perhaps a body lying on the steps? Ah, false image, treacherous image, vanished, indestructible."

76. "thousands of worms, moths and minute insects of all kinds which flourished inside."

77. "Now, it is now that I speak"

78. "I was not alone; I was an ordinary man."

79. "It seems that you do not want to interrupt for a minute the thread of aphorisms and maxims. The way your mind works has been strongly shaped by public offices."

80. "One day or another, you will slip."

81. "But all of a sudden, the expression on her face froze, and her arm sprang forth so violently that I leapt up against the partition, shouting: 'Now, it is now that I speak.'"

82. "His fist sprang forth with fascinating speed; I collapsed on the ground."

83. "This spot was unusual in that it was only a spot. It did not represent anything, was colorless, and except for the dusty permeation, nothing made it

visible. Was it even visible? It did not exist underneath the paper; it was formless but resembled something dirty and spoiled as well as something clean."

84. "the reminder of a lie, of an endless fraud, an insinuation made to degrade noble sentiments" . . . "there was neither a beginning nor an end, that history constructed nothing"

85. "a gurgle" . . . "a watery murmur"

86. "a thick, black water similiar to that which had once already seeped through the walls"

87. "papers covered with ink stains."

88. "You took some leaves of absence. You didn't feel like your normal self. With your free time, you were able to associate with various people. You got worried. You threw yourself into a search for something as if everything had not already been given to you. And then what typically happens? In the end, you are overcome by dizziness; you think that history has left you behind, that it is following its course without you; and you start to make judgments, to talk, and even to write with the stupor of a man who is always running after his boots."

89. Iche, which suggests the pronoun I in German, is an appropriate name for a dedicated, efficient member of the bureaucracy of a state whose principal occupation is the reduction of the Other to the Same: "Le moi est . . . une formule qui règle . . . la prétention du Même à la primauté" (*PAD* 12). ["The self is . . . a formula which regulates . . . the pretention of the Same to primacy" (*SNB* 4).] I will explore the constitution of the *moi* with respect to the regional and general economies in the next chapter.

90. "a schoolboy's assignment. I understood that as soon as I saw it, a task fulfilled by writing. You know, when one tries out a new pen, one resorts to sentences of a special type, ridiculous sequences of words, grammatical examples. All the same, in the future, be careful. Choose for your compendium less conspicuous formulas."

91. "that rag of a letter"

92. "This rag was a bright red piece of cloth . . . and I saw it mixing dangerously, curled up, shiny, and untouchable, with the refuse in the garbage pail."

93. "hope still remained, and the day stayed intact as well."

94. "I had only to hear the sound of the water penetrating the material to feel that it encountered something shamefully damp, much wetter than it, a sticky thickness, a repository saturated with moisture that could never be dried out. This sound drove me insane. It was that of a liquid being corrupted, losing its transparency, becoming something even wetter that was secreted by a denied existence, a cold, thick, black stain."

95. "what made this situation so dangerous was that with every drop that fell, the cloth continued to present the same dry, bright appearance, the same shiny, inalterable shade of red. That was the cursed ruse of this story."

96. "I was not allowed to be ignorant of how this shameless red color, which enclosed in its perpetually dry envelope a reserve of stagnant water, pulled me by the arm, drew my body toward it, caused me to lean forward, and made my fingers truly drunk at the thought that they would have only to wring out this piece of material, so visible and clear, in order to express its latent intimacy by making

the liquid flow forth and by spreading it out forever in an indelible thick, black stain."

97. "I felt how much the humiliating nature of my existence surpassed that of all other existences because I had to read, to write, and to think."

98. "the formless weight of being, present in absence" (*SL* 258)

99. "solitude's gaze, . . . vision which is no longer the possibility of seeing, but the impossibility of not seeing, the impossibility which becomes visible and perseveres—always and always—in a vision that never comes to an end" (*SL* 32).

100. "Entertain this dreadful thought: that I am, in many respects, merely a figure. A figure? Can you grasp what a dangerous, perfidious, and hopeless mode of living such a word implies? I am a mask. I am a stand-in for a mask, and in this capacity, I play the role of a lie in this universal narrative who spreads on the all-too-complete humanity of the law—as one would apply a coat of varnish—a cruder, more naive humanity, a reminder of earlier stages in an evolution which, having arrived at its end, vainly attempts to go back in time."

101. "the more the world is affirmed as the future and the broad daylight of truth, where everything will have value, bear meaning, where the whole will be achieved under the mastery of man and for his use, the more it seems that art must descend toward that point where nothing has meaning yet, the more it matters that art maintain the movement, the insecurity and the grief of that which escapes every grasp and all ends. The artist and the poet seem to have received this mission: to call us obstinately back to error, to turn us toward that space where everything we propose, everything we have acquired, everything we are, all that opens upon the earth and in the sky, returns to insignificance, and where what approaches is the nonserious and the nontrue, as if perhaps thence sprang the source of all authenticity" (*SL* 247).

102. "the opaque, empty opening onto that which is when there is no more world, when there is no world yet" (*SL* 33).

103. "No, . . . why? It is not a fable. It is an incident from ny youth. I see that you have brought in some new furniture."

104. "it was false, but didn't this happen because I was the same as he, and how could I make it understood that my silence was perhaps only the echo of his?"

105. "because we shared the same first name, and, moreover, watching him on certain days motionless at his desk, his forehead bent over registers in which he wrote nothing, I imagined him as being prey to the same kind of disarray that I had experienced and struggling to overcome difficulties posed by his work."

106. "I at once understood the conspiracy against me that this young man was involved in. I stood up slowly and stared at him: on this sickly, closed, and ceremonious face, the lie had its place, a lie which turned the comedy into an equivocal, repulsive scene that had a vague odor of delation about it. Then something else occurred to me. Maybe he wasn't in on anything. Swamped with work, he really needed my help."

107. "every time I had offered him my services, he had flatly turned them down."

108. "That paralytic, I suspected as much. He rummaged through my desk; he did it on purpose."

109. "one of the versions of the imaginary offers its lesson: man—is it man?— can make himself in accordance with the image, but this means that he is still more apt to unmake himself in accordance with his image" (*WD* 126).

110. "the formless weight of being, present in absence" (*SL* 258).

111. "The water in which Narcissus sees what he shouldn't is not a mirror, capable of producing a distinct and definite image. What he sees is the invisible in the visible—in the picture the undepicted, the unstable unknown of a representation without presence, which reflects no model" (*WD* 134).

112. "of an evasive death that consists entirely in the repetition of a mute misapprehension" (*WD* 126).

113. "the perpetuity of that which admits neither beginning nor end" (*SL* 261).

114. "he dies (if he dies) of being immortal, of having the immortality of appearance—the immortality which his metamorphosis into a flower attests: a funereal flower or flower of rhetoric" (*WD* 128).

115. "one of these means of defense, effectively conceived to avert the danger"

116. "to attract, while turning it away, the speaking boundlessness; to be a jetty thrust out in the middle of the agitated sand, and not a charming, little rampart visited by people on their Sunday strolls."

117. "in the poem, where the poet writes himself, he does not recognize himself, for he does not become conscious of himself. He is excluded from the facile, humanistic hope that by writing, or 'creating,' he would transform his dark experience into greater consciousness. On the contrary: dismissed, excluded from what is written—unable even to be present by virtue of the nonpresence of his very death—he has to renounce all conceivable relations of a self (either living or dying) to the poem which henceforth belongs to the other, or else will remain without any belonging at all. The poet is Narcissus to the extent that Narcissus is an anti-Narcissus: he who, turned away from himself—causing the detour of which he is the effect, dying of not recognizing himself—leaves the trace of what has not occurred" (*WD* 135).

118. Jeanne Galgat's name calls to mind Golgotha, a place of sacrifice. Sorge is the victim of a sacrifice performed by her which, unlike the crucifixion, fails to render death humanly possible.

119. "I find it hard to believe that such a thing could happen on a given day. Is it possible? Will anyone ever be able to say: 'From this day forth . . .'"

120. "Perhaps the dreams of your inkwell will give us some trouble, but it doesn't matter. We won't let them go to waste. We will pursue them for as long as it takes to express their value and turn them to our advantage."

121. "The cruelty of language is a consequence of the fact that it unceasingly evokes its death without ever being able to die."

122. "It is forbidden to die" (*SNB* 96)

123. "I don't have time to read"

124. "But I hate ideas."

125. "Abroad I studied quite a bit. I also did some writing."

126. "The events are at hand; everyone must now take part in the conflict."

CHAPTER SIX
FLAGRANTS DÉLITS: CAUGHT IN THE ACT OF SELF-READING

1. "In the Elegies, the affirmation of life and that of death are revealed as one" (*SL* 132).

2. "we like to substitute interesting ideas for the pure poetic movement" (*SL* 133).

3. "as if, in the anguish of words which he is called upon to write and never to read, he wanted to persuade himself that in spite of everything he understands himself; he has the right to read and comprehend" (*SL* 133).

4. "it is in this that his thought rises to a greater height" (*SL* 138)

5. "a prohibition that has always let itself be violated already" (*VC* 62).

6. "when the book in question is one whose purpose is to elucidate, there is a kind of methodological good faith in stating toward what point it seems to be directed: here, toward the pages entitled 'Orpheus's Gaze.'"

7. "Upon reading these sentences from years ago" (*WD* 59)

8. "Why this recollection? Why is it that . . . these words seem to need to be taken up again, repeated, in order to escape the meaning that animates them, and to be turned away from themselves, from the discourse that employs them?" (*WD* 59).

9. "But, taken up anew, they reintroduce an assurance to which one thought one had ceased to subscribe. They have an air of truth; they say something—they aspire to coherence. They say: you thought all this long ago; you are thus authorized to think it again. They restore this reasonable continuity which forms systems" (*WD* 59).

10. "there is not, to begin with, law, prohibition, and then transgression, but rather there is transgression in the absence of any prohibition, which eventually freezes into Law, the Principle of Meaning" (*WD* 75).

11. "a story from before Auschwitz" (*VC* 69).

12. "impossible not to think of the ridiculous work carried out in the concentration camps" (*VC* 66)

13. "'The Idyll' can be interpreted as the reading of an already menacing future" (*VC* 67).

14. "I do not know, but I know that I am going to have known."

15. In *The Step Not Beyond*, on pages 106, 112, and 124.

16. "the lack of a subject . . . capable of bearing this knowledge in the present" (*SNB* 114).

17. "Blanchot's last narrative work."

18. "the beginning of the book appears to place it within the narrative tradition"

19. De Man's "lead" is just that and nothing more. He makes no attempt to pursue it or to demonstrate the validity of his theory regarding *L'Attente l'oubli* or of this much broader claim which has ramifications for Blanchot's work taken

in its entirety: "A circular movement seems to take the writer, at first alienated in the work, back to himself, by means of an act of self-interpretation. In Blanchot, this process first takes the form of his critical reading of others, as preparatory to the reading of himself. It can be shown that Blanchot's criticism prefigures the self-reading toward which he is ultimately oriented. The relationship between his critical work and his narrative prose has to be understood in these terms, the former being the preparatory version of the latter. A complete study of Blanchot should illustrate this by means of several examples" (67). De Man whets our appetite with his thought-provoking hypothesis which unfortunately promises more than it delivers. He fails to convince us why the rapport between Blanchot's criticism and fiction "has to be understood in these terms" simply because he makes no mention of Blanchot's fiction, other than his statement about *L'Attente l'oubli* that I quoted. What I propose to do in this chapter, therefore, is to test de Man's hypothesis about *L'Attente l'oubli*.

20. "Here, and on this sentence which was perhaps also intended for him, he was obliged to stop."

21. "It was practically while listening to her speak that he had written these notes."

22. "He still heard her voice while writing."

23. "the first paragraph seemed to her to be the most faithful and so did the second somewhat, especially at the end."

24. "he could see her when she reclined on the spacious balcony, and he had made signs to her shortly after his arrival."

25. "Who is speaking?"

26. "But never did she recognize her words in mine."

27. "She sensed an error that she could not put her finger on . . . She sadly threw down all the pages. She had the impression that although he had assured her that he would believe her implicitly, he did not believe her enough, with the force that would have rendered the truth present."

28. "To be faithful, this is what was being asked of him: to take hold of this slightly cold hand which would lead him, by way of unusual meanders, to a place where she would disappear and leave him alone. But it was difficult for him not to look for the person to whom this hand belonged. He had always been like this. He thought about that hand, about she who had held it out to him and not about the itinerary. Therein without a doubt lay his mistake."

29. "It is that voice which was entrusted to him. What an astonishing thought! He picked up the sheets of paper and wrote: 'It is her voice that is entrusted to you, not what she says.'"

30. "She asked him what he had just written. But it was something that she must not hear."

31. "instead of the beginning, a kind of initial void, an energetic refusal to let the story commence."

32. "Act in such a way that I can speak to you."

33. "It is as if she had waited for him to give her a detailed description of this room which, however, she was occupying with him."

34. "she did not stop asking him, with a silent persistence, to describe it [the room] to her again and again, as if for the first time."

35. "With his youthful vigor, he had not hesitated then to respond. It was a brillant period when everything still seemed possible and when he threw caution to the wind, randomly taking note, always with sovereign rectitude, of the essential detail and entrusting the rest to his flawless memory."

36. "to speak truly, one must think according to the measure of the eye" (*IC* 27).

37. "because she had the feeling that this description would call forth this same room inhabited by someone else."

38. "that she would make his obligation to carry through to the end and which must have as the outcome its progressive movement toward a goal."

39. "Language makes neither the event of waiting nor that of forgetting present; it does not turn such an event into an actual episode that is or can be named. This event is undoubtedly nothing other than what happens to language itself."

40. "Wasn't she trying, and he along with her, to create for herself at the heart of this story a shelter so as to protect herself from something that the story also helped to attract?"

41. "When she spoke, she gave the impression of not knowing how to reestablish a bond between her words and the richness of a preexisting language. They had no history, no connection with the past of everyone else, not even a relationship to her own life or to anyone else's."

42. "Although she was apparently not very learned, she always seemed to prefer abstract words, which evoked nothing."

43. "Well, therein lies the secret: I had already told you everything."

44. "It is not a fiction, although he is incapable of pronouncing the word 'truth' in connection with it. Something happened to him, and he can neither say that it was true, nor the contrary. Later, he thought that the event consisted in this manner of being neither true nor false."

45. "Through the words a bit of daylight still passed."

46. "There is nothing to expect from the conversation except—given that everything has been said—that which precedes all saying, and its horizon, the dissolution of all totalizing speech."

47. " 'Act in such a way that I can speak to you.' —'Yes, but do you have any idea of what I should do to accomplish that?' —'Persuade me that you hear me.' —'Well then, begin, speak to me.' " The shift in the form of address used by the male interlocutor at the end of this quotation catches his companion off guard, and she registers her surprise while electing to remain with the formal pronoun: "Pourquoi ce tutoiement? Vous ne tutoyez jamais personne" (14). On rare occasions, they both use "tu" when speaking to each other, but "vous" is the pronoun that is predominantly employed throughout. I must confess that I am at a loss when it comes to explaining such abrupt shifts from "vous" to "tu" when they do occur.

48. "in your statements there is something that speaks constantly of this place where we are. Why? What happens there? You must say."

49. "It is up to you to know, since it is already said in my words that you are alone in hearing." In passing, it is worth noting that the absence of an "e" at the end of the word *seul* confirms that she has said this and not he. It is an attentive-

ness to this kind of detail that each reader must develop in order to determine who says what, but clues such as this one are not always present.

50. "'Who are you really? You cannot be you, but you are someone. Who?'. . . 'Don't have any doubts,' he said softly. 'I choose to be that which befalls me. I am indeed what you just said.' —'Who?' She is almost shouting. 'Yes, what you just said.'"

51. "'You asked it of me because it is impossible.' —'Impossible, but possible, if I was able to ask it of you.' —'Everything thus depends on that, if you really asked it of me?' —'Everything depends on that.'"

52. "He realized that . . . ," "He perceived that . . . ," "He has always known that . . . ," "He wonders if . . . ," "He often had the impression that . . ."

53. "When he understood that she was not trying to tell him how things had transpired . . . he felt afraid for the first time. To begin with, he would know nothing (and he saw how much he had wanted to know); moreover, he would never perceive at what moment he would be on the verge of finishing. What a serious, frivolous existence would be the consequence; as for his relationship with her, a perpetual lie."

54. "'I ask, however, for very little, admit it.' —'Too little for my life to be adequate to the task.' She was standing almost beside him, looking straight ahead: 'Naturally, if I were to die, you would not fail to call me back to life in order to make me respond again.' —'Unless,' he said smiling, 'I die first.' —'I hope not; that would be worse.'"

55. "he experiences the cold jubilation of the hunter, when the trap has worked and hands over, in a now certain proximity, the anticipated captive."

56. "she is merely complying with the customary usage of the place if it is true, as he has reason to believe, that a section of the hotel is reserved for such comings and goings. This idea does not displease him."

57. "But I would not want you to see me for the simple reason that I am visible."

58. "If we are visible by means of a power which precedes us, then he saw her outside this power, by a right without light which evoked the idea of a transgression, an extraordinary transgression."

59. "the work of art, the literary work is neither finished nor unfinished: it is. What it says is exclusively this: that it is—and nothing more" (*SL* 22)

60. "the writer never reads his work" (*SL* 23)

61. "And yet, with the patience which is particular to him, he thinks that if he could, responding to her, elicit from her the measureless regularity of the murmur and master it, a kind of measure of regularity would be established between their utterances capable of making more expressive and more silent, to the point of quieting it, the incessant affirmation."

62. "Death, considered as an event that one anticipates, is incapable of putting an end to the waiting. Waiting transforms the fact of dying into something that one does not merely have to anticipate in order to cease waiting. Waiting is what allows us to know that one cannot anticipate death."

63. "The question of waiting: waiting bears a question which is not asked. Between the one and the other, there is in common the infinite which is in the smallest question as well as in the feeblest expectation. As soon as one questions, there is no answer that would exhaust the question."

64. "It is her voice that is entrusted to you, not what she says."

65. "I am being, and seeing myself; seeing myself see myself, and so on."

66. "What you have written holds the secret. She does not have it any more; she gave it to you and because it escaped you, you were able to transcribe it."

67. "With what melancholy and yet with what calm certainty he felt that he would never again be able to say 'I.'"

68. "From the first instant, you spoke to me intimately, extraordinarily. I will never forget these first moments when everything was already said between us. But I regretted not knowing. I was never able to learn anything except what I knew."

69. "'I wanted to help you.' —'By wanting to lead me to myself?' —'I wanted nothing except to help you.' —'Yes, a little help does some good.' —'I had only a modest role, you know. I was the wall of this room whose purpose was to send back to you what you would have liked to say.' —'A modest role. And yet you waited, you waited all the time.'"

70. "When you approached . . ."

71. "Why are you speaking in the past tense?"

72. "'She is, therefore, no longer turned toward you?' . . . 'But you, where are you?' . . . 'At what moment did you decide to go over there?' . . . 'And weren't you afraid of frightening her?' . . . 'When you grabbed her by the shoulders, didn't she stiffen?' . . . 'Weren't you too sure of yourself?'"

73. "I think that I sat down next to her, but a little behind her, since she is at the end of the sofa, and close enough to touch her shoulders which the curved nape of her neck leaves exposed."

74. "He remembers that she remains there, motionless, and while he helps her remove some of her clothing . . . he draws her toward him, holds her; his eyes sweep across her face, whereas she lets herself slide, her eyes calmly open, motionless presence turned away from presence. Only her hand, a hand that she submissively abandoned to him, is still withheld." In "Orphée, Don Juan, Tristan," Blanchot establishes a link between eroticism and the approach of alterity when he says that "la passion du dehors . . . est la relation érotique par excellence" (*EI* 285) ["the passion of the outside . . . is the erotic relation par excellence" (*IC* 191)], a dimension much more fully explored by Georges Bataille.

75. "How did they come to speak to each other?"

76. ". . . why would he have suddenly been surprised to hear her?" and ". . . why was he certain that she demanded of him a confidence that he succeeded in returning only with difficulty, in spite of his attentiveness?"

77. "'Yes, I know, it was already her manner of struggling against her presence.' —'Oh, she doesn't struggle.' —'That is true; she understood that extraordinarily, that she must neither resist nor consent but rather slip indecisively between the two, motionless in her haste and her slowness.' —'She did nothing except respond to you.' —'But no more to me than to any other.' —'To you as to no one: this is what is extremely attractive.' —'Thus attracted as if drawn out of her presence.' —'Attracted, but, nevertheless, not yet, by the attraction of that which always attracts but not yet.' —'By the attraction which forces, rejects, and occupies every distance.' —'Attracted in her, in this place of attraction that she feels herself becoming.' —'Present everywhere.' —'Present without presence.'"

78. "'There is still a long road ahead.' —'But not one that will take us far

away.' —'One that will take us to what is nearest.' —'When that which is near is farther away than the farthest place.'"

79. "The event that they forget: the event of forgetting. And thus, all the more present insofar as it is forgotten. Giving the forgetting and giving itself forgotten, but not being forgotten. Presence of forgetting and in the forgetting. The power to forget without end in the event which is forgotten. Forgetting without the possibility to forget. Forgetting—forgotten without forgetting." This fragment contains a perfect example of the rhetorical figure of paronomasia, the stringing together of words of different word types which, however, belong to the same stem. In the third chapter of his *Heidegger and Derrida: Reflections on Time and Language* (Lincoln and London: University of Nebraska Press, 1991), Herman Rapaport discusses the importance this figure has as a key to understanding Heidegger's famous "turn" and the problem of temporality associated with it, and he shows how Blanchot was the first to anticipate this turn in his essay entitled "La parole 'sacrée' de Hölderlin" (in *La Part du feu*). Rapaport also demonstrates how important a mediating figure Blanchot is for Derrida's understanding of Heidegger.

80. "What she was saying—he did not fail to call it to her attention—did not stop struggling valiantly, obscurely. 'Against what?' —'That we may be able to discover it is also without a doubt the price of this struggle.' —'But against what?' —'You must continue to struggle in order to know that.'"

81. "There is no explosion except a book."

82. "the secret law of narrative"

83. "mysteriously waits for the end to come to her as the gift of his death" or ". . . as the gift of her death to him."

84. "Orpheus's gaze is Orpheus's ultimate gift to the work. It is a gift whereby he refuses, whereby he sacrifices the work, bearing himself toward the origin according to desire's measureless movement—and whereby unknowingly he still moves toward the work, toward the origin of the work" (*SL* 174).

85. "This is our superiority over them: as if we were their secret."

86. "How little you speak, you who make the last sign."

87. "When I am alone, I am not alone, but, in this present, I am already returning to myself in the form of Someone. Someone is there, where I am alone . . . Someone is what is still present when there is no one. Where I am alone, I am not there; no one is there, but the impersonal is" (*SL* 31).

88. "Someone in me converses with myself.
Someone in me converses with someone. I do not hear them. However, without me to separate them and without this separation that I maintain between them, they would not hear each other."
"She speaks to him, but he does not hear her. However, it is in him that she makes herself understood by me.
I know nothing of him; I make no room for him inside or outside of me. But if she speaks to him, I hear her in he who does not hear her."
"She speaks to him; he does not hear her; I hear her in him."

89. "it is not identity that the Self in myself brings me. This self is merely a formal necessity; it simply serves to allow the infinite relation of Self to Other. Whence the temptation (the sole temptation) to become a subject again, instead

of being exposed to subjectivity without any subject, the nudity of dying space" (*WD* 53).

90. "the privilege of the central place" (*SNB* 4)

91. "(he/it) thus doubles itself in redoubling itself indefinitely: the subject he/it that has this function in launching the sentence, is like the alibi of another he/it, which would not play any role, would fill no function, except that of putting itself out of work in repeating itself invisibly in an infinite series that analysis tries to catch and to take hold of again, after the fact, each time. But for that it seems necessary that there had been, at one end of the chain, to give itself the task of acting out the rule of identity, a myself capable of being there only to say 'I'" (*SNB* 20).

92. "fractured in advance" (*SNB* 6)

93. "since the day that the sky opened upon its void" (*SNB* 2)

94. "The relation to the 'he/it': the plurality that the 'he/it' holds is such that it cannot be marked by any plural sign; why? 'They' [*ils*] would still designate an analyzable, and thus maniable, whole. 'They' is the way in which ('he/it') frees him-/it-self from the neuter by borrowing from the plurality the possibility of determining itself, thus returning conveniently to indeterminacy, as if (he/it) could find the mark adequate to fix it a place—that very determined one in which every undetermined inscribes itself" (*SNB* 3).

95. "In the final analysis, once the work is finished, the one who completed it finds himself expelled from it, sent outside, and from that moment on incapable of gaining access to it, no longer desiring, moreover, to have access to it. It is only in the course of the task of creating the work, when the ability to read is still located completely within the work that is being created, that the author, still nonexistent, can double himself into a reader yet to come and attempt, from the angle of this hidden witness, to confirm what would be the movement of words apprehended by someone else who still would only be himself, that is, neither the one nor the other, but rather the sole truth of the doubling."

96. Blanchot's tendency to engage in critical activity in his works of fiction does not go unnoticed by Evelyne Londyn in her book *Maurice Blanchot Romancier* (Paris: Nizet, 1976), but whereas I have stressed that a transgressive rapport of circularity between the exigencies of writing and reading is constitutive of any act of literary creation, Londyn views the presence of the critical voice in the narrative work as an intrusion that is detrimental to the overall aesthetic qualities of a work. See, for example, her discussion of the final chapter of *Thomas l'Obscur*, in her eyes a "superfluous" chapter which has the effect of causing the "poème" to degenerate into a "roman à thèse" (135). In making such a value judgment, Londyn situates Blanchot's criticism with respect to his fiction in terms of the following hierarchical opposition: that "critical" writing is secondary and inferior to "creative" writing, a prejudicial distinction that Blanchot questions in *L'Attente l'oubli* and elsewhere.

97. "When commentators have not yet imposed their reign (as, for example, at the time of the epic), this work of redoubling is accomplished within the work itself and we have the rhapsodic mode of composition; that perpetual repetition from episode to episode, an interminable amplification of the same unfolding in place, which makes each rhapsode neither a faithful reproducer nor an immobile

rehearser but the one who carries the repetition forward and, by means of repetition, fills in or widens the gaps, opens and closes the fissures by new peripeteia, and finally, by dint of filling the poem out, distends it to the point of volatilization" (*IC* 390).

98. "There where, according to the general law, a perfect suture hides the secret of the joining together, the secret here, in the manner of a tear, shows itself in its hidden aspect. Of this void they are both, in accordance with their respective paths (voices) the witnesses."

CONCLUSION
BLANCHOT'S POSTMODERN LEGACY

1. "The Roman columbarium no longer conserves anything except the ashes of the deceased, just as the concept is merely the 'residue' of metaphors. Ashes are the complete obliteration of any effigy, the volatilization of all individuality: to conserve nothing more of life than ashes is to reduce differences to the extreme."

2. "what was written in the past will be read in the future, without any relation of presence being able to establish itself *between* writing and reading" (*SNB* 30). In the opening section of the sixth chapter, I cited a sentence from *Le Pas au-delà* that gives rise to a flagrant violation of the *noli*: "Je ne sais pas, mais je sais que je vais avoir su." The incident of self-interpretation occurs in a lengthy fragment in which Blanchot foregrounds the impossibility of absolute knowledge in a grammatical analysis of this sentence whose structure and significance hinge, interestingly enough, on the use of the future ("je vais") anterior ("avoir su").

3. "In those days, I dreamt of being Blanchot."

4. "It is true that Blanchot is the one who made all discourse on literature possible."

5. "It is strange, but this is precisely where the depth of the law appears: each individual must fade away and not be there in person but rather in general, in an invisible way."

6. "behind every worker is a delegate who embodies in flesh and blood the idea of the worker's job. In principle, the delegates are there to provide technical and moral assistance, but, in fact, they are also there to control the workers' activities."

7. "Thus Socrates recommends that this type of speech be avoided as much as possible, as if it were a dangerous illness, and that one confine oneself to true language, which is spoken and in which speech is assured of finding a living guarantee in the presence of the one who speaks."

8. "at the most capable of recording works or events of knowledge for posterity, without having any part whatsoever in the labor of their discovery."

9. "the opaque, empty opening onto that which is when there is no more world, when there is no world yet" (*SL* 33).

10. "there is not, to begin with, law, prohibition, and then transgression, but rather there is transgression in the absence of any prohibition which eventually freezes into Law, the Principle of Meaning" (*WD* 75).

11. "It is true that Ulysses conquered them, but in what way? He did so thanks to his obstinacy, his prudence, and his treachery, which enabled him to

enjoy the Sirens' performance without taking any risks or accepting the consequences. His pleasure was cowardly, uninspired, untroubled, and measured—entirely appropriate for a Greek of the decadence who never deserved to be the hero of the *Iliad*."

12. "an internal pocket larger than the whole."

13. In the final section of the preceding chapter, I classified *L'Attente l'oubli* as a rhapsody, another kind of "infragenre."

14. "as if perhaps thence sprang the source of all authenticity" (*SL* 247).

BIBLIOGRAPHY

PRIMARY SOURCES

Blanchot, Maurice. *Aminadab*. Paris: Gallimard, 1942.

———. *L'Amitié*. Paris: Gallimard, 1971.

———. *Après Coup*. Paris: Éditions de Minuit, 1983.

———. *L'Arrêt de Mort*. Paris: Gallimard, 1948.

———. *L'Attente l'oubli*. Paris: Gallimard, 1962.

———. *Au moment voulu*. Paris: Gallimard, 1951.

———. *La Bête de Lascaux*. 1957. Montpellier: Fata Morgana, 1982.

———. *Celui qui ne m'accompagnait pas*. Paris: Gallimard, 1953.

———. *Comment la littérature est-elle possible?* Paris: José Corti, 1942.

———. *La Communauté inavouable*. Paris: Éditions de Minuit, 1983.

———. *Death Sentence*. Translated by Lydia Davis. Barrytown, N.Y.: Station Hill Press, 1978.

———. *De Kafka à Kafka*. Paris: Gallimard-Idées, 1981.

———. *Le Dernier Homme*. Paris: Gallimard, 1957.

———. *L'Ecriture du désastre*. Paris: Gallimard, 1980.

———. *L'Entretien infini*. Paris: Gallimard, 1969.

———. *L'Espace littéraire*. 1955. Paris: Gallimard-Idées, 1968.

———. *Faux Pas*. Paris: Gallimard, 1943.

———. *La Folie du jour*. Montpellier: Fata Morgana, 1973.

———. *The Gaze of Orpheus*. Translated by Lydia Davis. Barrytown, N.Y.: Station Hill Press, 1981.

———. *The Infinite Conversation*. Translated by Susan Hanson. Minneapolis: University of Minnesota Press, 1993.

———. *Lautréamont et Sade*. Paris: Éditions de Minuit, 1949.

———. *Le Livre à venir*. 1959. Paris: Gallimard-Idées, 1971.

———. *The Madness of the Day*. Translated by Lydia Davis. Barrytown, N.Y.: Station Hill Press, 1981.

———. *Michel Foucault as I imagine him*. Translated by Jeffrey Mehlman. In *Foucault/Blanchot*. New York: Zone Books, 1987.

———. *Michel Foucault tel que je l'imagine*. Montpellier: Fata Morgana, 1986.

———. *La Part du feu*. Paris: Gallimard, 1949.

———. *Le Pas au-delà*. Paris: Gallimard, 1973.

———. *The Space of Literature*. Translated by Ann Smock. Lincoln: University of Nebraska Press, 1982.

———. *The Step Not Beyond*. Translated by Lycette Nelson. Albany: State University of New York Press, 1992.

———. *Thomas L'Obscur*. Paris: Gallimard, 1941.

———. *Thomas L'Obscur* (nouvelle version). Paris: Gallimard, 1950.

———. *Le Très-Haut*. Paris: Gallimard, 1948.

———. *The Unavowable Community*. Translated by Pierre Joris. Barrytown, N.Y.: Station Hill Press, 1988.

Blanchot, Maurice. *Vicious Circles.* Translated by Paul Auster. Barrytown, N.Y.: Station Hill Press, 1985.

———. *When the Time Comes.* Translated by Lydia Davis. Barrytown, N.Y.: Station Hill Press, 1985.

———. *The Writing of the Disaster.* Translated by Ann Smock. Lincoln: University of Nebraska Press, 1986.

SECONDARY SOURCES

Aron, Jean-Paul. *Les Modernes.* Paris: Gallimard, 1984.

Bataille, Georges. *L'Erotisme.* Paris: Éditions de Minuit, 1957.

———. *La Littérature et le mal.* 1957. Paris: Gallimard-Idées, 1980.

———. *Oeuvres complètes.* 12 vols. Paris: Gallimard, 1970–1988.

Baudelaire, Charles. *Oeuvres complètes.* Edited by Y.-G. Le Dantec and Claude Pichois. Paris: Gallimard-Pléiade, 1961.

Baudrillard, Jean. *Selected Writings.* Edited by Mark Poster. Stanford: Stanford University Press, 1988.

Beaujour, Michel. *Miroirs d'encre.* Paris: Éditions du Seuil, 1980.

Bellour, Raymond. *Le Livre des autres.* Paris: Union générale d'éditions, 1978.

Bogue, Ronald. *Deleuze and Guattari.* New York: Routledge, 1989.

Bruns, Gerald. "Language and Power." *Chicago Review* 34.2 (1984): 27–42.

Caillois, Roger. *L'Homme et le sacré.* 1950. Paris: Gallimard-Idées, 1963.

Carroll, David. *Paraesthetics: Foucault, Lyotard, Derrida.* New York: Methuen, 1987.

Collin, Françoise. *Maurice Blanchot et la question de l'écriture.* Paris: Gallimard, 1971.

Deguy, Michel. "*L'Attente l'oubli.*" *Nouvelle Revue Française* 118 (1962): 710–14.

Deleuze, Gilles. *Foucault.* Paris: Éditions de Minuit, 1986.

———. *The Logic of Sense.* Translated by Mark Lester with Charles Stivale. New York: Columbia University Press, 1990.

De Man, Paul. *Blindness and Insight.* New York: Oxford University Press, 1971.

Derrida, Jacques. *Dissemination.* Translated by Barbara Johnson. Chicago: University of Chicago Press, 1981.

———. *Of Grammatology.* Translated by Gayatri Chakravorty Spivak. Baltimore: Johns Hopkins Press, 1976.

———. *Margins of Philosophy.* Translated by Alan Bass. Chicago: University of Chicago Press, 1982.

———. *Parages.* Paris: Éditions Galilée, 1986.

———. *Positions.* Translated by Alan Bass. Chicago: University of Chicago Press, 1981.

Descombes, Vincent. *Modern French Philosophy.* Translated by L. Scott-Fox and J. M. Harding. Cambridge: Cambridge University Press, 1980.

Doubrovsky, Serge. "Critique et existence." In *Les Chemins actuels de la critique.* Paris: Union générale d'éditions, 1968. 215–29.

———. *Pourquoi la nouvelle critique?* Paris: Mercure de France, 1966.

Eribon, Didier. *Michel Foucault.* Paris: Flammarion, 1989.

Foucault, Michel. *Discipline and Punish: The Birth of the Prison*. Translated by Alan Sheridan. New York: Pantheon, 1977.

———. "Maurice Blanchot: The Thought from Outside." Translated by Brian Massumi. In *Foucault/Blanchot*. New York: Zone Books, 1987.

———. "Nietzsche, Freud, Marx." Translated by Alan D. Schrift. In *Transforming the Hermeneutic Context: From Nietzsche to Nancy*. Edited by Gayle L. Ormiston and Alan D. Schrift. Albany: State University of New York Press, 1990.

———. *L'Ordre du discours: Leçon inaugurale au Collège de France prononcée le 2 décembre 1970*. Paris: Gallimard, 1971.

———. *The Order of Things: An Archaeology of the Human Sciences*. New York: Random House, 1970.

———. "Préface à la transgression." *Critique* 195–96 (1963): 751–69.

———. *Raymond Roussel*. Paris: Gallimard, 1963.

Gallop, Jane. *Intersections: A Reading of Sade with Bataille, Blanchot, and Klossowski*. Lincoln: University of Nebraska Press, 1981.

Gasché, Rodolphe. *The Tain of the Mirror: Derrida and the Philosophy of Reflection*. Cambridge: Harvard University Press, 1986.

Gregg, John. "Theoretical and Fictional Portrayals of Reading in Blanchot." *Dalhousie French Studies* 20 (1991): 75–87.

Hartman, Geoffrey. "The Fullness and Nothingness of Literature." *Yale French Studies* 16 (1955–1956): 63–78.

———. "Maurice Blanchot: Philosopher-Novelist." *Chicago Review* 15.2 (1962): 1–18.

———. Preface. In *The Gaze of Orpheus*. By Maurice Blanchot. Translated by Lydia Davis. Edited by P. Adams Sitney. Barrytown, N.Y.: Station Hill Press, 1981.

Heidegger, Martin. *Poetry, Language, Thought*. Translated by Albert Hofstadter. New York: Harper and Row, 1971.

Hubert, Henri, and Marcel Mauss. *Sacrifice: Its Nature and Function*. Translated by W. D. Halls. London: University of Chicago Press, 1964.

Klossowski, Pierre. *Un si funeste désir*. Paris: Gallimard, 1963.

Kofman, Sarah. *Nietzsche et la métaphore*. Paris: Payot, 1972.

Kojève, Alexandre. *Introduction à la lecture de Hegel*. Paris: Gallimard, 1947.

Laporte, Roger. *L'Ancien, l'effroyablement ancien*. Montpellier: Fata Morgana, 1987.

Laporte, Roger, and Bernard Noël. *Deux lectures de Maurice Blanchot*. Montpellier: Fata Morgana, 1973.

Lévesque, Claude. *L'Etrangeté du texte*. Paris: Union générale d'éditions, 1978.

Levinas, Emmanuel. *De l'existence à l'existant*. 1947. Paris: J. Vrin, 1984.

———. *Ethique et infini: Dialogues avec Philippe Nemo*. Paris: Fayard-Radio France, 1982.

———. "La Réalité et son ombre." *Revue des Sciences Humaines* 185 (1982): 103–17.

———. *Sur Maurice Blanchot*. Montpellier: Fata Morgana, 1975.

Libertson, Joseph. *Proximity: Levinas, Blanchot, Bataille and Communication*. The Hague: Martinus Nijhof, 1982.

Londyn, Evelyne. *Maurice Blanchot Romancier*. Paris: Nizet, 1976.

Lyotard, Jean-François. "Answering the Question: What is Postmodernism?" Translated by Régis Durand. In *The Postmodern Condition*. Minneapolis: University of Minnesota Press, 1984.

―――. *The Postmodern Condition: A Report on Knowledge*. Translated by Geoff Bennington and Brian Massumi. Minneapolis: University of Minnesota Press, 1984.

―――. *The Postmodern Explained*. Translated by Don Barry, Bernadette Maher, Julian Pefanis, Virginia Spate, and Morgan Thomas. Minneapolis: University of Minnesota Press, 1993.

Madaule, Pierre. *Une Tâche sérieuse?* Paris: Gallimard, 1973.

Mallarmé, Stéphane. *Oeuvres complètes*. Edited by Henri Mondor and G. Jean-Aubry. Paris: Gallimard-Pléiade, 1945.

Marshall, Donald G. "The Necessity of Writing Death and Imagination in Maurice Blanchot's *L'Espace littéraire*." *Boundary 2* 14.1–2 (1985–1986): 225–36.

Mehlman, Jeffrey. *Legacies of Anti-Semitism in France*. Minneapolis: University of Minnesota Press, 1983.

―――. "Orphée scripteur: Blanchot, Rilke, Derrida." *Structuralist Review* 1.1 (1978): 42–75.

Morin, Edgar. *L'Homme et la mort*. 1951. Paris: Éditions du Seuil, 1970.

Nancy, Jean-Luc. *The Inoperative Community*. Translated by Peter Conner, Lisa Garbus, Michael Holland, and Simona Sawhney. Minneapolis: University of Minnesota Press, 1991.

Nietzsche, Friedrich. *The Gay Science*. Translated by Walter Kaufmann. New York: Random House, 1974.

―――. *Philosophy and Truth: Selections from Nietzsche's Notebooks of the early 1870's*. Translated and edited by Daniel Breazeale. Atlantic Highlands, N.J.: Humanities Press, 1979.

Paulhan, Jean. *Oeuvres complètes*. 5 vols. Paris: Cercle du Livre Précieux, 1966–1970.

Pefanis, Julian. *Heterology and the Postmodern: Bataille, Baudrillard, and Lyotard*. Durham: Duke University Press, 1991.

Poulet, Georges. *La Distance intérieure*. Paris: Plon, 1958.

―――. "Maurice Blanchot as a Novelist." *Yale French Studies* 8 (1959): 77–81.

―――. "Maurice Blanchot, critique et romancier." *Critique* 229 (1966): 485–97.

Préli, Georges. *La Force du dehors: Extériorité, limite et non-pouvoir à partir de Maurice Blanchot*. Fontenay-sous-Bois: Collection Encres-Recherches, 1977.

Rapaport, Herman. *Heidegger and Derrida: Reflections on Time and Language*. Lincoln: University of Nebraska Press, 1991.

Readings, Bill. *Introducing Lyotard: Art and Politics*. New York: Routledge, 1991.

Roth, Michael S. *Knowing and History: Appropriations of Hegel in Twentieth-Century France*. Ithaca: Cornell University Press, 1988.

Sartre, Jean-Paul. *Critiques littéraires: Situations I*. 1947. Paris: Gallimard-Idées, 1975.

Schrift, Alan D. *Nietzsche and the Question of Interpretation: Between Hermeneutics and Deconstruction*. New York: Routledge, 1990.

Shaviro, Steven. *Passion and Excess: Blanchot, Bataille, and Literary Theory*. Tallahassee: Florida State University Press, 1990.

Smock, Ann. *Double Dealing*. Lincoln: University of Nebraska Press, 1985.

Sollers, Philippe. *Writing and the Experience of Limits*. Translated by Philip Barnard with David Hayman. New York: Columbia University Press, 1983.

Stoekl, Allan. *Politics, Writing, Mutilation: The Cases of Bataille, Blanchot, Roussel, Leiris, and Ponge*. Minneapolis: University of Minnesota Press, 1985.

Strauss, Walter A. *Descent and Return: The Orphic Theme in Modern Literature*. Cambridge: Harvard University Press, 1971.

Todorov, Tzvetan. *Literature and its Theorists: A Personal View of Twentieth-Century Criticism*. Translated by Catherine Porter. Ithaca: Cornell University Press, 1987.

Ungar, Steven. "Night Moves: Spatial Perception in the Place of Blanchot's Early Fiction." *Yale French Studies* 57 (1979): 124–35.

———. "Paulhan before Blanchot: From Terror to Letters between the Wars." *Studies in Twentieth Century Literature* 10.1 (1985): 69–80.

———. "Waiting for Blanchot." *Diacritics* 5.2 (1975): 32–36.

Valéry, Paul. *Oeuvres complètes*. 2 vols. Edited by Jean Hytier. Paris: Gallimard-Pléiade, 1957–1960.

Warminski, Andrzej. "Dreadful Reading: Blanchot on Hegel." *Yale French Studies* 69 (1985): 267–75.

Wilhem, Daniel. *Maurice Blanchot: La voix narrative*. Paris: Union générale d'éditions, 1974.

INDEX

alterity, 54, 140, 154, 163–65, 169, 174, 182, 184, 187, 189, 195–96, 198, 200
L'Attente l'oubli, 5, 6, 132–72, 182, 184
autobiography, 5, 35, 37–41, 44. *See also* journal
autoportrait. See self-portrait

Bataille, Georges, 3, 5, 10–17, 31, 33, 34, 35, 39, 42, 46, 48, 50, 53–55, 67, 127, 140, 169, 184, 188, 210n.21, 227n.74
Baudelaire, Charles, 7
Baudrillard, Jean, 6, 174, 184–88
Beaujour, Michel, 40–42, 118
being, 23, 25, 27, 29, 31, 32, 60, 92, 102, 103, 105, 113, 114, 118, 146, 175, 186, 189, 191
Bellour, Raymond, 188
Bogue, Ronald, 184
book, 36, 58–61, 64, 70, 79, 92, 93, 175, 177, 181, 191, 199,

Caillois, Roger, 13
Camus, Albert, 3
Carroll, David, 9, 190
The Castle, 5, 64–66, 116, 130, 145
Char, Rene, 3, 193
Charon, 45
circular exigency: of reading, 68–70, 143, 170–71; of writing, 37, 48–49, 121–24, 143, 160, 170–71
circularity, 8, 30, 52, 106–8, 165, 170–71, 182
closure. *See* totalization
Collin, Francoise, 27, 62
community, 14–15
concept, 175–78, 195, 200

Da Vinci, Leonardo, 3
death, 5, 10–17, 27, 34, 35–38, 41–45, 46, 58, 59, 61, 62, 69, 119, 121–25, 145, 150, 160–61; dual status of, 13, 16, 17, 40–41, 58, 115, 177
deconstruction, 6, 193–97
Deguy, Michel, 133
Deleuze, Gilles, 6, 25, 26, 31, 174, 183–84, 185, 188, 199, 200

de Man, Paul, 132, 134, 137, 168–71, 223–24n.19
Derrida, Jacques, 6, 27, 174, 192–97, 198, 199, 200, 201n.2
Descombes, Vincent, 10, 11
des Forets, Louis-Rene, 168
difference, 26–27, 183–84
dissimulation, 25, 59, 63, 113, 143, 149, 181, 185, 186, 192, 196, 198

Eribon, Didier, 188
error, 36, 38, 47, 61, 62, 64, 66, 89, 114, 175, 197
Eurydice, 46–56, 57, 58, 62, 64, 68, 69, 70, 122–23, 130, 138, 145, 156, 160–61, 165, 182
event, 180–81
excess negativity, 12, 17, 27, 31, 40, 53, 60, 89, 90, 97, 98, 111, 113, 121, 123, 124, 177, 186, 190
existentialism, 174
expenditure, 16, 53, 54, 70, 97, 111

failure, 9, 15, 35, 47, 50, 51, 53, 55, 64, 69, 70, 97, 145, 165, 197. *See also* worklessness
fascination, 28–29, 36, 38, 47, 49, 56, 106, 118, 139, 145, 148, 149, 157, 165, 182
fascism, 187
flagrant délit, 136, 159–62, 170
Foucault, Michel, 6, 133, 150, 162, 174, 178, 188–92, 198, 199, 200, 218n.68
fragmentation, 5, 74, 98–108, 120
Freud, Sigmund, 10, 178

Gasche, Rodolphe, 194, 195
general economy, 15–16, 27, 39, 51, 53–54, 60, 61, 89, 92, 96, 98, 102, 106, 111–15, 117, 119, 123, 129–30, 146, 165, 181, 182, 185, 186, 187, 190, 191, 192, 193, 195, 196, 197
Giono, Jean, 3

Hartman, Geoffrey, 174
Hegel, Georg Wilhelm Friedrich, 5, 8, 10, 11, 12, 27, 30, 31, 46, 58, 62, 175, 202n.5

Hegelianism, 179
Heidegger, Martin, 5, 22, 23, 57, 58, 114, 133, 175, 193
history, 5, 29–30, 31, 32–34, 80–82, 88, 90, 109, 110, 121, 174
Holderlin, Friedrich, 3
Homer, 172, 199
Hubert, Henri, 13
hyperreal, the, 186–88

identity, 26–27, 29, 54, 164, 166, 183, 184, 187, 196, 200
Igitur, 42–43
il y a, 25, 27, 29, 30, 31, 32, 129
image, 22, 23, 29, 59, 104, 118, 182
imaginary, the, 27–28, 29, 118, 119, 185
impatience, 50–53, 55, 136, 145, 182
impersonality, 9, 16, 29, 38, 39, 163, 166, 182, 184

Jesus Christ, 5, 41–42, 46, 56, 57, 58, 62, 69, 197
Joubert, Joseph, 39
journal, 5, 38–39, 73–75, 96–97, 106, 139, 140

Kafka, Franz, 3, 5, 19, 35, 37, 38–39, 64, 66, 67, 207n.13
Kant, Immanuel, 4, 7
Klossowski, Pierre, 213n.2
Kofman, Sarah, 177
Kojeve, Alexandre, 10, 11

language, 5, 18–23, 30–34, 40, 45, 55, 80, 82–83, 86, 87, 108, 119, 123, 125, 140–43, 144, 146, 152, 176, 189
Laporte, Roger, 133
Lautreamont, 39
law, 39, 40, 47, 48, 50, 60, 64, 65, 66, 68, 74, 75, 76, 81, 85, 86, 89, 91, 93, 94, 96, 114, 118, 124, 140, 171, 197, 199
Lazare veni foras, 42, 58–60, 63
Lazarus, 5, 42, 46, 57, 58, 59, 62, 69, 177, 186
Leiris, Michel, 41–42, 128
Levinas, Emmanuel, 23, 31, 152
Libertson, Joseph, 25, 48, 50, 53, 67, 141, 173, 202n.13
limits, 105–6. *See also* law
Londyn, Evelyne, 79, 201n.2, 229n.96
Lyotard, Jean-Francois, 6, 174, 179–83, 188, 199, 200

Mallarmé, Stéphane, 3, 5, 18–20, 30, 41, 42, 56, 57, 70, 189, 205n.34, 208nn.21, 26
Marx, Karl, 178
mastery, 9, 10, 11, 15, 16, 38, 43, 47, 50, 52, 54, 62, 67, 69, 112, 145, 177, 179, 182, 199. *See also* power; regional economy
Mauss, Marcel, 13
metanarratives, 179
metaphor, 175–78, 195, 200
moment, 180–81
Morin, Edgar, 10
le mourir, 15, 17, 27, 33, 36, 38, 40, 41, 43, 45, 61, 119, 123, 124, 125, 175. *See also* death; *il y a*; excess negativity
murmur, 30–31, 52, 57, 140, 143, 144, 150, 159, 176, 190, 196, 198, 200

Nancy, Jean-Luc, 14
Narcissus, 115, 118–21, 124
negativity, 10, 11, 12, 36, 37, 40, 51, 61, 69, 75, 87, 89, 91, 113, 142, 177, 181
neuter, 22, 25, 36, 54, 60, 61, 65–68, 109, 115, 118, 125, 129–30, 142, 152, 166, 174, 180, 186, 197, 198
Nietzsche, Friedrich, 3, 6, 25, 30, 43, 174–78, 183, 188, 189, 200, 208n.28
noli me legere, 6, 8, 56, 58, 59, 60, 63, 66, 70, 85, 92, 116, 118, 127–32, 136, 137, 138, 139, 143, 144, 160, 162, 168–70

Oedipus, 5, 62–64, 65, 66, 151, 175, 197
Oresteia, 102
origin, 24, 28, 60, 101–5, 197, 198; of language, 21, 45, 55, 144, 150, 159, 176, 190; of the work, 4, 30, 39, 46, 137–38, 168, 182
Orpheus, 5, 9, 46–56, 57, 58, 60, 61, 62, 64, 65, 68–71, 106, 122, 123, 128, 130, 136, 138, 139, 145, 152, 154, 156, 160–61, 164–65, 175, 182, 197, 198, 199

Pascal, Blaise, 3, 83
patience, 50–53, 55, 145, 182
Paulhan, Jean, 19–21, 58
Pefanis, Julian, 186
pharmakon, 27
Plato, 26, 28, 186, 193
Platonism, 25–29, 89, 183, 188
Ponge, Francis, 32, 33, 206nn.41, 44

postmodern condition, 6, 174, 179–83, 188

Poulet, Georges, 42–43

power, 9, 11, 15, 16, 36, 47, 48, 49, 50, 51, 52, 54, 55, 61, 62, 64, 67, 69, 79, 89, 90, 92, 102, 112, 114, 139, 142, 145, 152, 165, 174, 177, 187, 189–92, 198. *See also* mastery; regional economy

Preli, Georges, 52, 89, 143

primary text, 6, 135–37, 144, 157, 158, 170

Rapaport, Herman, 228n.79

Reading, 5, 16, 42, 56–71, 75–80, 78, 84–85, 91–93, 127–32, 144, 158–62, 167, 168–71, 177, 182. *See also* circular exigency of reading

Readings, Bill, 180

recit, 199

regional economy, 9, 15–16, 27, 51, 54, 60, 61, 62, 79, 90, 92, 102, 112–15, 119, 123, 129–30, 139, 142, 163, 164, 181, 182, 185, 186, 187, 188, 191, 192, 193, 195, 196, 197

reinscription, 194–97, 199

repetition, 99–101, 103

representation, 5, 6, 87–97, 123, 174, 181, 183, 185. *See also* Platonism

ressemblance, 24–29, 59, 89, 90, 96, 97, 118, 149, 181, 183–86, 188, 196

resurrection, 5, 41, 57, 69

return. *See* circularity

reversal, 26, 53, 55, 139, 153–59, 180, 194–97, 199

rhapsody, 171–72, 231n.13

Rilke, Rainer Maria, 39, 127, 128

Rimbaud, Arthur, 168

Roth, Michael S., 202n.3

Rousseau, Jean-Jacques, 14

sacrifice, 12–15, 17, 53–56, 70, 160–61

Sartre, Jean-Paul, 6, 33, 174, 218n.68

Schrift, Alan, 177

secondary text, 6, 135–37, 144, 157, 158, 170

self-portrait, 40–42, 139

Shaviro, Steven, 201n.2

silence, 30, 31, 34, 140, 142, 198

simulacrum, 6, 26, 174, 183–86, 188, 195

simulation, 184–88

Smock, Ann, 70

Socrates, 28, 41, 42, 95, 193

Sollers, Philippe, 41, 43

Stoekl, Allan, 72

structuralism, 174

subject, 118, 119, 121, 164, 166, 172, 178, 182, 184

subjectivity, 16, 164, 167, 169, 192, 198

subversion, 40, 74, 75, 106, 108, 118, 121, 124, 140, 145, 174, 188, 190, 197

suicide, 35–36, 41, 42–44, 61, 62, 75, 145

surplus negativity. *See* excess negativity

temporality, 29, 49, 70, 121, 134, 180–83

totalization, 5, 10, 11, 31–34, 62, 80, 86, 94, 98, 120, 121, 177, 179, 187, 188, 193

transgression, 5, 15–17, 44, 47–56, 60, 64, 65, 66, 68, 69, 70, 78, 87, 98, 114, 117, 129–30, 142, 152, 159–62, 165, 167, 168–71, 182, 197

Le Tres-Haut, 5–6, 72–127, 133, 175, 178, 181, 184, 187–88, 190–92

Ulysses, 160, 198–200

Valery, Paul, 21, 32, 37, 151

Veyne, Paul, 188

Wagner, Richard, 7

Watergate, 187

Wilhem, Daniel, 140

work, 36, 58–61, 64, 70, 79, 92, 93, 175, 177, 181, 191, 199

worklessness, 9, 35, 37, 89, 97, 111, 152, 192. *See also* failure

writing, 5, 16, 28–30, 35–45, 52, 73–75, 96–97, 108–15, 123–24, 144, 154, 158–62, 168–71, 182, 193. *See also* circular exigency of writing